CRITICAL ESSAYS ON ALDOUS HUXL
EY

MECKIER, JEROME

PR6015.U9Z5956 1996

SE

Critical Essays on
ALDOUS HUXLEY

CRITICAL ESSAYS
ON
BRITISH LITERATURE

Zack Bowen, General Editor
University of Miami

Critical Essays on

ALDOUS HUXLEY

edited by

JEROME MECKIER

G. K. Hall & Co.
An Imprint of Simon & Schuster Macmillan
New York

Prentice Hall International
London Mexico City New Delhi Singapore Sydney Toronto

G. K. Hall & Co.
An Imprint of Simon & Schuster Macmillan
866 Third Avenue
New York, New York 10022

Library of Congress Cataloging-in-Publication Data

Critical essays on Aldous Huxley / edited by Jerome Meckier.
     p.   cm. —(Critical essays on British literature)
   Includes bibliographical references and index.
   ISBN 0-8161-8873-4 (alk. paper)
   1. Huxley, Aldous, 1894–1963—Criticism and interpretation.
I. Meckier, Jerome.   II. Series.
PR6015.U9Z5956   1995
823'.912—dc20   95-12209
                                                             CIP

The paper used in this publication meets the minimum requirements of
American National Standard for Information Sciences—Permanence of
Paper for Printed Library Materials, ANSI Z39.48-1984. ∞ ™

10   9   8   7   6   5   4   3   2   1

Printed in the United States of America

In memory of
Jerome Thomas Meckier, Sr.
1915–1995

Contents

◆

General Editor's Note

◆

The Critical Essays on British Literature Series provides a variety of approaches to both classical and contemporary writers of Britain and Ireland. The formats of the volumes in the series vary with the thematic designs of individual editors, and with the amount and nature of existing reviews and criticism, augmented, where appropriate, by original essays by recognized authorities. It is hoped that each volume will be unique in developing a new overall perspective on its particular subject.

Jerome Meckier's preface makes the case for Huxley's multifaceted stature and place in the vanguard of twentieth-century British letters, while Meckier's introductory essay and subsequent selection of essays provide a redefinition of Huxley and the "novel of ideas." The selected essays contain only those published in academic journals after 1977 and include many not readily available in the United States and none reprinted in earlier collections. Materials were gathered from Canada, Germany, Israel, India, Australia, and New Zealand as well as the United States, supporting Meckier's contention that Huxley's influence was indeed international and cross-cultural.

ZACK BOWEN
University of Miami

Publisher's Note

◆

Producing a volume that contains both newly commissioned and reprinted material presents the publisher with the challenge of balancing the desire to achieve stylistic consistency with the need to preserve the integrity of works first published elsewhere. In the Critical Essays series, essays commissioned especially for a particular volume are edited to be consistent with G. K. Hall's house style; reprinted essays appear in the style in which they were first published, with only typographical errors corrected. Consequently, shifts in style from one essay to another are the result of our efforts to be faithful to each text as it was originally published.

Preface

◆

More than 30 years after his death, Aldous Huxley retains a hold on the popular imagination; he enjoys a public as well as an academic reputation despite his repeated insistence that he wrote only for the small segment of society that thinks. When, for example, members of a soon-to-be-famous rock-and-roll band searched for an identity, inspiration came from *The Doors of Perception* (1954), not William Blake. At the Bourbon Burlesque on Bourbon Street in New Orleans, a reporter for *Esquire* discovered a stripper called "Gio," who took her stage name from an Aldous Huxley story[1] ("The Gioconda Smile," 1921). During the controversial case of "Baby M" (1987), New Jersey Superior Court Judge Sorokow defended noncoital reproduction as a means to genetic fulfillment for infertile couples; "We are not dealing with Huxley's *Brave New World*," the judge insisted.[2]

It was hardly surprising when Isaiah Berlin hailed Huxley as one of the century's "major emancipators," or when Kenneth Clark praised Huxley's "liberating books" for bringing readers since the 1920s a sense of Stephen Spender's "freedom from"—from conventions, humbug, taboos, etc.[3] Equally predictable was André Maurois's characterization of Huxley as "the most intelligent writer of our generation."[4] But what of this encomium? "Aristotle shocked people. Charles Darwin outraged people. Aldous Huxley scandalized millions!" Finishing third behind Aristotle and Darwin as a consternating force is not bad for a bookish intellectual who prided himself on being triphibian (philosopher-scientist-artist). The year was 1960. The speaker: Malcolm X, defending his outspokenness against charges of extremism.[5]

In an age of ever-increasing specialization sparked by incessant change, Huxley personified a vanishing inclusiveness in which the scientific genius of his grandfather, T. H. Huxley, complemented the cultural, artistic, even religious interests inherited from his mother, a niece of Matthew Arnold. Aldous never tired of trying to build bridges between different cultures and rival disciplines. His brother Julian termed him "a truly whole man" who may well have been "the greatest humanist of our perplexed era."[6] Huxley's mental scope and development have been likened to a record of the modern period's intellectual interests. Within a single volume, he could discuss Conrad, Ossian, *Ulysses*, *Kunstforschers* (culture vultures), Balzac, the environment, Breughel, Freud, Piero della Francesca's painting of the "Resurrection," and Felix the Cat (see *Along the Road*, 1925).

Acerbic satirist and saintly seer, Pyrrhonist and perennial philosopher, this polymath began as a poet, triumphed as a novelist, and yet is considered by some to have excelled chiefly as an essayist. In nearly 50 years of anatomizing the human situation, Huxley rolled several careers into one: bourgeois-baiter, art critic, world-traveller, dystopian, pacifist, student of mystical experience, dramatist, expatriate Hollywood screenwriter, LSD-taker, environmentalist, etc. An extraordinary human being, Huxley continually brought his precocious sensitivity to bear on subjects that soon turned controversial: drugs, population control, the planet's dwindling natural resources, for example. He can still be read as a one-man avant-garde.

Through it all, like many great teachers, Huxley conveyed both a sense of genius and the impression that he was still learning. In retrospect, he seems the most unconceited of Brahmins. Eventually, history may regard Huxley as the modern Dante or the new Goethe—that is, the twentieth century's foremost equivalent of the truly monumental, multifaceted artist. Such a writer-thinker constitutes the formative mind of his generation, its central intelligence. His intellectual journey supplies the era with a crucial paradigm.

To celebrate Huxley's many-sidedness, I focus on the novels, most of which are discussed at least once in the dozen essays that follow. Always busy, Huxley published at least one book each year between 1920 and 1933. Despite an astonishing multiformity, however, he averaged a novel every four years in the 41 between his first and final novels. A twelfth was in progress when he died. *Crome Yellow* (1921) made him famous at age 27; his fourth novel, *Point Counter Point* (1928), earned a handsome sum—not to mention a place of distinction for Huxley among modern experimentalists. *Brave New World* is the best-known and most widely read novel about the future. Hearing the title, one thinks first of Huxley, then of Shakespeare.

In one idea-laden novel after another, Huxley exposed the interrelated dilemmas of the modern age; he gave not just utterance but flesh and blood to life's perennial counterpoints and the modern era's cacophony of competing theories, each character the exponent of an attitude toward life. Initially, Huxley provided an ironic record of the ridiculously eccentric things being thought and said during the postwar decade. Gradually, as a believable authorial voice emerged, select individuals in Huxley's later fictions began to mature in accordance with his salvationary hypothesis. Thirty years after

Brave New World (1932), when Huxley strove in *Island* to offset his negative prognosis with a positive proposal, he still relied upon the novel.

Simultaneously farsighted, topical, and timeless, Huxley's rereadable novels conduct a careerlong meditation that ranges from the follies of present circumstances to a consideration of Man's Final End. Wonderfully elastic, these novels utilize most of the genres in which Huxley worked: besides notebooks and diaries, they incorporate poems, short stories, drama, essays, history, (auto-) biography, lecture, even a film script. As a result, Huxley's novels of ideas best reflect his broad extent of aesthetic and philosophic pursuits. They may be designated the principal place where the man of intellect, the creative artist, and the aspiring mystic regularly meet. The discussion novel of ideas was Huxley's preferred medium, the vehicle to which he always returned and in which he experimented most successfully. Huxley's lifelong preoccupation with the fictionalization of ideas stands out as the common denominator in his bibliography; it also serves as a recurrent motif for this collection, first as the key note sounded in my Introduction, then as the thread on which several of the essays are strung.

I have not excerpted chapters from books. At Huxley's death, only two book-length treatments of his work were in print in English: John Atkins, *Aldous Huxley: A Literary Study* (1957) and Sisirkumar Ghose, *Aldous Huxley: A Cynical Salvationist* (1962). During the Huxley Revival in the late 1960s and early 1970s, upwards of half a dozen useful studies appeared. But I have chosen to concentrate on essays published in academic journals since that outburst—either by authors of the groundbreaking studies or scholars indebted to them. *Critical Essays on Aldous Huxley* is intended to occupy a place on one's shelf alongside the book-length analyses whose insights it strives to extend without duplication.

To gather materials for this collection, I have tapped a multiplicity of sources—journals or authors in America, Canada, England, Germany, Israel, India, New Zealand, and Australia. I reprint no essay originally published earlier than 1977; half are from the 1980s. The results further demonstrate my opening contention—namely, that Huxley remains a living voice. Still internationally influential, he continues to be a cross-cultural spokesperson whose readership is worldwide. Collectively, the essays in this anthology prove that high-quality Huxley scholarship has proceeded steadily during the three decades since his death, a good omen one year after the centenary of his birth. 1977–78 is roughly the cut-off date for the last full-scale Huxley bibliography: Eben E. Bass, ed., *Aldous Huxley: An Annotated Bibliography of Criticism* (New York: Garland, 1981). *Critical Essays on Aldous Huxley* thus updates as it commemorates. For articles earlier than those assembled here or listed by Bass, one should consult Claire John Eschelbach and Joyce Lee Shober, eds., *Aldous Huxley: A Bibliography 1916–1959* (Berkeley: University of California Press, 1961).

Gavin Keulks toiled indefatigably as my editorial assistant during preparation of this volume: hunting down difficult-to-find journals, photocopying articles, petitioning interlibrary loan, proofreading, and indexing. I must also acknowledge the unfailingly helpful staff of the University of Kentucky's M. I. King Library, especially the interlibrary loan department. For Keulks's invaluable services, I thank Dr. Richard Edwards, Dean of the College of Arts and Sciences at the University of Kentucky, who granted me a research assistant, and Professor David Durant, Chair of the English Department, who supported my request for one.

Notes

1. See *Esquire* for December 1993, 140.
2. This remark prompted Valerie Hartouni to exclaim: "it is largely against or in terms of Huxley's dystopic vision that issues raised by the new technologies [especially for human genetics and reproduction] are framed." See *"Brave New World* in the Discourses of Reproduction and Genetic Technologies," in Joan Bennett and William Chaloupka, eds., *In the Nature of Things: Language, Politics, and the Environment* (Minnesota: University of Minnesota Press, 1993), 87. Proof of Hartouni's observation quickly materialized. Without having to mention Huxley, *Life* ran an article about growing embryos in the lab and maturing them by machine in the year 2020: "The Brave New World of Babymaking," December, 1993, 88; or see "Brave New Embryos," *Time* (29 August 1994), 60–61.
3. Julian Huxley, ed., *Aldous Huxley: A Memorial Volume 1894–1963* (New York: Harper & Row, 1965), 144, 17, 19.
4. Julian Huxley, 62.
5. Alex Haley, *The Autobiography of Malcolm X* (New York: Ballantine, 1991; first pub. 1964), 454.
6. Julian Huxley, 21, 25.

Introduction: Aldous Huxley and the Congenital Novelists: New Ideas about the Novel of Ideas

JEROME MECKIER

The novel of ideas—"that strange mutt of literature"[1]—has generally attracted slander instead of critical inspection. Johnson's *Rasselas*, Voltaire's *Candide*, and Peacock's underrated novels have been used to deride the novel of ideas as an unsatisfactory form. Yet Doris Lessing, introducing *The Golden Notebook*, insists that "to attempt a novel of ideas is to give oneself a handicap,"[2] by which she means an additional requirement the superior novelist imposes upon himself. This view of the novel of ideas as something more, not less, than ordinary fiction, is central to the aesthetic of Aldous Huxley, especially in *Point Counter Point*, his finest contribution to the genre.

Point Counter Point supplies the first of two critical texts. A much misunderstood passage from Philip Quarles's Notebook is actually a manifesto cunningly disguised as a definition full of self-reproach:

> Novel of ideas. The character of each personage must be implied, as far as possible, in the ideas of which he is the mouthpiece. In so far as theories are rationalizations of sentiments, instincts, dispositions of soul, this is feasible. The chief defect of the novel of ideas is that you must write about people who have ideas to express—which excludes all but about .01 per cent. of the human race. Hence the real, the congenital novelists don't write such books. But then I never pretended to be a congenital novelist.[3]

The second crucial text, a magnificently comic letter to E. S. P. Haynes nearly twenty years later, begins where Quarles leaves off. Huxley's favorable opinion of the novel of ideas depends on an elaboration of the tantalizing

Reprinted from the *Southern Review* 13 (1980): 203–22, with permission of the author.

distinction his alter ego starts to draw between the congenital and non-congenital novelist. To Haynes Huxley wrote:

> . . . I remain sadly aware that I am not a born novelist, but some other kind of man of letters, possessing enough ingenuity to be able to simulate a novelist's behaviour not too unconvincingly. To put the matter physiologically, I am the wrong shape for a story teller and sympathetic delineator of character within a broad social canvas. The fertile inventors and narrators and genre painters have all been rather burly genial fellows. Scott looked like a farmer. Balzac and Dumas were florid to the point of fatness. Dickens was athletic and had a passion for amateur theatricals. Tolstoy was an intellectual moujik. Dostoevsky was physically tough enough to come through imprisonment in Siberia. Conan Doyle was a barrel, Wells is a tub. Dear old Arnold Bennett was a chamber pot on spindly legs. . . . So what chance has an emaciated fellow on stilts? And of course this is no joke. There is a real correlation between shape and mind.[4]

A self-serving definition camouflaged as a confession of inferiority and an epistle composed with tongue in cheek seem remarkably cautious and oblique; but the indirection is ironic, an instance of guile rather than tact or temerity. It must not obscure Huxley's underlying conviction that only the novelist of ideas can be a seminal and synthesizing intelligence: the mind of his age.

For Quarles the "chief defect" of his specialty becomes part of the satire. Few people have ideas or want to read about those who do—this is the perennial shortage Quarles confronts whenever he picks up his pen. Only ".01 per cent." of the participants in the human fugue, a precious minority in any generation, possess significant minds. This chronic deficiency appears to be a basic defect in the human condition, one which no amount of satire can correct. Despite a modicum of self-depreciation, Quarles's definition is an elitist's jibe at plebeian tastes. It reinforces the unflattering animal imagery Huxley employs throughout *Point Counter Point* as part of his anti-evolutionary satire.[5] If 99.9 per cent of the human race, at any given moment, lack ideas worth expressing, the progress of the species is an idea even less deserving of serious attention.

Having dispatched the mindless majority, the novelist of ideas is severely handicapped when choosing real-life models for his characters. He must turn his observations toward a fictional simulation of the atypical fraction that nonetheless constitutes the most important segment of the community: its so-called thinkers. In *Point Counter Point* Huxley sits in judgement on the procrustean theories and eccentric behaviour of the scientists, artists, politicians and their patrons who bestow directing ideas on British society. By criticizing this often misguided and irresponsible percentile of the human race, novelists of ideas (in the role Webley's British Freemen try to usurp) "keep the world safe for intelligence" (55).

The protection of intelligence is an additional burden the novelist of ideas assumes. Woefully incomplete theories about life, Huxley suggests, are the peculiar province of the modern British intelligentsia, whose inadequate notions provide the novelist of ideas with his primary source of material. As the ideas of his talkative characters collide with and confound one another, Huxley depicts a babel of conflicting attitudes towards modern life and designates the resulting sense of being rudderless as the prominent characteristic of the post-war decade. The novel of ideas is one of the obligatory modern forms, perhaps the most efficient means of gauging the extent of philosophical confusion in an age of unprecedented relativity.

Throughout Huxley's fiction, the human comedy becomes one of ideas. The deplorable nature of things, human nature included, forces the satirical novelist to reject the insufficient explanations of life his characters egotistically adopt. These ideas never fit all the wearisome facts, and their exponents reveal themselves to be perpetrators of self-enhancing rationalizations. Fascinated by the power of ideas, Huxley mistrusts the self-centred world of the intellect in which they originate, often without regard for the apparent inexplicability of complex modern reality. He exposes a counterpoint of mind against matter. In a seemingly pointless world, the viability of ideas, whether new or traditional, is the idea about which Huxley's satirical novels remain most sceptical.

Rampion's Greco-pagan vitalism, Quarles's efforts to see life whole by musicalizing his fiction, Walter Bidlake's Shelleyan idealism, Lord Edward's monistic biology, Illidge's Communism, Webley's Fascist tendencies, Spandrell's Baudelairean diabolism, John Bidlake's unadulterated sensualism, and Lucy Tantamount's amoral hedonism are only some of the insufficient aesthetic, philosophical, and scientific attitudes towards modern life that fail to explain fully the nature of things and, instead, contradict each other through *Point Counter Point*. Ideas, it seems, have no mandatory existence outside the minds of those who conceive them. This surmise gives Huxley's novels of ideas an additional dimension, ontological and epistemological, which enables him to quarrel with life itself.

The "chief characteristic" of the novel of ideas, according to one foe of the genre, is that interest focuses "on the ideas expounded" by the characters, not on their feelings and relationships.[6] Lurking behind this derogatory definition is the implication that the novelist of ideas has no interest in his characters and small aptitude for creating them. But again the novelist of ideas is actually making things harder for himself. Characters in Quarles's projected novel and Huxley's completed one seldom deteriorate into mere mouthpieces for ideas. Quarles's Notebook describes a new approach to the revelation of character at a time when new methods of character depiction were an obsession in modern fiction. Throughout *Point Counter Point* characters are only as worthwhile as their ideas and ideas only as commendable as the characters who hold them.

Huxley's novels do not ignore feelings and relationships. In Quarles's opinion, feelings contribute to the ideas upon which human interaction depends. Ideas, Huxley contends, determine conduct. The discontinuity separating people stems from the discord among the one-sided ideas that govern their images of themselves. Ruptures to the events in which Huxley's characters participate—concerts, dinner parties, marriage, parent-child relations—are the inevitable consequence. As Quarles points out, theories are seldom pure. In large part they are "rationalizations of sentiments, instincts, disposition of soul." Huxley remains sensitive to the feelings and ego as irrational bases for the mental fabrications his self-centred characters rely on to justify their lives.

Instead of neglecting human intercourse, Huxley examines it closely as a possible modern ideal. But the deficient philosophies of life the characters espouse in *Point Counter Point* turn the novel into an anti-Bloomsbury satire on the value and efficacy of human relationships.[7] Unable to agree about the scheme of things and the wisest manner in which to live, members of Huxley's parodic community prove incapable of harmonious connectivity and become illustrations of counterpoint. An emotional Elinor collides with a cerebral Philip, a scientific Lord Edward with a political Webley, a heartlessly modern Lucy with a romantic Walter, a cockney Illidge with the upper-class coterie at Tantamount House, and a religious hypocrite like Burlap with the pagan life-worshipper in Rampion.

Huxley never loses sight of his special responsibilities: not only depicting character but tracing the effect ideas have on those who voice them and on the society created by their utterances. The value of an idea in *Point Counter Point* depends on the time and place it is expressed and the success or failure of the speaker's previous and subsequent activities, a situation unusual for Peacock's novels and foreign to the prose narratives in *Rasselas* and *Candide*. Ideas in *Point Counter Point* are always tested by incidents. Philosophers, essayists, and lesser practitioners of the novel of ideas cannot introduce many of these. Their interest centres exclusively on specific ideas, whereas Huxley's concern extends to the value of ideas in general and the role they play in modern life, which are essentially a novelist's preoccupations. They become especially important in a pluralistic, experimental age, when a host of intellectual disciplines, each presuming to prescribe for society, competes contrapuntally for the attention communal overviews once enjoyed.

In *Point Counter Point*, where ideas discredit characters and *vice versa*, denigration is often mutual and simultaneous. Ideas have fates and fortunes, just as characters do; the fate of a character determines, and is determined by, ideas he holds.[8] When Walter and Marjorie strive to relive *Epipsychidion*, they demolish Shelley's Romantic idealism (9–11). Leaving London behind for a rustic Berkshire cottage, they are "alone with one another, month after month, among the bare downs." Soon overcome by acute boredom, they discover the counterpoint Huxley continually posits not only between mind and matter but also between art and life. The failure of Marjorie and Walter's experimental life-style unveils the inapplicability of Romantic attitudes in modern contexts, a theme that pervades *Point Counter Point*. It also reveals personal inadequacies—Walter's baseness as he tires of her, Marjorie's vapidity as she fails to inspire him.

Even Rampion's attractive philosophy of life, his emphasis on attentiveness to body as well as mind, does not go unscathed. The humanistic stance of the life-worshipper, which Huxley borrows admiringly from D. H. Lawrence, rebukes the circumscribed views of Mark's one-pointed fellow talkers, victims of self-division, who seem to dread integrity and inclusiveness. But it holds no answers for Webley, a murder victim, and offers little consolation to John Bidlake, who contracts stomach cancer. The nature of things, Huxley satirically implies, may be oriented more towards death than life. Spandrell's disconcerting pessimism and the epigraph from Fulke Greville about the wearisomeness of the human condition survive the novel almost as persuasively as Rampion's vitalism.

Huxley's novels of ideas thus deliberately fail to resolve themselves. They thrust the reader into modernity, a world of mutually exclusive choices, none of which seems totally satisfying. Since the ideas of one personage regularly undercut those of another, it is perilous to locate the novelist's philosophy in a single character or to assume that ideas in the novel of ideas are portable, discrete, or detachable. Huxley frequently discredits everybody. At the climax of *Brave New World*, for example, Mond and the Savage debate to a standoff unfavourable to them both and to the competing world views of Wells and Lawrence, whose ideas they personify. To compromise all parties, Huxley often parcels out his allegiance along with his erudition. He displays sympathy for Blakean elements in Rampion's philosophy, adopts portions of Quarles's modernist aesthetic in writing *Point Counter Point*, and is sorely troubled by Spandrell's diabolical pessimism. Like *Brave New World*, *Point Counter Point* cannot be classified with Plato's dialogues, Lamb's occasional essays, Swift's prose polemics, or Landor's imaginary conversations. As Quarles assumes the extra obligations novels of ideas impose, he never doubts, even in the privacy of his Notebook, that he is devising a novelistic form.

In the letter to Haynes, Huxley regrets that he is not "a born novelist," which is different from not being a novelist at all. The born or congenital novelist is an incessant spinner of tales largely for their own sake. A non-congenital novelist or modern satirical novelist of ideas is an intellectually superior being who successfully simulates the behaviour of a novelist to dramatize his themes and gain a greater audience. Huxley's comments to Haynes insinuate that novelists decrease in value the closer they approximate an imaginary nadir of grotesquerie: the totally mindless storyteller. Novels, as E. M. Forster laments, must tell stories, yet being gifted with a knack for telling them, Huxley feels, is poor compensation if one is not especially endowed intellectually, if one is not metaphysically inclined to compare different hypotheses about life, ponder the mysteriousness of the nature of things, or speculate about man's ultimate purpose.

Like Quarles's declaration that he "never pretended to be a congenital novelist" (410), Huxley's missive to Haynes winds up by awarding its author a badge of merit; it is not a *mea culpa*. The letter corroborates several important revelations Huxley makes at different stages of his career. The common denominator behind these statements is Huxley's conviction that something more important than the narrative is always simultaneously in progress in genuine novels of ideas. "I feel about fiction," Huxley wrote in 1933, "as Nurse Cavell felt about patriotism: that it is not enough. Whereas the 'born story teller' obviously feels that it is enough."[9] "The congenital novelist," Huxley lectured the *Paris Review*, "doesn't have other interests. Fiction for him is an absorbing thing which *fills up his mind* and takes all his time and energy, whereas someone else with *a different kind of mind* [italics added] has these other, extracurricular activities going on."[10] The superiority of the novelist of ideas stems from the greater curiosity of its author, his broader, more versatile mind with interests in philosophy, religion, and science, and his determination to do several things simultaneously—such as recount in chapter nine of *Point Counter Point* an engrossing love story that also lyrically examines the Lawrentian ethos and refutes the tragically corrupt attitude towards women and love broached in chapter eight by the unsavory Spandrell and illustrated thereafter by his depressing life and violent death.

Novelists of ideas can write like traditional novelists if they choose— or at least Huxley can, even if, according to Elinor, Quarles cannot. During their idyllic courtship in chapter nine, Mark and Mary Rampion, like Mellors and Connie Chatterley, bring each other back to life. Theirs is the one instance in Huxley's novel of a relationship that is complementary, not contrapuntal. Huxley also succeeds with the melodramatic murder of Webley in chapter thirty-three and the revenge the British Freemen exact from a suicidal Spandrell. In these scenes, however, Huxley is always more than a congenital novelist, not less. He does not write each scene to determine what philosophical implications arise, nor does he focus on a set of implications and devise each scene with them in mind. Thanks to the capacity for "extracurricular" activity in the "different kind of mind" Huxley claims to possess, he invents interlocking stories about Rampion and Spandrell, begins to examine ideas each man holds, and envisions a working-out of the emphatic contrasts between their attitudes simultaneously in the same creative act.

Rampion's Lawrentian thesis that civilization is harmony and completeness (144) underwrites the healthy love that rapidly unites him with Mary. His Blakean championing of "relevant human truth" (555) over abstract scientific concepts designates their "spontaneous, natural, untroubled way of living" (153) as the only commendable life-style in a novel crammed with less wholesome experiments. Spandrell's assassination of Everard Webley, suspenseful *per se*, serves as the ultimate test for his ill-fated Baudelairean theories, especially the hypothesis that one can pursue good through evil because "things exist only in terms of their opposites" and "The devil implies God" (560). Incidents contrasting Rampion's happiness with Webley's sudden death and Spandrell's subsequent desolation contribute to Huxley's underlying preoccupation, throughout *Point Counter Point*, with the diversity of fates awaiting different individuals and their ideas in the modern struggle for dominance between life-enhancing outlooks and death-oriented philosophies.

Excellent storytelling, chapters nine and thirty-three also contain Huxley's evaluation of the divergent theories proposed by two philosophical poets from different quarters of the nineteenth century. Far from becoming types, allegedly the fate of characters in novels of ideas, Rampion and Spandrell seem interesting in themselves. They represent opposing principles (life against death, optimism against pessimism) and, like many of the characters in *Point Counter Point*, they have contemporary models—Lawrence and Philip Heseltine—as well as historical ones—Blake and Baudelaire.[11] Huxley takes on the added challenge of a twofold *roman à clef*. As can be shown with other chapters, these two exist point counter point to divulge the consequences of two oddly similar quests by mutually antagonistic temperaments for a reliable first principle upon which to base a satisfying way of life.

Rampion and Spandrell unfold their contrasting attitudes in chapters eight and ten, but the idyllic romance in the intervening chapter supports Rampion. In chapter thirty-four, following the murder of Webley, Rampion confronts the novel's anti-completeness perverts (Quarles, Burlap, Spandrell) and casts Huxley's vote for integrity. Despite a plethora of characters who illustrate the manifold varieties of self-division, the enlightened cultivation of body and mind, once practised by the sane, harmonious Greek, is Huxley's provisional definition, in 1928, of wholeness and health. Chapters nine and thirty-three are framed or followed by discussion sequences that form part of a larger contest in which Rampion, Huxley's modern version of Socrates, vanquishes his opposition. Unlike Plato's *Dialogues*, which are mainly discussions of ideas, *Point Counter Point* is a novel in which strategically placed discussion scenes (the main ones occur in chapters eight, ten, sixteen, twenty-one, and thirty-four) contribute to the demolition of old values and the sceptical search for new ones.

With the exception of Dickens, whose genius Huxley habitually undervalued, the congenital novelists in the letter to Haynes are carefully chosen: Balzac, Dumas, Bennett, Wells, Conan Doyle, but not Forster or Mrs Woolf and certainly not Lawrence, all of whom were frequently better storytellers than Huxley, yet hardly unintellectual. Writers Huxley omits clearly have important ideas to express, but do not produce novels of ideas. Like George Eliot, they may be said to put ideas into their novels. Generally, they dramatize only their own conceptions, seldom testing them at length against the notions of other thinking novelists. They cannot really be credited with writing *about* ideas because they never ponder the accuracy of ideas *per se* in the material world.[12]

Lawrence's enthusiasm for Birkin's theories in *Women in Love* or for Lilly's in *Aaron's Rod* is never seriously in doubt. Values Mrs Ramsay personifies in *To the Lighthouse* coincide with ideals cherished by Mrs Woolf. In *Howards End*, when the Schlegel sisters admonish other characters to connect, they speak unequivocally for Forster. Most novelists of consequence, Huxley realizes, have ideas to propose. But none of them becomes the mind of the age simply by voicing his own necessarily incomplete attitudes towards modern life. To do so is merely to augment the babel of competing voices in an era of contrapuntal value systems. Forging the conscience of one's race entails being a judge or referee. The bona fide novelist of ideas does not simply chide empty-headed storytellers; he also functions as a clearing-house for the philosophies of novelists who put ideas into their novels.

Novelists *with* ideas supply the novelist *of* ideas with many of his finest targets. In *Point Counter Point* Huxley assesses the case for a modern humanism. He compares the Lawrentian thesis and the ideals of Bloomsbury; then he measures both against less sanguine views of the human condition. Novels that proclaim the philosophy of the life-worshipper or exalt human relationships as the goal of earthly existence do not impress Huxley as final answers. They must take their place alongside the crotchets of the Garsingtonians (*Crome Yellow*), the worn-out idealism of Wordsworth and Shelley (*Those Barren Leaves*), and the theories of Pavlov, Freud, and J. B. Watson (*Brave New World*) as unsatisfactory phenomena for the non-congenital novelist of ideas to digest and dramatize when he mirrors the disturbingly inconclusive intellectual turmoil of the modern age.

Huxley recruits his undesirable novelists from the previous century and the Edwardian era. He treats congenitals unjustly, disparaging them too severely for supposedly ignoring the paramountcy of ideas, just as Mrs Woolf unfairly downgrades Bennett, Galsworthy, and Wells for their allegedly excessive obsession with externals. Congenital novelists are Huxley's equivalent for writers whom Stephen Spender dubs "contemporaries" and Mrs Woolf brands "materialists."[13] They capture something of the outward life of the century, Huxley concedes; but, along with most modern poets, they include "precious little of its mind."[14] They do not portray the intellectual condition of the age, nor do they critically examine very many of its controlling ideas and guiding principles. Identifying himself as a non-congenital novelist of ideas does not dissociate Huxley from a genre. On the contrary, it is his way of claiming to be modern.

"Burly," "athletic," "physically tough"—congenitals with these traits are made to seem more at home in the world, by contrast with Huxley's ontological discontent. "An emaciated fellow on stilts," the six-foot four-inch Huxley repudiates "jolly optimistic fellows" like Dickens, "who assure us humanity is all right" because it exhibits a few "merely animal virtues."[15] He assumes, instead, the lean and hungry look of someone born to be dissatisfied. The modern novelist of ideas, a compulsive satirist, emerges as a non-congenial as well as non-congenital fictionist. Quarles is not only displeased with human nature but upset by life's "bewildering diversity," its inexplicability in terms of art, science, and religion, or by any apparent combination of these different layers of reality. He pursues "a new way of looking at things" (265), but his attempts to "make the familiar seem fantastically mysterious" result in deliberate parody of both the Words-worthian sense of wonder and Bennett's romantic realism. Quarles finds the nature of things exceedingly "queer"; his idea of modern life emphasizes its "astonishingness" (342), its capacity to provoke amazement while frustrating rational explanation. Like Quarles, non-congenital novelists are inclined to raise unanswerable questions about human behaviour and the life process or promote ideas that overturn accepted values; whereas congenitals, Huxley suggests, seldom portray reality in radically unexpected ways, and so avoid extensive experimentation. The novel proves useful to them as they find it because its principal task, they feel, is not to perplex the reader but to show him the life he already knows.

The unflattering self-portrait with which the epistle to Haynes com-mences quickly becomes secondary once the irrepressible satirist starts to downgrade his competition. Huxley's brilliant character-sketches, as good as the caricatures Rampion shows Burlap during the latter's visit to his studio (289–90), treat congenital novelists as ludicrous fossils and impugn their intellectual ability: Scott is called a farmer, Tolstoy a peasant, Dickens an athletic amateur actor, Conan Doyle a barrel, Wells a tub. Huxley enlists a spindley-legged chamber pot to represent Bennett. A statement that began as a revealing concession is cleverly converted into a useful war club.

Having read Dr William Sheldon's *The Varieties of Human Physique* and *Varieties of Temperament*, Huxley admits that he lacks "the right temperament" and possesses "the wrong shape" to be a congenital novelist. But the regret is largely feigned. Like Quarles's conception of the idea-laden novel, Huxley's modern theory of humours confesses to minor inadequacies within the appar-ent object of investigation—here the intellectual novelist—in order to point out more serious deficiencies in others. Assuming a correlation between physical shape and mental scope, Huxley implies that the unattractive bodies of "genial fellows" like the fat and "florid" Balzac signify heavy, misshapen minds. The meatier the physique, the hoax goes, the less nimble the intellect. If a lean, long-limbed satirist is not right for story telling, oddly contoured congenital novelists are the wrong shape for serious thought. They were not made to be novelists of ideas. "And of course," Huxley adds the final stroke, "this is no joke"—or, rather, it is an excellent one with an extremely serious point. Using poetic license, Huxley borrows from Sheldon to give scientific flavor to an aesthetic discrimination he believes is valid.[16]

In his statement to the *Paris Review* Huxley combines ideas from Quarles's Notebook with the revelations to Haynes: "I don't think of myself as a congenital novelist—no . . . Some people are born with an amazing gift for story telling; it's a gift which I've never had at all. . . ."[17] This is considerably humbler than the insistence, in the same interview, on "a different kind of mind" which mere storytelling is insufficient to fill. But the "amazing gift," Huxley apparently feels, can be meticulously acquired or at least simulated, whereas the mental scope necessary for the novelist of ideas to become the Rhadamanthus of the intellectual life of his era must be ruled strictly a question of favourable genes. "People are not interested in ideas by choice," Huxley informs Robert Nichols. "They are predestined to ideas as they are predestined to a Roman nose."[18]

Clearly, Huxley considers it a congenital blessing to have been born Aldous Huxley instead of Arnold Bennett. He abides by this opinion even though his assessment of the human predicament in *Point Counter Point* consequently involves hints of psychological and physiological determinism that compromise the call for a philosophy of wholeness and dispute Rampion's right to be considered the guiding light of his age. Since Quarles has Huxley's pride in being predestined to ideas, *Point Counter Point* must cling to the anti-Lawrentian fear that temperament, life-style, and the individual's theories about the way life operates are sometimes dictated by uncontrollable factors, such as body structure and social origins.[19] This depressing possibility modifies the counterpoint of chapters nine and thirty-three by giving added credence—but not acceptance—to the dismaying fatalism Spandrell expresses in chapter twenty-one, his belief that "Everything that happens is intrinsically like the man it happens to" (389).

Defending *Antic Hay*, Huxley terms it a faithful recollection of "the life and opinions of an age."[20] He outlines *Those Barren Leaves* as "a discussion and fictional illustration of different views of life."[21] "The mere business of telling a story," Huxley continues, "interests me less and less. I find it very difficult to understand the mentality of a man like Bennett who can sit down and spin out an immense realistic affair about life in Clerkenwell (his latest, *Riceyman Steps* is that). When it was first done that sort of thing had a certain interest; I suppose it was Balzac who first exploited the curious subject. But it is a purely factitious interest. The only really and permanently absorbing things are attitudes towards life and the relation of man to the world." "Attitudes towards life," the "opinions of an age," man's ideas about his "relation" to the world—these overriding philosophical concerns go beyond mere storytelling to become "really and permanently absorbing things," which the novelist of ideas, Huxley thinks, is uniquely equipped to handle. In addition to being at least a passable storyteller, he is also, the letter to Haynes claims, "some other kind of man of letters." Huxley does not specify what kind, but seems to regard the novelist of ideas as the modern successor to the great poet-philosophers who examined conflicting views of life, synthesized the ideas of their eras, and served as spokesmen for their age.

Dante, Goethe, and Lucretius, whom Huxley praises highly in the "Subject Matter of Poetry,"[22] were congenitally blessed with capacious intellects. They made themselves conversant with the leading philosophical and scientific theories of their times. Having surveyed the age, these polymaths characterized its state of mind and reflected its diverse intellectual activity. They were also formative intelligences who offered universal laws, divine plans, or cosmic frameworks to explain the wearisomeness of being human. As the epigraph from Fulke Greville indicates, Quarles, representing Huxley, is struggling to summarize the human condition, thereby patterning himself on the major shaping intelligences from the past. "Before the rise of science" with its lack of concern for human values, Huxley points out in *Literature and Science*, "the only answers" to life's conundrums—"Who are we? What is our destiny? How can the often frightful ways of God be justified?"— "came from the philosopher-poets and poet-philosophers."[23] Congenital storytellers attempt unsuccessfully to take their place; novelists of ideas, like Quarles and Huxley, succeed as replacements even if, in the chaos of the immediate post-war world, they can only do so parodically.

The non-congenital novelist of ideas aspires to complexity as a combination of satirist and sage. This unusual dual role is the heaviest additional burden Huxley wants the novelist of ideas to shoulder. Congenital novelists like Bennett and Balzac merely further the withdrawal from wisdom begun by Descartes. Once the seventeenth-century thinker insisted that all knowledge be as firm as mathematics and geometry, poet-philosophers, with imaginative explanatory hypotheses that took science into account but were not provable by scientific observation and experiment, forfeited some of their credibility. At first, in the "Subject Matter of Poetry," Huxley speaks only of poet-philosophers, but later he expands his ideal to the poet-philosopher-scientist, a triphibian with artistic ability to propagate a philosophy that is not scientifically absurd. Quarles is an experimental novelist, a student of philosophy (Rampion's in particular), and an expert, if amateur, zoologist. Followers of Balzac, so-called realists like Bennett, strike Huxley as heirs of Descartes, whereas novelists of ideas allegedly trace their ancestry to Lucretius, Dante, and Goethe.

In *The Old Wives' Tale* Bennett produces an arithmetic demonstration: youth plus the passage of time equals the tragedy of old age. He imposes a restrictive pattern on the nature of things, achieving unity of vision by unfair means. Sophia beholds the withered corpse of Gerald Scales and utters Bennett's lugubrious explanatory hypothesis: youth, vigour, beauty, "Everything came to that."[24] Powerful though his climactic passage is, Bennett's attitude toward life hardly seems more profound than John Bidlake's reduction of the females in his paintings to pure sensuality (60) or Lord Edward

Tantamount's confidence that life "comes down to chemistry in the end, of course" (49). For Huxley, Bennett is as one-pointed as the lop-sided egotists in his discussion-novels, eccentric conversationalists whose ideas about life frequently resemble fixations or crotchets. The puzzlement Quarles exhibits at the variety of fates individuals and their ideas can meet is intended to counteract the impoverishing influence of so-called *natural* storytellers who often function mechanically as accomplices of a modern materialistic scientism.

Huxley comes down hardest on the "mentality" of professed realists like Balzac and Bennett because he considers the "immense," "purely factitious" descriptions of life they put forward merely pseudo-scientific accounts, not the long-awaited modern synthesis. In *The Old Wives' Tale*, more than in *Riceyman Steps*, Bennett presumes to show readers his idea of "What Life Is." But he transcribes only one aspect of the nature of things: the process of change, "the earth's fashion of renewing itself" (451). An oversimplifier, he boils life down to common denominators—the passage of time, the inevitability of aging, the finality of death—and invites readers to put aside religious and philosophical considerations in order to experience, along with Sophia, the "pure and primitive emotion" (530) a detailed analysis of these phenomena evokes.

After digesting *The Old Wives' Tale*, the reader still does not know how best to regard life. He suspects that, for Bennett, life is a kind of martyrdom that individuals are capable of bearing heroically, but he has not discovered what it *means*. *The Old Wives' Tale*, an epical summation of community feeling and social values in the industrial Midlands, fails to answer life's basic conundrums. To ask Bennett "What must I do to be saved?" is a waste of breath. Applied to the epics by Dante and Goethe, however, the question makes more sense. It is posed tacitly throughout *Point Counter Point*, but the parodic formative intelligence at the novel's centre, Quarles speaking for Huxley, gives voice to a nonplussed generation by suggesting that no totally reliable answer is to be found.

In *Point Counter Point*, Huxley has an abundance of explanations of what life is. His point is that he can see through them all. From the biological standpoint, ideals such as art and beauty, so essential to Romanticism, seem impossible to authenticate. From the philosopher's vantage point, science seems to have reduced man to a soulless propagating animal controlled by a nervous system of easily conditioned reflexes. Darwin, Einstein, and Freud leave little room for Wordsworth and Shelley, and vice versa. The historian's explanations are no sounder than the chemist's, a religious attitude no more complete than one that is predominantly economic or political. Consequently, the non-congenital novelist of ideas in Huxley discounts positive explanatory hypotheses even as Quarles seeks them. He becomes the mind of his age ironically. Only a Pyrrhonist or Jesting Pilate, it seems, can speak for the twenties. Huxley has it both ways: the failure of a genuine poet-philosopher to emerge remains part of the satire he directs against modern life; at the same time, the mind for the age does appear, in parodic form, as the archly satirical contrapuntist, a sceptic who deals in permanent paradoxes or absolute oppositions, not in naturalistic reductions, like Bennett's, or fanciful reconciliations. He balances Rampion's view of life as sane harmoniousness against Spandrell's conception of it as "the essential horror," a "bad and tedious jape" too "absurd" to qualify as "tragical" (542). He is as realistic as Bennett, as vitalistic as Lawrence, romantic like Blake, yet vitriolic and cynical: in short, a burlesque chameleon poet, overtaxed to reflect an amorphous age.

Having assessed the quality of contemporary intellectual discussion, Huxley finds no completely satisfactory attitude toward life in operation anywhere. The majority of men have no genuinely healthy "relation . . . to the world." Quarles is obliged to make these painful conclusions into parodic first principles, thereby achieving and frustrating coalescence simultaneously. The framework *Point Counter Point* posits in 1928 is satiric and negative: modern life as a musical piece badly played, a contrapuntal travesty of good composition, an exercise in cacophony. Huxley is forced to parody poet-philosophers he would rather emulate. As conflicting opinions disable one another in a series of discussion scenes, the eighteen hundred million self-centred instruments in the "human fugue" (32), Quarles's satiric image for modern life, make Wordsworth's "still, sad music of humanity" sound even sadder.

Seeing into life's discords, the "diverse laws" that lie absurdly at the heart of things, does more than determine authorial procedure. Counterpoint becomes an anti-Romantic idea about the basis of things, a satiric proposition about life, as well as Huxley's dominant structural technique. *Point Counter Point* is a paragon of the novel of ideas in that it is governed, thematically and structurally, by an idea of its author: one of the novel's major ideas, counterpoint, furnishes the concept around which the book itself is constructed.[25] The invention of a poet-philosopher-scientist, counterpoint gives musical dimension to philosophical dilemmas arising from the modern era's foremost scientific theory: relativity and the consequent accumulation of contradictory, diverse truths. The thoughts of the atypical minority with ideas to express resist rewarding synthesis by a would-be orchestrating intelligence. Quarles's narrative techniques fail to produce a triumphant positive overview yet prove satirically appropriate to reveal the constantly proliferating diversity of modern life.

In *Point Counter Point*, the only guiding hypothesis offered is universal counterpoint: idea against idea, head against heart, body against mind, mind against matter, art against life, husband against wife, parent against child. Formless multiplicity becomes the most feasible accommodation for the nature of things. Multiformity of plot, character, mood and idea is Quarles's unifying principle. Synthesis Huxley accomplishes parodically by enclosing in one enormous structure all the friction, contradictions, and contrapuntal clamour that preclude—and therefore replace—positive governing laws. Seeing life whole in 1928 means cataloguing the ubiquity of discontinuity and self-division. The only absolute Huxley puts forth in the twenties is that there appears to be none. The only point worth making about modern life is its apparent pointlessness.

Huxley discovers that the human situation is even more fragmented than the poet-philosopher-scientist Lucretius imagined. Based on such findings, his best novel of ideas imitates *De Rerum Natura* even as he parodies it. By eliminating the fear of divine punishments, Lucretius compensates the readers he thrusts into a godless universe. In Huxley's epic novel, Fulke Greville's ideas about the human predicament are reasserted with contemporary examples. Huxley demolishes outmoded Romantic and Victorian attitudes, ridicules experimental life-styles, and frustrates the mind's desire for absolutes. Nevertheless, disturbing as the results are, he also confers upon his audience the joys of a sceptic's intellectual independence, the consolations of an enlightened, misanthropic pessimism.

Rampion's pursuit of perfect balance for body and mind is admittedly superior to Lucy Tantamount's desire for ever intenser pleasures, just as Quarles's hope of gaining omniscience by looking with everyone's eyes at once outranks his father's ambition to write the world's largest book on democracy. Yet, like Lord Edward in his search for a chemical solidarity beneath life's discontinuities, Rampion and Quarles are seekers of impossible absolutes, idealists embarked on parodically Faustian quests. Despite Rampion, imbalance predominates; the multiplicity of aspects Quarles sees never adds up. Goethe to the contrary, Huxley deflates his aspiring Fausts to offer additional proof for his thesis that no explanatory hypothesis, except incompleteness itself, encompasses all the facts, no passing moment of illusory synthesis is strong enough to last forever. At the same time, however, Quarles's plans for an aesthetics of simultaneity, his ideas about "The musicalization of fiction" (408), and his eagerness to confront the many different layers of reality with a "Multiplicity of eyes" (266) permit Huxley's novel of ideas to refute the inept notions he contends most conventional novelists have about writing realistic novels.

When Beatrice and the despicable Burlap take their baths together in the novel's final scene, Huxley passes stern judgement on the moral stature of his contemporaries. The novel's concluding exclamation: "Of such is the Kingdom of Heaven" (601), a sarcastic invocation of the Beatitudes, means its opposite. *Point Counter Point* defies the reader to construct a heavenly kingdom from its characters and proclaims itself, as well as the London it describes, a modernized, parodic version of Dante's *Inferno*. Even with Rampion as his Virgil, Quarles finds no exit.

Despite his cynical modernity, Huxley is old-fashioned enough to want to enlist the novelist of ideas in the great but unfortunately suspended tradition of poet-philosopher-scientists. Beginning in the twenties, he complains regularly that a certifiable mind for the modern age has yet to come forward. With Quarles too cold, Spandrell too bitter, and Rampion too atavistic and unscientific, *Point Counter Point* is about this failure. Huxley's satire in *Point Counter Point* and *Brave New World* often seems engrossed in discrediting the ideas of incompetent thinkers who must not be mistaken for the central intelligence the modern century desperately needs. Compared with Milton and Blake, scientists like Freud and Pavlov and technologists like Henry Ford lack the philosophical breadth, the humanistic understanding, to become the requisite polymath, while Eliot, Pound, and Yeats are criticized for not contemplating "lyrics of relativity" instead of refurbishing old myths.[26]

The twentieth century, Huxley complains "still awaits its Lucretius, awaits its own philosophical Dante, its new Goethe. . . . Will they appear?"[27] Huxley seems to have had doubts. With himself and Quarles as parodic versions of the mind for the modern age, he supplies the need at first in the only manner he thinks still possible. Simultaneously, he begins to groom himself to play the role in earnest. He plunders a variety of thinkers, classical as well as contemporary, for ideas he can assimilate into a "guiding hypothesis," "some kind of over-all understanding of the world."[28] Searching for this sort of comprehension, he continually experiments with the novel of ideas, devising new aspects that refute the charge that the form is monolithic.

In *Brave New World*, where the nature of happiness and the idea of freedom undergo severe scrutiny, Huxley employs the novel of ideas to satirize the related notions of several influential thinkers who work independently but constitute a latent conspiracy. The extra task the non-congenital novelist of ideas accepts in this case is to uncover hitherto unsuspected connections between current intellectual trends. Where *Point Counter Point* reveals a world of incommensurabilities, *Brave New World*, equally contrapuntal, exposes several prominent scientific and economic philosophies as invidious variations on the same themes. Huxley criticizes specific fallacies in the thinking of Freud, Ford, Pavlov, and J. B. Watson, whose ideas turn out to be compatible programs for the dehumanization of man. Constructing the brave new world in obedience to their complementary teachings, Huxley predicts awful consequences from the potential confluence of their mechanistically oriented aberrations.[29] Huxley revises the novel of ideas to combat a conglomeration of philosophies with another set he admires. Moving toward total awareness, Helmholtz Watson, an embryonic mystic and budding poet-philosopher, begins to mature contrary to Freudian and Pavlovian theories but in accord with precepts for spiritual growth in middle age that are borrowed respectfully from Gerald Heard, Maine de Biran, Cardinal Newman, and F. W. H. Myers.

The later Huxley writes less successful novels of ideas in which he expounds at length positive proposals of his own. He uses discussion scenes that encourage his ideas and the speakers representing them to win out over less appealing choices. In *Eyeless in Gaza* Huxley supports the socio-religious ideas of a character named Miller, a composite of Gerald Heard and F. M. Alexander. In *After Many a Summer Dies the Swan* Mr Propter, yet another rendition of Heard, enlarges on theories already familiar to readers from Miller. In a third example from the category of later Huxley novels, *Time Must Have a Stop*, the perennial philosophy of Bruno Rontini triumphs more decisively than Rampion's Greco-paganism did.

Rontini's disciple, Sebastian Barnack, appears on the verge of becoming the first full-fledged poet-philosopher in Huxley's fiction. At the end of the novel, he starts to formulate Rontini's Westernized version of Vedanta's *philosophia perennis*. This distillation of tenets common to most major religions he further condenses into a "Minimum Working Hypothesis," not reductive but expansive, that calls for a broadening of awareness. In the novel's "Epilogue," Barnack stipulates that man has a spiritual destiny. The Vedantic precept *tat tvam asi* ("That art thou") asserts that the immanent eternal self (Atman) in every man is identical with the Absolute Principle of all existence (Brahman), also called the divine Ground.[30] With Barnack offering reassurances of continued interplay between temporal and eternal, the "Minimum Working Hypothesis," however tentative the title sounds, seems intended as Huxley's equivalent for Milton's idea of the *felix culpa* and Goethe's confidence in salvation for indefatigable strivers. Evolutionary as well as salvationary, Barnack's explanatory thesis assumes that man-in-general may be able to expand his consciousness until he achieves participative unity with the divine Ground, something only a select number of gifted individuals throughout history—the mystics—have hitherto enjoyed. Huxley borrows from East and West for a master synthesis that bolsters occidental scientific theory and Romantic confidence in man's unconquerable mind with concepts from oriental philosophy.

Island epitomizes and virtually exhausts the kind of novel of ideas the later Huxley writes. To create the imaginary community of Pala, Huxley heroically amalgamates all the ideas he admires, his own and those of others, into a total paradigm for living based on assumptions Vedanta makes about man's Final End. Pala is a society in which all the details have been worked out in the light of Huxley's guiding hypothesis. The novel is meant to embody Huxley's long-sought "over-all understanding" of the world. It is his prescription for humanity, his answer to life's conundrums, such as what life is, what man is for, and how it is wisest for him to live. At the close of an illustrious career, Huxley, like Dr MacPhail, who is Pala's Prospero, finally tenders his era the kind of blueprint for salvation supplied more successfully to more fortunate periods by poet-philosophers like Dante and Goethe.

The Old Raja's treatise, *Notes on What's What*, is Pala's philosophy handbook.[31] With an allusion to Lucretius in its title, this spiritual guide takes an affirmative approach to human nature and the nature of things. A refinement on Barnack's remarks in the "Epilogue," the *Notes* justify God's ways to man by locating the real utopia within the individual soul, where every man supposedly harbours a particle of the divine. Will Farnaby is instructed that he can travel to this internal spiritual kingdom, the paradise within, even if the external state of affairs deteriorates, as indeed it soon does. It is conceivable that Farnaby will continue maturing, despite the annexation of Pala by Rendang, until he becomes the mind of his age and a living example of the next evolutionary stage for mankind.

Were men able to evolve a society that perfectly reenforces their essential spirituality, Huxley predicts Pala would be the result. For his excellent island, he combines ideas from sources as disparate as Margaret Mead's Samoans, the Oneida Community of John Humphrey Noyes, and Indo-European societies that worshipped divinely inebriating mushrooms.[32] In the pliable literary utopia the poet-philosopher discovers an ideal format for a religious hypothesis about the nature of man, to which he believes the mutually corroborative testimony of mystics throughout the ages gives a kind of scientific validity. Describing his conception of paradise regained, Huxley confirms an affinity between the novel of ideas and fictional accounts of ideal societies. Huxley imagines an enlightened community and, in the process, defines utopia as a society organized according to all the best ideas. Huxley must have hoped, too optimistically it turns out, that *Island* would be hailed as a successor to *The Divine Comedy* and *De Rerum Natura*, just as *Point Counter Point* was intended as their ironic antithesis.

Unfortunately, Huxley's most novel idea about the novel of ideas— that it must serve as the modern surrogate for ancient compendiums of wisdom—has not been generally accepted. The perennial philosophy remains timeless but has yet to become universal. And Huxley himself had reservations about the viability of Pala.[33] To speak as the formative mind for the modern age may be too great a handicap for anyone. Huxley's penchant for didacticism, evident alike in Rampion's discourses and Dr MacPhail's, makes him vulnerable to the charge that he comes to resemble the Victorian and Edwardian "obfuscators" he began by satirizing, when, actually, he hoped to succeed where he felt Wordsworth and Tennyson failed.[34] Either Huxley's guiding hypothesis has not been sufficiently persuasive or his ideal, the novelist of ideas, is a victim of processes he was not able to reverse: the accelerating breakdown of unity into diversity, which is ultimately a synonym for secularization, and the continuing preference for know-how over wisdom.

Conceivably, Huxley is the last of the polymaths, the last modern with the ability and audacity to pattern his career on the great poet-philosophers. The novel of ideas is in danger of becoming a museum piece like the epic poems it was scheduled to replace. Huxley's life-long quarrel with congenital novelists and his development of the novel of ideas as a corrective for their fiction may be the final attempt in this century to train a philosophical mind on an era's dominant scientific and religious theories via the storyteller's art. Huxley tends to urge and admonish. Unlike in every other way, congenital novelists and post-moderns share a reluctance to do this. They eschew the novel of ideas because they dare not imitate the later Huxley's confidence in the Old Raja's optimistic professions, a confidence that was once the goal of every modern with a sense of lost values and the desire to rehabilitate them. The Old Raja boasts that he possesses something the Pyrrhonist in the early Huxley also has but only in a negative, pessimistic sense: "a clear idea about what's what" (38).[35]

Notes

1. George Catlin delivers this judgement while reviewing *After Many a Summer Dies the Swan* in the *Saturday Review of Literature*, 27 Jan. 1940, p. 5.

2. Doris Lessing, *The Golden Notebook* (New York: Bantam Books, 1973), p. xiv.

3. Aldous Huxley, *Point Counter Point* (London: Chatto & Windus, 1928), pp. 409–10. Subsequent references to the first edition appear by page numbers in parentheses.

4. Letter for 25 March 1945 in Grover Smith, ed., *Letters of Aldous Huxley* (London: Chatto & Windus, 1969), p. 516.

5. See Jerome Meckier, "Quarles Among the Monkeys: Huxley's Zoological Novels," *Modern Language Review*, 68 (1973), 268–82.

6. Douglas Hewitt, *The Approach to Fiction* (Totowa, New Jersey: Rowan and Littlefield, 1972), pp. 147–48. Throughout this essay, I take issue with chapter eight of Hewitt's study, "Entertaining Ideas: *Crotchet Castle*." Hewitt states negatively several opinions previously expressed more sympathetically by Frederick Hoffman. His analysis of Huxley's "unusual and interesting adaptation of a respectable art form" contends that ideas in Huxley's fiction become his characters. See "Aldous Huxley and the Novel of Ideas," William Van O'Connor, ed., *Forms of Modern Fiction* (Bloomington: Indiana University Press, 1959), pp. 189–200.

7. Anti-Bloomsbury themes are discussed in Jerome Meckier, "Philip Quarles' Passage to India: *Jesting Pilate*, *Point Counter Point* and Bloomsbury," *Studies in the Novel*, 9 (Winter, 1977), 445–67.

8. A dramatizer of ideas, Huxley consistently ranks "the novel form" above the treatise because "the fictionally embodied idea" seems "different from, and much more alive than, the 'same idea' in the abstract." See the letter to Henry S. Canby for 9 May 1929, in *Letters*, p. 312.

9. Letter to Eugene Saxton for 24 May 1933, in *Letters*, p. 371.

10. George Wickes and Ray Frazer, "Aldous Huxley," in *Writers at Work: The Paris Review Interviews*, Second Series, ed. George Plimpton (New York: Viking Compass, 1965), p. 206.

11. In a letter to Canby for 17 January 1929, Huxley admits that models for characters in *Point Counter Point* are both contemporary and "historical." *Letters*, p. 312, n. 288a.

12. Hewitt's argument that novelists with ideas are innately superior to novelists of ideas and render them superfluous is unacceptable. See "Novels of Ideas and Ideas in Novels," chapter nine of *The Approach to Fiction*.

13. Stephen Spender distinguishes "moderns" from "contemporaries" in an excerpt from *The Struggle of the Modern* in *The Idea of the Modern in Literature and the Arts*, ed. Irving Howe (New York: Horizon Press, 1967), pp. 43–49. Mrs Woolf castigates "materialists"

in "Modern Fiction," in Mark Schorer, ed., *Modern British Fiction* (New York: Oxford University Press, 1961), pp. 3–9.

14. Aldous Huxley, "Subject Matter of Poetry," in *On the Margin* (London: Chatto & Windus, 1923), p. 36.

15. Francis Chelifer delivers these comments for Huxley in *Those Barren Leaves* (London: Chatto & Windus, 1925), pp. 96–97.

16. Huxley's borrowings from philosophy and the sciences are often intended for imaginative use (whether satiric or utopian) and need not denote literal belief on the part of the appropriator. Thus the disfavour Sheldon fell into with his fellow scientists never bothered Huxley as much as it should have.

17. *Paris Review Interviews*, p. 205.

18. Letter for 18 January 1927, in *Letters*, p. 281.

19. Quarles blames the childhood accident that crippled his foot for the sedentary, cerebral cast of a life intensely private and withdrawn. Rampion is an exception, a refugee from the lower classes who overcomes physical and social infirmities, but "the little carroty" Illidge (48), a part-time anarchist, remains the prisoner of a cockney upbringing and an unimpressive physique. In a universe of "diverse laws," men are commanded to be sound by vitalists like Rampion but created sick like Spandrell, who never outgrows Oedipal anxieties about his mother.

20. Letter for 26 November 1923, in *Letters*, p. 224.

21. Letter for 29 April 1924, in *Letters*, p. 228.

22. This essay in *On the Margin* (pp. 26–38) is central to Huxley's philosophy of art.

23. Aldous Huxley, *Literature and Science* (New York: Harper and Row, 1963), p. 82.

24. Arnold Bennett, *The Old Wives' Tale* (New York: Signet, 1963), p. 530. Subsequent references are by page numbers in parentheses.

25. See Jerome Meckier, *Aldous Huxley: Satire and Structure* (London: Chatto & Windus, 1969).

26. *On the Margin*, p. 30, and *Literature and Science*, pp. 59, 112.

27. *On the Margin*, p. 38.

28. Letter to Victoria Ocampo quoted in Sybille Bedford, *Aldous Huxley: A Biography*, Vol. II, *1939–1963* (London: Chatto & Windus, 1974), p. 74.

29. See Jerome Meckier, "Our Ford, Our Freud and the Behaviorist Conspiracy in Huxley's *Brave New World*," *Thalia*, 1 (Spring, 1978), 35–59.

30. Aldous Huxley, *Time Must Have a Stop* (London: Chatto & Windus, 1945), pp. 287 ff., and *The Perennial Philosophy* (London: Chatto & Windus, 1946), p. 8.

31. Aldous Huxley, *Island* (London: Chatto & Windus, 1962), pp. 38–39, 132. Subsequent reference is by page number in parentheses.

32. See Jerome Meckier, "Coming of Age in Pala: The Primitivism of *Brave New World* Reconsidered in *Island*," *Alternative Futures*, 1 (Summer, 1978), 68–90; and R. Gordon Wasson, *Soma: Divine Mushroom of Immortality* (New York: Harcourt Brace Jovanovich, 1968), pp. 175–76.

33. See Jerome Meckier, "Cancer in Utopia: Positive and Negative Elements in Huxley's *Island*," *Dalhousie Review*, 54 (Winter, 1974–75), 619–33.

34. Harold H. Watts denies Huxley full modernity in "The Viability of *Point Counter Point*," *Studies in the Novel*, 9 (Winter, 1977), 414. Similarly, Anthony Powell confesses that Huxley's brilliance still impresses him but not the Huxley who teaches moral lessons. See *Infants of the Spring* (London: Heinemann, 1976), p. 145.

35. On the other hand, Huxley's novels of ideas leave their mark on authors as diverse as Waugh, Burgess, Powell, Murdoch, and Lessing. Throughout *The Golden Notebook*, for example, Lessing benefits enormously from Quarles's suggestion that the novelist of ideas put into his novel a novelist who is also writing a novel.

The Fire of Prometheus: Romanticism and the Baroque in Huxley's *Antic Hay* and *Those Barren Leaves*

ROBERT S. BAKER

In *Jesting Pilate*, published in 1926, the year following the appearance of *Those Barren Leaves*, Aldous Huxley observed that "the fire of Prometheus is put to the strangest uses,"[1] a judgment that could easily serve as an epigraph to the early novels, particularly to what Jerome Meckier has described as the "natural trilogy"[2] of *Crome Yellow* (1921), *Antic Hay* (1923), and *Those Barren Leaves* (1925). Huxley's critics have neglected the repeated references to prophecy and apocalypse in *Those Barren Leaves*, particularly as they pervade the novel's atmosphere, gradually adumbrating its central themes and linking it to *Antic Hay*, a work equally concerned with romantic Prometheanism. Huxley regarded romanticism as identical in style and substance with baroque painting and architecture, arguing that both modes were cultural aberrations from a norm established by artists like Sir Christopher Wren. In the early novels and essays he consistently associated what he referred to in *Along the Road* as the "extravagant baroque, romantic style"[3] with a dead end of philosophical and aesthetic extremes, with a passion for theatrical display and histrionic self-mythologizing. But Huxley's criticism of romanticism is only in part an aesthetic issue. Its primary significance lies with its historical implications, with Huxley's interpretation of modern history and the intimate connection, in Huxley's view, between the restiveness of a postwar society that seemed to pursue, if not endorse, the fragile and fragmentary apocalypses of a Lilian Aldwinkle or a Maurice Spandrell, and the cultural roots of that society extending back to the formative experiences of the romantic period.

Sanford Marovitz has suggestively observed that "even in his earliest fiction, Huxley's references to painting and artists generally do serve a distinctive thematic or satiric purpose."[4] Huxley's interest in art history, however, shaped his approach to the art of fiction to a greater degree than Marovitz allows for. The early novels are filled with references to painting, sculpture,

Reprinted from *Texas Studies in Literature and Language* 19 (Spring 1977): 60–82, with permission of the author and the University of Texas Press.

and architecture, and especially to romantic Prometheanism, to prophecy and "revelation"[5] as well as to the major romantic poets, Shelley, Wordsworth, Keats, and Byron. Huxley's interest in romantic poetry and baroque architecture and his condemnation of its underlying aesthetic and epistemological assumptions is inseparable from his endeavor to probe and anatomize the intellectual and psychological matrices of postwar culture. He was intent on not merely holding up a mirror to an increasingly divisive society but on comprehending its historical roots, particularly as they extend back to the "Romantic Revival" (*TBL*, 37) and its Promethean aspirations. At the same time, once the significance of these allusions to romantic and baroque art is understood, particularly as they are used to inform specific symbolic settings within the early novels, then the issue of the aesthetic unity of the early novels can be, if not resolved, at least placed on a more comprehensible footing.

The problem of narrative structure in *Those Barren Leaves* is a case in point, having occupied a number of Huxley's critics, most of whom appear to be united in their condemnation of the novel's thematic complexity. Most recently Keith May has described the book as comprised of "heterogeneous elements" that yield a fictive structure "less unified"[6] than *Antic Hay* or *Crome Yellow*. Laurence Brander finds it a "strangely lengthened novel" padded out with digressive subplots and "much irrelevant material,"[7] while George Woodcock simply asserts that the novel "has several themes."[8] Peter Firchow, however, argues that, while the novel has "virtually no plot," it does exhibit "tight thematic unity,"[9] and Jerome Meckier discovers the organizing principle in the various love stories that display both "similarity in situation and simultaneity in action."[10] As both Firchow and Meckier have noted, Huxley has a more cogent and holistic grasp of his materials than has often been admitted, although I would argue that the unity of *Those Barren Leaves* proceeds from a different but related source first defined in *Antic Hay* and the essays of *On the Margin*.

The various characters and subplots of *Those Barren Leaves* are drawn together by means of a skillfully managed web of interrelated motifs dealing with journeys, acting, and the possibility of reaching the threshold of some kind of final prophetic disclosure. All three of these motifs are elaborated within the more general context of Huxley's criticism of "baroque romantic" art; indeed, they are symptomatic of a culture that has not freed itself of "the cult of the emotions" that "began in the nineteenth century" and its attendant quest for prophetic vision. Lilian Aldwinkle waits patiently for "the one supremely important, revealing, apocalyptic thing" (*TBL*, 63) and, like the youthful Francis Chelifer, she hopes for a "revelation" (*TBL*, 122) as a consequence of her ambition to "think the one apocalyptic thought" (*TBL*, 64). Mrs. Aldwinkle will fail to impose her "mythopoeic faculties" (*TBL*, 300) on a recalcitrant world much as Chelifer's Shelleyan idealism "revealed . . . apocalyptically" (*TBL*, 130) what was, in fact, merely a self-imposed delusion. Mary Thriplow searches for "emotional revelations" (*TBL*, 266) while the "eloquently prophetical" Mr. Falx (*TBL*, 61), the embittered socialist, also confesses his willingness to play the "prophetic part" (*TBL*, 189). Even the idiot, Grace Elver, is busy "conjuring up fairy palaces" (*TBL*, 242), and her brother, Philip, boasts of his own sinister ability to "prophesy" (*TBL*, 235). Irene, Mrs. Aldwinkle's niece, looks "prophetically forward" (*TBL*, 355) to a new life apart from her aunt, who in turn provides Chelifer with an architecturally contrived "moment of revelation" (*TBL*, 170) at her villa, the Cybo Malaspina, the counterpart to Chelifer's earlier and equally disappointing "divine revelation" (*TBL*, 122) on the summit of Wordsworth's Snowdon. To comprehend the range and depth of these allusions, however, it is necessary to examine Huxley's attitude towards romantic Prometheanism, its connection with baroque art, and finally Huxley's use of Sir Christopher Wren and Shelley as the representatives of two contending impulses.

In *On The Margin*, published in 1923, Huxley commented on the centenaries of both Wren's death (in 1723) and Shelley's (in 1822). In "Centenaries," written while Huxley was in Italy (on the Viareggio where, as he notes, Shelley's body was cremated), he described the function of a centenary as an occasion for reassessment "that we may see precisely where, in relation to their achievement, we stand at the present time, that we may appraise the life still left in their spirit and apply to ourselves the moral of their example."[11] Huxley's assessment of Shelley, unlike his straightforward endorsement of Wren, is significantly ambivalent. Shelley is praised as a "literary innovator" but gently chided as the author of "strangely childish poetry"; on the one hand, he is described as a "dangerous young man" but, on the other, condescendingly characterized as "beautiful and child-like" (*OM*, 2). The essay on Wordsworth in the same volume sheds further light on Huxley's reservations concerning Shelley's achievement and that of the "Romantic Revival" in general.

Huxley defined romanticism as a movement based on "theories" that were not only "emotional on principle" (*OM*, 188) but that attempted the "conversion of emotions into intellectual terms" (*OM*, 156) and then proceeded to erect "a whole cosmogony" (*OM*, 157) on what, from Huxley's point of view, was a demonstrably irrational basis. Such a judgment strikes at the very foundation of Wordsworth's *Prelude*, of his attempt to record his emotional growth as, in M. H. Abrams's words, "an evangelist of a new redemption"[12] and to describe his apocalyptic revelations in the valley of the Gondo and on the summit of Snowdon as well as his identification of the visionary imagination with "Reason in her most exalted mood." The *Prelude* plays a key role in *Those Barren Leaves*, and Huxley linked it with what he understood to be one of the defining traits of the romantic sensibility, the "dangerous" faith in "inenarrable emotions" (*OM*, 157) that lay at the basis of the romantic theory of the imagination. His general conception of romanticism, however, was complicated by both his interpretation of the painting and architecture of the baroque period and the appearance of what he termed "new" or "inverse romanticism."

In "Sir Christopher Wren," Huxley celebrated the ideal artist whose work is equally antithetical to the poetry of Shelley and the engravings of Piranesi. The artists who figure in the thematic structure of *Antic Hay* and *Those Barren Leaves* are precisely those who, in the essays, are cited as representatives of two opposing aesthetics. Wren, like the "innovative" Shelley, is an "artist of profoundly original mind" (*OM*, 178), whose "most characteristic quality . . . is . . . rather moral than aesthetic" (*OM*, 179). What Huxley finds so commendable in Wren's work is his rejection of the triumphal sublimity of the baroque, an ornate and mannered theatricality that in Huxley's view had divested itself of everything human. Wren's art is founded on "reason and order" and his distrust of the "extravagance and excess" (*OM*, 179) of the baroque style: "Wren, the restrained and dignified gentleman, stands out most clearly when we compare him with his Italian contemporaries. The baroque artists of the seventeenth century were interested in the new, the startling, the astonishing; they strained after impossible grandeurs, unheard-of violences." Baroque art was not only atectonic but inherently illusory: "The architectural ideals of which they dreamed were more suitable for embodiment in theatrical cardboard than in stone. And indeed, the late seventeenth and early eighteenth century was the golden age of scene-painting in Italy" (*OM*, 179–80). Wren's art of "sober restraint" is "never theatrical" while his masterpiece, St. Paul's cathedral, is in essence "a country gentleman's house." If Wren's St. Paul's is a "monument of temperance and chastity," the work of his successors was "infected by a touch of the baroque *folie de grandeur*," as a consequence of which the "architects of the eighteenth century built houses in imitation of Versailles and Caserta— huge stage houses, all for show and magnificence and all but impossible to live in" (*OM*, 180). Mrs. Aldwinkle's Cybo Malaspina, as I shall show later, is such a huge stage house, a romantic palace of art associated with baroque theatricality and prophetic illusion.

The connection between baroque spectacle and romantic subjectivity forms a continuous thread in Huxley's early work. In *Along the Road*, published in the same year as *Those Barren Leaves*, he continues to evolve the rough typology of styles begun in *On the Margin*, characterizing the essential nature of what he now refers to as "the baroque style and the kindred romantic style" as marked by a "mistrust of realism"[13]—the same charge that he will level at modern art (as symptomatic of the "new romanticism") in *Music at Night*. He also insists that "almost all baroque art and almost all the kindred romantic art of a later epoch are grotesque because the artists (not of the first order) are trying to express something tragic in terms of a style essentially comic" (*AR*, 174). Abjuring the disciplined restraint of Wren's art and laboring for illusory effects, the baroque-romantic style is always associated in Huxley's mind with both violent deformation and histrionic emotions. In *Those Barren Leaves*, Huxley employs the realist Cardan as a spokesman for his condemnation of the Romantic Revival: "Romanticism, of which the seventeenth-century baroque is a queer sub-species, makes violent gestures; it relies on violent contrasts of light and shade, on stage effects; it is ambitious to present you with emotions in the raw" (*TBL*, 207). In the early novels, Huxley's houses are symbolic settings that generally align themselves with one of the antithetical aesthetics represented by Wren or Shelley. Crome, for example, is seen by Mr. Scogan, another sober realist, as primarily a human artifact based on an aesthetic that is explicitly compared to Shelley's: "The great thing about Crome . . . is the fact that it's so unmistakably and aggressively a work of art. It makes no compromise with nature, but affronts it and rebels against it. It has no likeness to Shelley's tower in the 'Epipsychidion.' "[14] The chthonic nature of Shelley's tower in the *Epipsychidion* and its dramatic emphasis on darkness and light is, for Scogan and Huxley, another piece of baroque scene-painting, a Piranesian miniature of obfuscating shadows and nebulous outline. Crome, although a sixteenth-century house, stands for the thoroughly credible values of Wren, for clarity and control, while Shelley's tower is a symbol of the Promethean histrionics embodied most fully in Casimir Lypiatt of *Antic Hay*.

Casimir Lypiatt is not, as Milton Birnbaum would have him, an endorsement of the "need for suffering"[15] on the part of the artist—a need that would be incomprehensible to Huxley's Wren. Lypiatt conceives of himself as a medium for the trumpeting imagination. Like Shelley (particularly in *Adonais*), he is fond of identifying himself with prophets and martyrs, including Cain, Christ, and Prometheus—and, surprisingly, Wren as well. The reader is first introduced to Lypiatt as an artist dwelling at the end of "a long *cul de sac*"[16] that, significantly, resembles the "entrance of one of Piranesi's prisons" (*AH*, 87). In *On the Margin*, Huxley cited Piranesi as a typical Baroque artist, unrestrained and theatrical. Accordingly, the "Piranesian arch" (*AH*, 87) that spans the entrance to Lypiatt's studio is not a gratuitous architectural detail but, rather, the fitting emblem of a cultural dead end, an aesthetic impasse that Lypiatt, despite his consciousness of having a "mission" (*AH*, 45), will fail to recognize. Indeed, he eventually commits suicide in his studio. As a crusading Promethean, he is associated with Veronese, a baroque master of *trompe l'oeil*, and is busily engaged in the creation of a "great Crucifixion . . . as big and headlong as a Veronese" (*AH*, 48). Referring to Shelley's *Adonais*, he insists that the man of genius "bears upon his brow a kind of mark of Cain" (*AH*, 48), and in the final chapters (before his suicide) he refers to himself as a "dead Christ" (*AH*, 273) lacking only the evidence of the stigmata. His baroque "Crucifixion" is, in essence, a self-portrait of the guilt-cursed romantic visionary filled with self-pity and self-exultation. He "sees himself as a misunderstood and embittered Prometheus" (*AH*, 88); and, as a self-proclaimed "prophet" (*AH*,

119) speaking with "the voice of Prometheus" (*AH*, 91), he chose as his text Shelley's "Ode to the West Wind," a poem that he repeatedly invokes as a romantic manifesto. Lypiatt's endorsement of "passion and feeling" (*AH*, 96) or the "inenarrable emotions" that Huxley repudiated in "Wordsworth" lead to his exuberant identification with Shelley in which he casts himself in the role of the poet's voice in the "Ode to the West Wind," rhapsodizing about the "great wind that is in me" and "the wild west wind" that he conflates with "life itself, its God" (*AH*, 94). For Lypiatt, the wind is the divine afflatus, the Promethean spirit of the artist who "rushes on the world, conquers it, gives it beauty, imposes a moral significance" (*AH*, 95). And while he claims to be "like Wren" an opponent of "abject specialization" (*AH*, 46), he nevertheless repudiates the basis of the latter's art.

Antic Hay is Huxley's celebration of Wren's bicentenary, and, in accordance with his definition of what a centenary should accomplish, it is a reappraisal "that we may see precisely where, in relation to . . . [his] achievement, we stand at the present time." Gumbril Senior, throughout the novel, is systematically associated with Wren's architecture and, not unexpectedly, is explicitly placed in opposition to the baroque style represented by Piranesi. In chapter 11, Gumbril Junior listens to his father expounding on his plans for the architectural renovation of London in which Wren's "dome of St. Paul's" (*AH*, 175) would be employed as the hub of a rationally ordered community: "Looking at him, Gumbril Junior could imagine that he saw before him the passionate and gesticulating silhouette of one of those old shepherds who stand at the base of Piranesi's ruins demonstrating obscurely the prodigious grandeur and the abjection of the human race" (*AH*, 177). In Gumbril Junior's mental picture, "Piranesi's ruins" are the charred remnants of old London after the great fire, a "disgusting chaos" (*AH*, 158) that his father, as a disciple of Wren, will reorder by means of an "intellectually ripened" aesthetic. Lypiatt, however, entrapped within one of "Piranesi's prisons" (*AH*, 87), prefers the baroque illusions of Veronese and eventually dies in his "*cul de sac.*"

In a letter to Mrs. Flora Strousse, written on 9 May 1929, six years after the publication of *Antic Hay*, Huxley criticized one of her short stories dealing with an insane artist, insisting that "it wd [*sic*] have been more interesting, because more cruel, if it had been about a less extreme case— not a madman but somebody like B. R. Haydon, sane, but with an infinite faith in himself completely unjustified by forty years of passionate and industrious self-expression. The fact that faith *can't* move mountains is one of the corner-stones of tragedy—also of comedy."[17] Huxley's portrait of Casimir Lypiatt is based in part on the life of the romantic painter Benjamin Haydon, an artist whose huge canvases and ambitiously conceived historical subjects failed to assure him the renown he so passionately sought. Haydon's suicide, like Lypiatt's, was a grotesquely nihilistic gesture that Huxley regarded as entirely characteristic of the romantic's inflation of both the artist's powers and, as an inescapable corollary, his expectations as well.

Lypiatt, then, is Huxley's satirical portrait of "romantic bardism" (MN, 282). Living under a Piranesian arch that "threw vivid lights and enormous architectural shadows" (AH, 87) exemplifying the baroque obsession with dramatic contrasts of light and dark, Lypiatt is a self-dramatizing illusionist who alternately adopts the highly emotional roles of outcast (Cain), savior (Christ), and visionary martyr (Prometheus). His "fantastic egoism" (AH, 46) leads him to believe that he lives more intensely, feels more deeply, than the average man, and that, consequently, his creations are somehow consecrated by a spirit of prophecy. But in Jesting Pilate, Huxley rejected "prophetic visions" or the "New Jerusalems of prophecy" (JP, 141) that could only thrive on a romantic aesthetic that conceived of art as "something sacred" (JP, 264) and the artist as a "priest" (JP, 265) or a "prophet of heroic grandeurs" (AH, 119).

In Music at Night, Huxley condemned what he saw as the "new romanticism,"[18] a style that, like the suicidal Lypiatt, was "headed straight towards death" (MN, 220). The new or "reversed romanticism," as a counterpart of the "old romanticism," betrayed a self-destructive impulse because "its subject-matter [was] arbitrarily simplified by the exclusion of all the great eternal obviousness of human nature" (MN, 30). The old romanticism, fundamentally egocentric, involved an "exaggeration of the significance of the soul and the individual" (MN, 220), while the new was founded upon a profoundly inhumane "disparagement of spiritual and individual values" (MN, 216). Lypiatt embodies both tendencies, but his painting of Myra Viveash is a crucial and instructive example of the growing predominance of the latter. As a conventionally romantic artist who believed in "the aristocratic individual" (AH, 90) and who based his work on "passion and feeling," he characteristically selected Promethean subjects, "Crucifixions, martyrs, and triumphs of great men" (AH, 96). But his portrait of Mrs. Viveash demonstrates his affinity with the "new romanticism" as well: "It was a stormy vision of her, it was Myra seen, so to speak, through a tornado. He had distorted her in the portrait, had made her longer and thinner than she really was, had turned her arms into sleek tubes and put a bright metallic polish on the curve of her cheek" (AH, 93). Lypiatt's deformative style is symptomatic of what in the essays Huxley refers to as "the Cubist dehumanization of art," a style marked by "a romantic . . . admiration for machines" (MN, 217). The term "romantic" had, by the time Huxley wrote "The New Romanticism," come to mean any style that, like the baroque, is "extravagant and one-sided (that is to say . . . romantic)," and "modern romanticism" was simply the "romanticism of Shelley" only "turned inside out" (MN, 212). Thinking probably of Ferdinand Leger or, as Marovitz has suggested,[19] of Modigliani, Huxley depicts Lypiatt's "stormy" portrait as the misguided attempt of a modern romantic "to reproduce the forms invented by engineers"

(*MN*, 217). The "sleek tubes" and "bright metallic polish" represent a turning away from "reason and order" (*MN*, 219), the same phrase Huxley had used earlier to characterize the art of Sir Christopher Wren in *On the Margin*, while the "tornado" that shaped the portrait is the modern counterpart of Shelley's west wind.

Similarly, Lypiatt's poem, "Look down, Conquistador" (*AH*, 95), is a parody of Keats's sonnet, "On First Looking into Chapman's Homer," a celebration of the artist's visionary power to discover new worlds and, like Lypiatt's poem, metaphorically structured around the Spanish exploration and conquest of Central America. Lypiatt's "coming man" is the romantic Promethean whose "golden dream," like Keats's "Realms of gold," is a long-awaited apocalyptic revelation. Looking down from the Promethean heights, the artist as conquistador (like Keats's Cortez) can see his vision, but, significantly, the poem ends abruptly in a manner that foreshadows Lypiatt's failure to realize his ambition and, as a consequence, his eventual suicide. Moreover, his obsession with the prophetic disclosure of a "reality more than human" (*AH*, 64) extends to the other characters, but in an increasingly debased form. Rosie Shearwater, fascinated by "fortune-teller's prophecies" (*AH*, 249), views the egocentric aesthete, Mercaptan, as "the definitive revelation" (*AH*, 264). The old anti-Semite that Gumbril Junior encounters on the train rants "like the prophet Jonah" (*AH*, 244), and Gumbril Junior himself feels like a "prophet in Nineveh" (*AH*, 80) where the only "revelation" (*AH*, 213) is the cacophony of jazz.

Huxley's interpretation of modern history aligns itself, to a surprising degree, with his ethical classification of styles in art. Rejecting Virginia Woolf's well-known observation that the mind of Europe had changed decisively around December 1910, he wrote in "Art and the Obvious" that "those who proclaim that human nature has changed since August 4th 1914, are merely rationalizing their terrors and disgusts" (*MN*, 31). In "Accidie," however, he admitted the undeniable impact of "the appalling catastrophe of the War of 1914" and lamented that "in no century have the disillusionments followed on one another's heels with such unintermitted rapidity as in the Twentieth" (*OM*, 25). But Huxley claimed that modern history, like modern art, does not represent a shift so radical that it must be viewed as absolutely unique. Rather, he insisted on the centrality of the romantic period, arguing "that something has happened is surely simply history since 1789" (*OM*, 23). The War of 1914 had, in Huxley's view, merely provided additional momentum for tendencies that had already come into play as a consequence of the revolution of 1789. The unfulfilled aspirations of the "Romantic Revival," particularly as they took the form of a quest for a fundamentally evasive apocalypse, whether aesthetic, religious, or political, were responsible for the destructive cleavages of postwar society. The early twentieth century was, for Huxley, a period of cultural drifting in which modern values and ideals remained historically enmeshed with the obsolescent conventions of both a traditional romanticism and a significant variation in the form of a new "reversed" romanticism. The result was a malaise first defined in "Accidie" and more carefully analyzed in "The New Romanticism." This preoccupation with the "baroque romantic" mode extends throughout the Huxley canon and is founded on a perception of a society constantly jeopardized by its confused allegiances to worn-out conventions: "The activities of our age are uncertain and multifarious. No single literary, artistic, or philosophic tendency predominates. There is a babel of notions and conflicting theories. But in the midst of this general confusion, it is possible to recognize one curious and significant melody . . . the tune of our modern romanticism" (*MN*, 212). In *Antic Hay* this tune is played with a vengeance by the histrionic Lypiatt, the "ridiculous actor of heroic parts" (*AH*, 274), while in *Those Barren Leaves* its final exhaustion is embodied in both Francis Chelifer, who will climb the sacred mountain of English romanticism, Wordsworth's Snowdon, and Lilian Aldwinkle, who will attempt to inspire Chelifer by introducing him to the mysteries of her baroque palace of art, the Cybo Malaspina.

The chief link between Lypiatt and Chelifer is Shelley and romantic accidie, while Lypiatt's Piranesian "*cul de sac*" reappears on a more grandiose scale in the form of Mrs. Aldwinkle's villa. Lilian Aldwinkle is more than a wealthy hostess. She is a restless promoter of the imaginative life, particularly as it endeavors to realize unpossessable ranges of experience. As a woman of "romantic yearnings" (*TBL*, 185), she radically distorts her world "through the dense refractive medium of her imagination" and feverishly endorses Lypiatt's romantic Prometheanism. Leading the "higher life" (*TBL*, 60) on the heights of the Cybo, she is the inhabitant, or, more precisely, the prisoner of an ivory tower. Like the poet Dennis in *Crome Yellow* who, at the novel's conclusion, is helplessly isolated in Crome's tower gazing down at life in the form of the charity bazaar, Lilian clings to her belief in the artist as a superior being, insisting that "through art man comes nearest to being a god . . . a god" (*TBL*, 60). In saving Chelifer, she believes that she has "rescued a poet from death" (*TBL*, 184) and, in restoring him to the Cybo, that she will place him in the one setting where "he should gather . . . new inspiration" (*TBL*, 180). Like Lypiatt, she dramatizes her role, conceiving her relationship with her new guest in terms of a baroquely theatrical painting by Augustus John: "She saw herself standing there on the beach between sea and sky, and with mountains in the middle distance, looking like one of those wonderfully romantic figures who, in the paintings of Augustus John, stand poised in a meditative and passionate ecstasy against a cosmic background" while Chelifer lies "at her feet, like Shelley" (*TBL*, 180). The monstrous inflation of the imaginary John is reflected in the Cybo itself, a world wholly defined by art and a baroque projection of her histrionic imagination. But Lilian, who searches forlornly for the "revealing, apocalyptic thing" (*TBL*, 63), is discouragingly inarticulate, having been endowed "with no power of self-expression" and even in ordinary conversation unable "to give utterance to what she wanted to say." Her language is a muddle of "fragments of sentences" (*TBL*, 58), yet she searches untiringly for the means to "utter the significant word or think the one apocalyptic thought" (*TBL*, 64). Her quest for the one "significant word," or what Wordsworth saw as the "Characters of the great Apocalypse" (the vision in the Vale of the Gondo that Huxley analyzed and sharply criticized in *Do What You Will* [20]), is a pursuit of "the *one* word" that Byron despaired of achieving in *Childe Harold's Pilgrimage*.[21] The sardonic empiricist, Cardan, in pursuit of a baroque sculpture later discovers a statue of Byron, or "what in the imagination of a monumental mason of 1830 figured as a poet," but this "slenderer Byron" holds out a "square tablet" that, significantly, is "a blank" (*TBL*, 251), while later in the novel "the house" of "Byron" is associated with "self-inflicted boredom" (*TBL*, 275). Mrs. Aldwinkle is a victim of romantic accidie, "a mixture of boredom, sorrow and despair" (*OM*, 22) that, according to Huxley, manifests itself in a desire to be "anywhere, anywhere out of the world" (*OM*, 22–23). Romantic accidie lies at the root of Huxley's treatment of romantic Prometheanism and its complementary baroque beguilement with the new and the marvelous. Lilian Aldwinkle's drifting peripatetic behavior is governed by a generalized anxiety that she has been "kept . . . away from the places where the exciting things were happening" (*TBL*, 16), a fear that reinforces her search for some kind of apocalyptic revelation.

The symbolic setting for much of the action in the early chapters of *Those Barren Leaves* is the Cybo Malaspina. If, as Huxley repeatedly argues, romanticism (old or new) is a matter of roles, posturings, and histrionics, then Mrs. Aldwinkle's villa is the most suitable stage for the enactment of such a "farce." Indeed, for Huxley, it is the "comic" as opposed to the cosmic lengths to which the romantic artists and poets were willing to go that most impressed him, and the Cybo is the concrete embodiment of "the grand theatrical flourish" so deeply and persistently admired by Huxley's romantics. The Cybo is a vast ensemble of gardens, stairways, and buildings, surrounded by allegorical and mythological sculpture, and designed to impress the visitor with its arcades that dramatically open onto complex architectural compositions. In concept and ambition the Cybo evokes both "Versailles and Caserta" although on a much reduced scale. Cardan, describing the characteristic effect of baroque[22] architecture, is, in fact, sketching the murkily dramatic features of the Cybo: "Look how all the architecture of the period is conditioned by the need for display. The architect was there to make backgrounds for the incessant amateur theatricals of his employers. Huge vistas of communicating saloons to march down, avenues for processions, vast flights to do the Grand Monarch descent from the skies" (*TBL*, 26). Huxley took great care in his description of the villa, introducing it through the eyes of Chelifer in a series of fragmented glimpses through the trees as he approaches by car. The most prominent feature of the Cybo is one that Huxley repeatedly stresses and that Chelifer notes immediately. As the car approaches, he spies a bewildering accumulation of features that suddenly arrange themselves into a dramatic spatial sequence (characteristic of the baroque) in the form of "a great flight of steps, set between cypresses, mounting up past a series of terraced landings to a carved doorway in the centre of the long facade" (*TBL*, 168). At the center of the Cybo's complex web of corridors, arcades, and immense grounds crowded with statues is a symbolic pattern of ascent towards a sacred temple, a symbol of Promethean aspiration and baroque spectacle that will find its counterpart in Chelifer's autobiographical fragments.

The villa is composed out of the gradual accretion of centuries of architectural ideas, but its most marked feature is its striving for dramatic effect by means of complex interwoven spaces. Mrs. Aldwinkle, who regards it as a "very fine specimen of early baroque" (*TBL*, 19), accompanies the unwilling Chelifer on a tour of the estate where, after walking through the house, they arrive at a "great quadrangle" (*TBL*, 169) formed by an inner court surrounded on three sides by the villa and on the fourth by an arcade. Mrs. Aldwinkle, obsessed with the Cybo as a patrician dwelling, leads Chelifer to the statue of one of the princes of Massa Carrara. "With the expression of one who is about to reveal a delightful secret," she excitedly ushers Chelifer into position at the foot of the statue and produces her "moment of revelation": "From the central arch of the arcade, a flight of marble steps climbed up to where, set against a semi-circle of cypresses, at the crest of the hill, a little round temple played gracefully at paganism" (*TBL*, 170). The architectural ensemble of statue, arcade, stairs, hill, and crowning temple is a baroque tableau that Chelifer repudiates as little more than one of the "pretty peep-shows" (*TBL*, 170) that were the hallmark of the baroque *trompe l'oeil* style. The Cybo, "infected by a touch of the baroque *folie de grandeur*," typifies the "stage houses" (*OM*, 181) that Huxley saw as a betrayal of Wren's aesthetic. Mrs. Aldwinkle's momentary apocalypse is a Piranesian vista, a complex of arches and flights of stairs, of "vaulted corridor[s]" and tunnels that recur endlessly in Piranesi's engravings where they typically arrange themselves in spatial sequences that conduct the eye towards dramatic culminations. It is a dynamic perspective that, like Casimir Lypiatt's taste for Veronese, a master of *trompe l'oeil*, is rooted in what Huxley viewed as a radically debased style.

The theatrical character of the composition, overwhelmingly evident to Chelifer, extends to the interior of the house as well. Mrs. Aldwinkle's own *trompe l'oeil* tendencies have transformed the "Saloon of the Ancestors," with its ceiling painting of "the rape of Europa" and a sculptured "group of marine deities" (*TBL*, 20) writhing furiously in its niche, into an artist's Mecca, that is, into "what it had never been except in Mrs. Aldwinkle's fancy" (*TBL*, 23). Her niece, Irene, whom Mrs. Aldwinkle is attempting to win over to her religion of art, is given a bedroom that had once been occupied by Cardinal Alderano Malaspina. The room is a setting for an elaborate fresco in the style of Veronese of the Cardinal's "apotheosis" (*TBL*, 259), a deification of the Cardinal who sits as an allegorical symbol of the spirit of art, surrounded by the "Nine Muses and three Graces" (*TBL*, 259). For Mrs. Aldwinkle, who believed that "through art man comes nearest to being a god" (*TBL*, 60), the *trompe l'oeil* apotheosis of the Cardinal is a suitably murky conflation of art and religion that embodies her belief that aesthetic creation is a lower form of mystical ecstasy.

If the Cybo is, as Cardan would have it, a baroque stage for "incessant amateur theatricals" (*TBL*, 26), its occupants have clearly imbibed the spirit of the place. Mary Thriplow observes that "life tends to become a bit operatic" in Italy and throughout the novel eagerly plays the "part assigned to her" (*TBL*, 52). She regards her affair with her dead cousin as a "comedy" (*TBL*, 82) and cultivates a role more suitable to a "comic opera by Offenbach" (*TBL*, 169). Cardan describes his confrontation with Mr. Elver as a "queer pantomime" (*TBL*, 231) that leads first to a "tragedy" that, in turn, eventually reveals itself as a "farce . . . in the worst of bad taste" (*TBL*, 334). Miss Thriplow maintains that "those in real life perform as much for an inward as an outward gallery" (*TBL*, 264), a judgment that corresponds to Cardan's cynical observation that, in life, it is "only the acting that matters" (*TBL*, 337). Similarly, Mrs. Aldwinkle falls in love with her idea of Chelifer and consequently "played the part assigned to her" (*TBL*, 326), shocking Chelifer by her assumption of a role that was "not in the programme" (*TBL*, 327). In short, the Cybo is a stage setting designed to symbolize the universal "love of a show" (*TBL*, 29) in which Huxley skillfully manages to integrate the themes of "baroque romantic" aspiration and its fundamental insincerity, its propensity for self-dramatization and artifice.

In *Those Barren Leaves*, the symbolic significance of the Cybo Malaspina is carefully developed in relation to a countervailing architectural setting, Gog's Court, a lower-class boardinghouse that in the *Fragments from the Autobiography of Francis Chelifer* is celebrated as "the navel of reality" (*TBL*, 98). The *Fragments* is a loosely structured *bildungsroman*, or, more accurately, a parodic version of a romantic *kunstlerroman*[23] based on Wordsworth's *Prelude* but designed to move in an opposite direction in keeping with Chelifer's role as a "reversed romantic" or, in Calamy's words, a "reversed sentimentalist" (*TBL*, 371). It closely parallels *The Prelude* in its choice of subjects. Chelifer records his childhood, his university years, his ascent to Mount Snowdon with his father, his experiences of war in France, his flirtation with political violence as an "ardent revolutionary" (*TBL*, 132) and a "democrat" (*TBL*, 86), his crisis as lover and artist, and, finally, his revelation of "the heart of reality" (*TBL*, 108) at Gog's Court. Consequently, and contrary to what Keith May has argued, the *Fragments*, as a modern *Prelude*, is not a pointless digression that raises "the technical problem of how to attach the

beliefs and life-story of Chelifer to a comedy set in Italy."[24] Chelifer, identi-
fied with both Wordsworth and Shelley, is the romantic Lilian Aldwinkle's
accomplice. Their accidie proceeds from similar sources; and, as Lilian falls
in love with Chelifer who, as a result, is forced to hide from her, they
become their own nemeses, punishing one another for their mutual sterility.
Mrs. Aldwinkle loves, not Chelifer, but an idea, a product of her "baroque
romantic" imagination, while Chelifer, "lacking a native enthusiasm for
Love" (*TBL*, 323), avoids human relationships, preferring to passively "slide"
through life. As romantic and "inverse romantic," they are, in Huxley's
eyes, superficially opposed but intrinsically identical, much as the Cybo
Malaspina is the obverse of Gog's Court.

Chelifer, rather than repudiating the blankness of life as it is conceived
at Gog's Court, actively embraces it as the only avenue to truth—as far
removed from the exclusive idealism of the Cybo Malaspina as he can make
it. Located in "Fetter Lane," Chelifer, as an inhabitant of Gog's Court, is a
reversed Prometheus who has deliberately sought out his place of bondage.
Obsessed with the idea of Shelley, he, nevertheless, repudiates the latter's
"millennial visions" (*TBL*, 93) as well as Calamy's belief in a "realm of
Absolute Art" (*TBL*, 99). The recovery of life's meaning is, for Chelifer,
somehow connected with a surrender to the "void" (*TBL*, 106), to the "one
unceasing slide through nothing" (*TBL*, 108), the origins of which are traced
in the autobiographical fragments.

Like Mrs. Aldwinkle, Chelifer suffers from "extravagant spiritual cravings"; yet he remains a cynical dilettante reading "a page of Wittgenstein"
and playing "a little Bach" in the midst of a "monotonous and tedious"
existence (*TBL*, 85). The autobiographical *Fragments* record the two formative
experiences that have contributed to his nihilistic passivity, satirizing along
the way Wordsworth's doctrines of the spots of time, of nature, and of the
poet as prophet. The *trompe l'oeil* "moment of revelation" engineered by Mrs.
Aldwinkle, the romantic muse of the Cybo, finds its earlier and more decisive
counterpart in the *Fragments* when the youthful Chelifer ascends Mount
Snowdon with his "Wordsworthian" father who "knew most of the *Prelude*
by heart." Climbing to "the top of Snowdon" (*TBL*, 120), "gazing at the
astonishing landscape" (*TBL*, 121), and listening with wonder to his father's
quotations from "Tintern Abbey," he rapturously surrenders to what "seemed
an oracle, a divine revelation" (*TBL*, 122). But, like his ascent into the
baroque spatial sequences of the Cybo, his experience remains vague and
elusive. All he remembers is the animal appetite of his father who, descending
the mountain and sniffing the air, cries out "Onions" (*TBL*, 122). This is an
ironic version of Mrs. Aldwinkle's "significant word," the "one apocalyptic"
utterance that the Cybo is designed to inspire and enshrine. Chelifer cannot
shake off this memory; and, just as Wordsworth's *Prelude* was intended to
affirm the renovatory power of memory, the powers of the imagination, and

the abiding reality of love, Chelifer's autobiography founders on precisely these issues.

The longer fragment dealing with the Barbara Waters affair is dexterously handled by Huxley as a further development of Chelifer's dreamy romanticism. He is hardly conscious of Barbara as a human being, but rather, like Mrs. Aldwinkle, he pursues an elusively nebulous phantom of his own creation, always associating her with fire (the romantic emblem of the imagination) and Promethean vision as a consequence of having first encountered her where "fire-bearing hands" moved round "a pyre" and "a new small universe" was "suddenly created." In *On the Margin*, Huxley had criticized Wordsworth for erecting "a whole cosmogony" on the basis of an obsession with "inenarrable emotions." Now Chelifer proceeds to do the same thing as "the leaping flame" reveals "apocalyptically" (*TBL*, 130) what he insists is "the embodiment of life itself" (*TBL*, 131), an image of "an intense and secret and unutterable happiness" (*TBL*, 130). He sees Barbara as an enigmatic symbol in the midst of alternating light and darkness, a typically baroque image, "flushed, bright and with an air of being almost supernaturally alive in the quivering, changing light of the flames" (*TBL*, 130). She is also transformed by Chelifer's hectic fancy into an emblem of the superiority of intuition to mere intellect: "I felt that I ought to have known that she wouldn't like reading. After all, what need was there for her to read? When one is life, one has no use for mere books" (*TBL*, 132). Chelifer's idealization of Barbara Waters explains the title of the novel, taken from "The Tables Turned" where Wordsworth had renounced books as mere "barren leaves." Chelifer, then, in spite of his experience on Snowdon, is still dealing in "Wordsworthian formulas" (*TBL*, 122) and ruefully confesses that he had loved (Barbara) only "as a symbol" (*TBL*, 190). Like the inarticulate Mrs. Aldwinkle's inability "to give expression to what she wanted to say" or the statue of Byron holding a "blank" tablet, Barbara Waters's imputed superiority to "mere books" is another strand in an interlacing pattern of references to what Huxley regards as a romantic belief in the supremacy of feeling, emotion, or intuition to reason and intellect (symbolized by books). For Huxley, however, it is not books that are barren but rather the Sybilline leaves of romantic prophecy. The title, then, is intentionally ironic, turning back on Wordsworth rather than endorsing the glib generalizations of "The Tables Turned."

Barbara, with her mysterious expression of secret joy, becomes consolidated in his mind as a Wordsworthian spot of time, "a memory of a kind of symbolic loveliness" that he retains for "years" (*TBL*, 135). This radiantly aureoled vision of "profound and lovely mysteries" somehow "incarnate in one face" (*TBL*, 140), like Wordsworth's revelation of the "one face" in the valley of the Gondo, is an illusion, a projection of Chelifer's "spiritual cravings": "I had not yet learned to reconcile myself to the fact that Barbara's higher nature was an invention of my own, a figment of my proper imagination" (*TBL*, 142). Chelifer's faith in Barbara's "higher nature" (like Mrs. Aldwinkle's "higher life" at the Cybo) is his last illusion. When it shatters, he becomes, like Lypiatt of *Antic Hay* and Maurice Spandrell of *Point Counter Point* (both repeatedly associated with Shelley[25]), intensely suicidal, cherishing a "little hand-grenade" (*TBL*, 146) in a hatbox and fantasizing about mass murder. Huxley underscores Chelifer's irrational submission to Barbara as a kind of romantic muse by means of Hans Baldung Grien's "Aristotle and Phyllis," an engraving also cited by James Joyce in *Ulysses*:[26] "There is a German engraving of the sixteenth century . . . which represents a naked Teutonic beauty riding on the back of a bald and bearded man, who she directs with a bridle and urges on with a switch. The old man is labelled Aristotle" (*TBL*, 147). His idealization of Barbara has reduced him "to a state of abjection at her feet" (*TBL*, 148), just as later, in the imagination of Mrs. Aldwinkle, he will lie "at her feet, like Shelley" (*TBL*, 180). But Chelifer, after his disillusionment with Barbara Waters, will reject Mrs. Aldwinkle and the "old romanticism" embodied in the Cybo Malaspina and embrace instead the "abyss" (*TBL*, 108) of Gog's Court. Shelley, the Cybo, and the possibility of a Promethean vision of Shelley's "Platonic eternity" are contemptuously dismissed as an escape "into the ideal" (*TBL*, 94). Indeed, he encounters Mrs. Aldwinkle at precisely the point at which he admits "I had no right to Shelley" (*TBL*, 153). Mrs. Aldwinkle, "living inside of one of Shelley's poems" (*TBL*, 92), retreats into the Cybo and takes Chelifer with her. Both fear "the pointless landscape" of a world that resists their naively ideal formulations, and, as a consequence, they express themselves in acts of regression or withdrawal, seeking out sharply demarcated sanctuaries like the Cybo Malaspina or Gog's Court that are really outward extensions of their inner fears, metaphors for the "state of mind" (*OM*, 25) that Huxley defined as romantic accidie. In Calamy's words, "the bad principle is the same in both cases—an excessive preoccupation with what is illusory" (*TBL*, 371).

Chelifer's poems are obliquely symptomatic of his intellectual and aesthetic predicament. At first glance, a sequence of poems on the Roman Caesars would appear to be at a far remove from the sordid "reality" of Gog's Court where Chelifer, after his final disillusionment at the hands of Barbara Waters, eagerly embraced "the difficult art of the exclusive concentration on the relevant." Yet, even at this stage in his life, he is busy casting his resentments and perversely subjective inclinations into erudite molds aimed, in part, at defining his own baroque-romantic impulse. The first lyric in the unfinished sequence, inspired appropriately by a baroque painting, is entitled "Caligula crossing the bridge of boats between Baiae and Puteoli. By Peter Paul Rubens (b. 1577; d. 1640)" (*TBL*, 123). The poem evokes a vast canvas, a composition whose historical drama and allegorical complexity would have appealed to Casimir Lypiatt of *Antic Hay*. The Caligula lyric is the first in a series of meditations on Promethean figures whose energies and aspirations have, in "romantic" fashion, imposed themselves on their surrounding worlds:

> And they have filled the vacant skies
> With waltzing Gods and Virtues, set
> The Sea Winds singing with their shout, ... (*TBL*, 123)

Bearing in mind that the Caligula poem, created by the poet Chelifer, celebrates a painting created by another artist, Rubens, whose allegorical meaning, at least in Chelifer's eyes, proclaims the inspired power of "Caesar's lifted fist," it becomes a series of reflecting mirrors in praise of Promethean power and, in particular, the power of "Beauty, like conscious lightning" to transform Caligula into a "God." The Nero lyrics continue to develop this theme. Chelifer celebrates Nero as a type of the artist, declaring his superiority to Christ and identifying his art with divinity:

> Christ died, but living Nero turns
> Your mute remorse to song; he gives
> To idiot fate eyes like a lover's,
> And while his music plays, God lives. (*TBL*, 127)

In retrospect, Chelifer regards his own poems as fundamentally spurious, governed by "romantic and noble sentiments" (*TBL*, 127), and, with the exception of the Tiberius poem, devoid of the epistemological integrity that the older Chelifer has come to value.

Chelifer's romantic pilgrimage is a spiritual journey that illuminates the structure of *Those Barren Leaves* by drawing the reader's attention to the centrality of the journey motif. All of the characters are seeking some form of "revelation," and all are drawn into a final hectic car race for Rome. Miss Thriplow pursues Calamy, hoping to achieve an authentic emotional relationship; Lilian Aldwinkle chases Chelifer in her desire to possess poet and lover in one; Cardan hopes to marry the idiot Grace Elver and finally realize his goal of financial security; Mr. Falx journeys to his socialist convention; Hovenden pursues Irene; and, finally, Calamy hopes to escape his increasing sense of intellectual and spiritual despair. The central symbol that stands at the end of the journey, gathering up the various threads of aspiration and disillusion that dominate the final chapters, is "the silhouette of St. Peter's" (*TBL*, 294). The dome of St. Peter's looks back to "the top of Snowdon" and the "round temple" of the Cybo Malaspina and forward to the "shining peak" (*TBL*, 380) of Calamy's mountain. Its symbolic meaning exceeds in range and depth that of Wren's "dome of St. Paul's" in *Antic*

Hay because it is not a "human symbol" (*AH*, 327) celebrating proportion and reason. Rather, each of the pilgrims reacts differently to the dome, described by Huxley in *Two or Three Graces*, published the year after *Those Barren Leaves*, as "the great symbolical dome of the world."[27] The "silhouette of St. Peter's" stands at the end of the journey to Rome as the culminating symbol of human diversity and, at the same time, of a final mystery that is inherently unknowable. Huxley accomplishes this by having his pilgrims react to St. Peter's in diverse but individually circumscribed ways. Mrs. Aldwinkle, as the book's representative romantic monist searching for "the one apocalyptic thing," is disappointed, lamely remarking "St. Peter's isn't much of a work of art" (*TBL*, 292). Chelifer, loyal to Gog's Court, disavows St. Peter's, exclaiming "what has it or he to do with us" (*TBL*, 294). Mr. Falx, the socialist, bristles angrily, denouncing the dome as a symbol of "the secular oppression of millions of human beings" and of "their degraded lives in order that St. Peter's might be what it is" (*TBL*, 291). The cynical hedonist, Cardan, opposes Mr. Falx and sees the dome as primarily an opportunity for aesthetic pleasure: "allow us to amuse ourselves with Michelangelo if we want to" (*TBL*, 294) while in the background "the Pilgrim's Chorus out of Tannhauser" (*TBL*, 295) is drowned out by a jazz band. The mingled political, aesthetic, and philosophical responses of the pilgrims are not resolved by Huxley because the dome of St. Peter's symbolizes the intractability of what Huxley will celebrate in *Do What You Will* as a world of "distinctions and relations" (*DWW*, 63), in which the soul's "principal food is the direct . . . physical experience of diversity" (*DWW*, 93) and "Shelley's . . . prophetic escape" (*DWW*, 99–100) is displaced by a belief that "knowledge is mostly a knowledge of diversity" (*DWW*, 91). There is a remarkable consistency to Huxley's intellectual development, and while, as Jerome Meckier[28] has shown, D. H. Lawrence's influence was clearly a formative one, many of the central ideas of *Do What You Will* can be traced back to *Antic Hay*, *Those Barren Leaves*, and the essays of *On the Margin* and *Along the Road*.

In "One and Many," Huxley closely equated human experience with the experience of diversity, but he also insisted that reality is inherently "unknowable." He rejected monism, declaring that "the One is the equivalent of the Nothing" (*DWW*, 12), but, at the same time, in "Spinoza's Worm," he held out the possibility of "apocalypses" revealing an "all-comprehending unity" (*DWW*, 63). In *Antic Hay* and *Those Barren Leaves*, Huxley vigorously denied such a mode of perception, particularly as it was often associated with art. But his attack on baroque self-aggrandizement and romantic Prometheanism did not extend to mysticism or preclude a mystical apprehension that transcends both language and plastic form. The Cybo's "round temple" and the *Fragments'* Mount Snowdon are inflated symbols that celebrate art as a sacred enterprise and the artist as an inspired prophet. But the "shining peak" that Calamy gazes at in the final chapter is not a consequence of an aesthetic experience or a romantic imposition of the imagination upon the external world.

In the final chapter Calamy rejects the cynicism of Cardan, who nostalgically looks back to "the Romantic Revival" (*TBL*, 37) as the "good old days" when there was "no seen reality; only imagination" (*TBL*, 36). Cardan admits that he "really and sincerely like[d] the baroque only," despite his awareness that its "essence is exaggeration" (*TBL*, 207). Cardan's quest for "extravagant, romantic, grotesqueness" (*TBL*, 209) ends when he carries off a living grotesque, the retarded Grace Elver, whom he hopes to marry. Cardan's allegiances, however, are easily overturned. His cynicism is, in part, the product of fear and confusion, and just as Chelifer seeks the security of Gog's Court and Mrs. Aldwinkle hides herself in the Cybo, Cardan idealizes the past, "the simple faith of nineteenth-century materialism" (*TBL*, 35). He opposes Calamy's patient openness to the world around him, particularly Calamy's "sense that everything's perfectly provisional and temporary" (*TBL*, 34). Cardan is not Huxley's spokesman in *Those Barren Leaves*; rather, he represents "the babble of notions and conflicting theories" (*MN*, 212) that Huxley saw as characteristic of modern culture. It is no accident that Cardan, who loved the baroque, achieves the final insight into the theatrical absurdity of life as it is led at the Cybo. He loses Grace Elver when she dies of food poisoning and is confronted with the same revelation of human vulnerability that he had encountered earlier on the plain of Maremma, "visions of disease, decrepitude, death" (*TBL*, 218). Life, according to Cardan, is a "farce" of mere "struttings and posturings" in which "it is only the acting that matters" (*TBL*, 337).

In *Antic Hay*, "the monster" in the night-club drama insists that "Brunelleschi's dome" (*AH*, 230) contains a spiritual meaning that validates his endeavor to "reach aloft" (*AH*, 231). In this parable of romanticism, the monster struggles to ascend only to fall head foremost to the floor, just as Chelifer collapses when confronted with the two hundred and thirty-two steps of Mrs. Aldwinkle's tower at the Cybo. The attempt to transcend the inescapable diversity of human experience by an ascent towards a monistic ideal is, for Huxley, an evasion of life lived on a human rather than a baroque scale. The "dome of St. Paul's" is a symbol of "human" achievement, revealing only human truths as opposed to Casimir Lypiatt's "reality more than human." In the trilogy of the early novels it stands in the shadows of the "silhouette of St. Peter's" as a symbol of order in a world of overwhelming darkness and diversity, and in opposition to "the top of Snowdon" as an emblematic repudiation of romantic Prometheanism. Yet the "shining peak" that Calamy confronts in the final chapter of *Those Barren Leaves* would seem to resurrect the already discredited "exclusive idealism" of "baroque romantic" art. Shimmering beneath the surface of the "great pinnacle" is the promise of apocalypse, of the divulgence of an "enormous secret" (*TBL*,

363) similar to Mrs. Aldwinkle's Cybo or Barbara Waters's mysterious smile. Calamy, however, is not a Casimir Lypiatt or a Francis Chelifer.

In *Crome Yellow*, the poet, Dennis, ascends the ivory tower of art that isolates him from the vitality of the charity bazaar on the grounds below Crome's tower. In *Antic Hay*, the Promethean Lypiatt commits suicide in a Piranesian *"cul de sac,"* and in *Those Barren Leaves* the cynical Chelifer, equally self-destructive after the failure of his idealization of Snowdon and Barbara Waters, buries himself in what he thinks is the reality of Gog's Court. In the three early novels Huxley has radically and uncompromisingly evoked the isolation, the self-destructiveness, and the misguided cynicism that inevitably follow once an artist surrenders to the "baroque romantic" mode and its hollow Prometheanism. Calamy, however, is *not* an artist and refuses to endorse either the posturing self-consciousness of a Lypiatt or the superficial despair of a Chelifer. In keeping with Wren's aesthetic, he calmly observes: "If one desires salvation, it's salvation here and now. The kingdom of God is within you" (*TBL*, 366). Turning his back on both conventional religion and the religion of art, he adopts a position of sensitive alertness to the landscape around him, open to its influence and "somehow reassured" (*TBL*, 380). Cardan, however, continues his life of dependency and aimless wandering with the restless Lilian Aldwinkle who has decided "to move on to Monte Carlo," while Chelifer anticipates his return to the "familiar horrors of reality" at Gog's Court (*TBL*, 379). Calamy has, at least, recognized the sterility of their lives and made the difficult decision to stop, to step outside the confinement of the illusory Cybos and Gog's Courts, and to look into his own soul. In doing so, he has made a step, albeit an inconclusive one, towards establishing "the human reality in the centre of a pointless landscape" (*TBL*, 127).

Notes

1. Aldous Huxley, *Jesting Pilate: An Intellectual Holiday* (New York: George H. Doran, 1926), p. 286. All subsequent references to *Jesting Pilate* will be to this edition with the abbreviation *JP*.

2. Jerome Meckier, *Aldous Huxley: Satire and Structure* (London: Chatto and Windus, 1969), p. 73.

3. Aldous Huxley, *Along the Road: Notes and Essays of a Tourist* (London: Chatto and Windus, 1925), p. 174. All subsequent references to *Along the Road* will be to this edition with the abbreviation *AR*.

4. Sanford E. Marovitz, "Aldous Huxley and the Visual Arts," *Papers on Language and Literature*, 9 (Spring 1973), 174.

5. Aldous Huxley, *Those Barren Leaves* (London: Chatto and Windus, 1969), p. 122. All subsequent references to *Those Barren Leaves* will be to this edition with the abbreviation *TBL*. Huxley's definition of "apocalyptic mystical experience" for the period of the early novels can be traced in the early essays as it evolves from a skepticism concerning the possibility of a genuine theophany in *Jesting Pilate* (pp. 216–17) and *Music at Night* (p. 19)

to the more positive attitude of *Do What You Will* (pp. 264–65). For the editions of these texts, see notes 1, 18, and 20, respectively. "The Essence of Religion," in *Proper Studies* (London. Chatto and Windus, 1927), while important, is less helpful.

6. Keith M. May, *Aldous Huxley* (London: Paul Elek, 1972), p. 61.

7. Laurence Brander, *Aldous Huxley: A Critical Study* (London: Rupert Hart-Davis, 1969), p. 128.

8. George Woodcock, *Dawn and the Darkest Hour: A Study of Aldous Huxley* (London: Faber and Faber, 1972), p. 127.

9. Peter Firchow, *Aldous Huxley: Satirist and Novelist* (Minneapolis: University of Minnesota Press, 1972), p. 82.

10. Meckier, p. 74.

11. Aldous Huxley, *On the Margin: Notes and Essays* (London: Chatto and Windus, 1923), pp. 174–75. All subsequent references to *On the Margin* will be to this edition with the abbreviation *OM*.

12. M. H. Abrams, *Natural Supernaturalism* (New York: Norton, 1971), p. 117.

13. *Along the Road*, p. 172. Huxley's aversion for modern art is a pervasive theme in his essays and fiction. He regarded baroque sculpture and painting as similarly antimimetic. A useful but sketchy index to his ideas on art history and the devolution of aesthetic taste can be found in the essay, "The Pierian Spring," in *Along the Road*.

14. Aldous Huxley, *Crome Yellow* (London: Chatto and Windus, 1969), p. 68.

15. Milton Birnbaum, *Aldous Huxley's Quest for Values* (Knoxville: University of Tennessee Press, 1971), p. 66.

16. Aldous Huxley, *Antic Hay* (London: Chatto and Windus, 1923), p. 87. All subsequent references to *Antic Hay* will be to this edition with the abbreviation *AH*.

17. Aldous Huxley, *Letters of Aldous Huxley*, ed. Grover Smith (London: Chatto and Windus, 1969), p. 311.

18. Aldous Huxley, *Music at Night and Other Essays* (London: Chatto and Windus, 1960), p. 211. All subsequent references to *Music at Night* will be to this edition with the abbreviation *MN*.

19. Marovitz, p. 176. Marovitz's essay is a valuable general discussion of Huxley's interest in art, but he does not place Lypiatt's painting in the context of the novel nor does he examine Huxley's concern with either baroque or romantic art.

20. Aldous Huxley, *Do What You Will: Essays* (London: Chatto and Windus, 1929); see esp. p. 119. All subsequent references to *Do What You Will* will be to this edition with the abbreviation *DWW*. Huxley also attacks Wordsworth's subjectivism in *Proper Studies* (London: Chatto and Windus, 1927), p. 233.

21. Byron's quest for the "*one* word" finds its most intense evocation in stanza XCVII, Canto III, of *Childe Harold's Pilgrimage*. See page 223 of *Byron: Poetical Works* (London: Oxford University Press, 1970).

22. Huxley's analysis of the baroque style aligns itself to a surprising degree with current scholarship. While the literature on this subject is extensive, the reader need only consult the two special issues of *The Journal of Aesthetics and Art Criticism* devoted to the baroque (5 [December 1946] and 19 [Spring 1961]). Huxley's description of the baroque is also in essential agreement with the article in the twelfth edition of the *Encyclopaedia Britannica*, the edition that accompanied him on his tours of Italy in the early twenties.

23. The definitions of *bildungsroman* and *kunstlerroman* that I am drawing on here are those advanced by Edward Engelberg in "James and Arnold: Conscience and Consciousness in a Victorian 'Kunstlerroman,'" *Criticism*, 10 (1968), 93–114.

24. May, p. 62.

25. For an analysis of this withdrawal motif, see my "Spandrell's 'Lydian Heaven': Moral Masochism and the Centrality of Spandrell in Huxley's *Point Counter Point*," *Criticism*, 16 (Spring 1974), 57–72.

26. An excellent reproduction of the Grien etching can be found in Richard Ellmann's *Ulysses on the Liffey* (London: Oxford University Press, 1972), following page 158.

27. Aldous Huxley, *Two or Three Graces and Other Stories* (New York: George H. Doran, 1926), p. 176.

28. Chapter 4 of Meckier's study (see note 2) contains a valuable examination of Huxley's relationship to Lawrence.

The Technique of Counterpoint

Murray Roston

Point Counter Point has seldom fared well with the critics. Some have applauded its amusing and irreverent parody of contemporary modes, but any claim to its being a serious literary work, to be placed among the major novels of the century, was dismissed by David Daiches and others some forty years ago.[1] The characters, it was argued, do not develop organically in the manner required by the novel genre, and the musical theme of counterpoint which forms the structural frame of the novel, contributes little to the central theme of the work. These strictures have been repeated so frequently in subsequent years as to become a veritable chorus of condemnation, with only a lone voice here or there attempting, usually very hesitantly, to defend the novel from total dismissal as a literary work.

The principles behind that condemnation are, however, more than a little strange when they are placed within the context of the era as a whole. In a period when all art-forms, including the novel, have been essentially innovative, breaking away from established patterns to deal with basically new challenges, it would scarcely seem justifiable to dismiss Huxley merely on the grounds of his failure to conform to convention. Neither *Orlando* nor *Finnegans Wake* could pass that test of organic, naturalistic development of character, yet because the latter were more obviously experimental, the test was never applied to them as either authenticating or invalidating their literary success. One has only to move to the pictorial arts in order to see the absurdity of condemning Braque or Kandinsky for failing to conform to the requirements of naturalism. Surprisingly, however, even Huxley's most energetic supporters have hesitated to defend him as an artistic innovator, but have rather sought for ways to justify his techniques on more traditional grounds.

In fact, one of the most impressive achievements of *Point Counter Point* lies within this very area of experimentation with form and its close integration with the central theme of the novel. By placing within the story a writer who is jotting down notes for an essentially new type of novel the author openly acknowledges this intention, and his well-known Quaker Oats

From *Studies in the Novel* 9 (Winter 1977): 378–88. Copyright © 1977 by North Texas State University. Reprinted by permission of the author and publisher.

image of a novel about a novelist writing a novel underscores the point. The series of figures on that packet, each holding a smaller packet in his hand can be read away into infinitesimal smallness, but the series can also be read in the reverse direction; for the small picture held by the Quaker depicts the outer packet on which he appears. In the same way, the novel being planned by Philip Quarles is actually the outer novel, *Point Counter Point*, in which he is a participant. Any innovations, therefore, which he suggests for his own projected book must be taken as applying directly to Huxley's own experiments with form.

The "multiplicity of viewpoint" which Philip decides to adopt for his novel has, of course, long been seen as in some way relevant to the main novel, but only in a very restricted sense, as helping to create those ludicrous juxtapositions and incongruous polarities which contribute to its wit. As Philip sits with Elinor on the deck of the homeward-bound ship and catches disconnected snatches of conversation from the passengers promenading past—a truncated remark about missionaries, a giggling denial of flirtatiousness, a protest at the quality of flannel underwear—Philip perceives a new way of structuring a novel which might prove more true to life than even the most realistic works of previous traditions. Elinor (forestalling some of Huxley's critics) wishes he would write "a simple, straightforward story about a young man and woman who fall in love and get married," but he brushes the suggestion aside as unworthy of consideration, and continues to investigate the possibilities offered by the new technique.

What precisely is that new technique? Since he calls it half-humorously the "musicalization of fiction," the primary focus has always been either on the parallelism in plot with its fuguelike reflection of similar situations,[2] or on the implications of the musical imagery of the novel. Jerome Meckier, for example, has used the latter as a starting-point for the theory that in this novel Huxley presents us with an orchestra in which each character insists on playing his own individual tune instead of working in unison with others, the resulting cacophony being the main object of the satire.[3] Peter Quennell, taking a similar, though less sympathetic line, castigates Huxley for offering us only eccentrics going to extremes and ignoring the possibility of a middle path. His characters "must either be exploring the heavens . . . or wallowing in the slime" with no hint of any marriage between heaven and hell.[4] It can, however, be argued that this polarity, the impossibility of finding a middle path, is, in fact, the main thrust of the novel. Huxley is neither satirizing his characters for their ridiculous idiosyncrasies, nor condoning them, but exploring the major problem confronting the intellectual of his day; and the tragic undertones of that exploration must not be missed. Once the full implications of his technique have been grasped, beneath the surface humor and mockery can be perceived a troubled search into the predicament of the twentieth-century artist, an enquiry into those very concerns which had produced T. S. Eliot's "Prufrock" and *The Waste Land*, though now in the setting of the novel.

Let us return to Philip's discussion with Elinor, and the idea which occurs to him of a novel offering a multiplicity of viewpoint. What at first seems merely comical suddenly grows more serious toward the end of the passage:

> "Multiplicity of eyes and multiplicity of aspects seen. For instance, one person interprets events in terms of bishops; another in terms of the price of flannel camisoles; another, like that young lady from Gulmerg," he nodded after the retreating group, "thinks of it in terms of good times. And then there's the biologist, the chemist, the physicist, the historian. Each sees, professionally, a different aspect of the event, a different layer of reality. What I want to do is to look with all those eyes at once. With religious eyes, scientific eyes, economic eyes, *homme moyen sensuel* eyes. . . ."[5]

The reason for Philip's enthusiasm is clear. Such an approach will enable him to explore the most perplexing element introduced by scientific thought—that, as the title of the novel suggests, no settled or controlling view seemed possible any longer. Each standpoint was cancelled out by a counter point.[6] For the biologist, art and beauty, so essential to the poet's belief, are mere titillations of the nervous system. For the Freudian psychologist, the noble human spirit has become a series of preconditioned reflexes dictated by heredity and childhood experience. For the religious mystic the Darwinian reduction of man to a propagating mammal devoid of the image of God is an obscenity. From one standpoint we are shown the absurd untenability of the second; then the process is reversed and from the second standpoint we are shown the utter irrationality of the first. The result is spiritual paralysis, the conflict of reason and emotion symptomatic of that age for which Huxley became a spokesman. Hence the epigraph for the novel from Fulke Greville who, experiencing a similar conflict between faith and the New Philosophy of the Renaissance, complained of the wearisome condition of man, torn between the incompatible claims of heart and intellect: "What meaneth nature by these diverse laws, / Passion and reason, self-division's cause?"

It is here that the brilliance of the counterpoint technique can be seen at its best. For instead of offering us a single Prufrockian character, longing to be a Michelangelo or John the Baptist but left pinned and wriggling on the wall by the formulated phrases of psychology or biology which his intellect must affirm, he offers us here a series of different characters, each adopting one of the various possible responses to that dilemma and each failing to achieve any harmony or integrity of viewpoint which could satisfy the author or, indeed, the reader. Moreover, a number of these characters are even more integrally related. There is, of course, an obvious element of self-portraiture in Philip Quarles, a novelist suffering from a physical disability which prevents him from indulging in sport or developing close human contacts. His proximity to Huxley's own situation invites comparison. But so too does Walter Bidlake, an assistant editor fuming at the exploitation he suffers at the hands of his employer Burlap, the literary portrait of Middleton Murry for whom Huxley had once slaved on *The Athenaeum*. Yet the most significant element here is not the similarity between these two self-portraits but the difference; for they serve as extrapolations of the two main elements within his own spiritual conflict.

On the one hand there is Philip the intellectual sceptic, painfully aware of his emotional inadequacies but condemned by his rationalism to see everything in analytical, scientific, or philosophical terms; on the other hand there is Walter, the Shelleyan romantic believing passionately in the soul and unable to fit in with the objective realities of the new age. Both fail as human beings, and their failures are highlighted by the parallel scenes of love. Elinor, still fond of her husband, tries desperately to elicit from him some small expression of warmth and affection, but to no avail. It is not that he is clumsy about it; he simply freezes all her approaches, often unintentionally, by invariably seeing their love relationship either in a physiological or statistical setting, drawing his parallels from his wide encyclopedic reading: "Even in Sicily there are twice as many births in January as in August. Which proves conclusively that in the spring a young man's fancy. . . ." Elinor listens with a kind of horror. An incident, she notes, "evoked from Philip a selection from the vital statistics of Sicily, a speculation about the relativity of morals, a brilliant psychological generalization. It was amazing, it was unexpected, it was wonderfully interesting; but oh! she almost wanted to scream" (111), and his empirical analyses gradually destroy their love, almost driving her into the arms of Webley.

For Walter's scene the roles are changed. Here it is he who is the passionate lover, longing for the warm word of affection, but confronted by the dictates of a cold rationalism personified by Lucy. Caught up in his romantic dream of love, he insists, as he lies in bed with her, on knowing whether she loves him, returning again and again to this same question. All his pleas for assurance are met, however, by the amused detachment of the New Woman, who reminds him how "absurdly unmodern" he is, to request love in the fast world of aeroplanes which leaves no room for the weighty, old-fashioned baggage of romanticism. "Not even for a heart?" he begs. No, she insists, there is not even room for that. To claim, as Peter Quennell does, that Huxley ought to have considered some happy mean between two such views is to misunderstand this central problem. For the intellectual of Huxley's era the tragedy lay precisely there—that no compromise seemed possible. If Darwin was right (and all evidence seemed to indicate that he was) then love *was* no more than a neurological itch urging the human toward the propagation of his species. The Shelleyan idea of man ennobled and elevated by love, splendid as it may be for the soul, simply could not coexist with the new biological theory. They cancelled each other out.

Incidentally, if this interpretation of Walter and Philip as twin extrapolations of Huxley's inner conflict seems at all far-fetched, in fact he offers us a broad hint in the text. As though to confirm our suspicions, there is the amusing scene of Burlap's first meeting with Romola Saville who had submitted a number of love poems for his perusal. The door opens to admit not one person, but two, one portly, one thin. It transpires that they are joint authors, the Jekyll and Hyde as they call themselves, who together form the poetess. It is a pointless incident in the novel unless it is intended to hint at a split in the novelist's personality too.

On a more serious level, however, one should note how integral Huxley's literary innovation was to the artistic setting of his period. At exactly the same time as Huxley was writing *Point Counter Point*, Picasso was introducing into modern painting that same multiplicity of viewpoint. We are now so familiar with the device that we tend to forget how revolutionary it was when he began to present the human face, for example, viewed simultaneously both frontally and in profile on the assumption that if the eye may see only one view at a time, the mind is aware that other equally valid angles exist. His *Still Life with Guitar* (1924), painted only four years before the publication of the novel, was one of the first paintings to view a scene from above and from the side; and in his *Girl Looking in a Mirror* (1932) the multiplicity of viewpoint was extended to include, in addition to the various spatial angles, the further dimension of the mythic or archetypal viewpoint which enters the mind of the viewer at the same moment as the spatial registers on the eye. Her breast has become the apple of Eden, her ribs evocative of her formation from Adam, and the egg-shaped oval in her womb a symbol of fertility. This was not, of course, mere whimsicality on the artist's part but an aesthetic response to the new concepts of the era. Like others he was learning to cope with the relativism of viewpoint implicit in the twentieth century and the challenge it posed to the traditional more unified approach.

Once this technique has been grasped, not only Walter and Philip but almost every character in the novel can be seen as representing a different facet of the book's central concern, a different way of responding to that shared problem. Some of these responses seem absurd, some seem initially legitimate; but together, the bewildering variety, the contradictions they produce, and their ultimate failure to offer a solution make the choice of any final satisfactory view quite out of the question. Lucy, for instance, is, as the reversal of roles in the love scenes suggests, a female counterpart to Philip, but with important variations. She, too, is the possessor of a sophisticated and analytical mind, and has long realized the change which the new science has wrought, that love is merely a physical act devoid of spiritual ennoblement. Unlike Philip, however, she needs love, and decides at the very least to enjoy the pleasures of sleeping around, free from any moral inhibitions. In the earlier scenes there is a certain attractiveness in her new-found liberty and her ability to enjoy that freedom to the full, but later her letter from Paris points ominously to the future which lies in store for her. To vary the basic tedium of a loveless life she will need to embark on a neurotic search for ever-new sensations—nymphomania, masochism, sadism—leading inevitably to a dismal end in some brothel or madhouse. John Bidlake places his faith in the flesh, in an instinctual response to life which scorns all intellectualism. A blend of Renoir and Augustus John, he delights in visceral vitality before which all prudery or scruples of marital fidelity evaporate. A booming laugh, a robust figure, a dominating presence, until the moment that death lays a warning hand upon him and finds him utterly unprepared. He reverts to childish superstitions, terrified avoidance of his grandson's sickroom, and pitiful refusal to confront his own condition. Lord Edward blithely engrafts a newt's tail on to its leg-stump, completely unconcerned by the implications of his experiments (which Huxley was to explore so devastatingly in *Brave New World*), while his brother hopefully searches for mathematical formulas to prove God's existence.

Such characters may themselves be unaware of the absurdity of their positions, but the reader is left in no doubt. Illidge adopts the materialist ideology of communism to which he is fiercely dedicated, the principle that the individual is as nothing compared to the needs of the body politic; yet his heart and sentiments prompt him secretly to send a weekly allowance to his aged mother. This dichotomy of heart and intellect is dreadfully exposed as Spandrell drives him to political murder. Burlap, in reversion to Victorian modes, chooses the heart over the mind, but in so self-serving a form, like so many of his Victorian predecessors, that Philip, though envying his ability to write from the heart, decides that if that is the only alternative, he will stay with the intellect. Marjorie, with Rachel Quarles's assistance, finds her way from despair to a peace that passeth all understanding and does achieve, through mystical contemplation, the answer to her quest. But Huxley was not yet ready for that solution, and within this novel Marjorie's escape is seen as slightly ridiculous. She lacks the intellectual apparatus necessary for a full awareness of the conflict and at the end her contemplation of the clouds leads her merely to forget to serve Walter's supper. Lastly, of course, there is the more formidable Rampion, by far the most positive character in the novel, who at times seems to have found the long-sought answer to Huxley's predicament. The Laurentian solution is to reintegrate the body and soul in a world which has divorced them, and he does achieve a wholesome and apparently satisfactory answer for himself. Yet gradually we perceive how limited it really is. His only response to the spiritual ideals of Christianity is to dismiss St. Francis contemptuously as a nasty, smelly little pervert who gets a thrill out of licking other people's ulcers (that very fixing in a formulated phrase which Prufrock had so abhorred); and what is worse, the objective experimentalism of science which occupies so central a place in the concerns of the novel is simply rejected as unworthy of consideration. Philip, though he admires Rampion for having achieved his own personal unity, ruefully recognizes toward the end of the novel that the latter's answer is not for him, and that he himself will need to struggle on further for a means "to transform a detached intellectual scepticism into a way of harmonious all-round living." By the end of the book, he is no nearer his goal.

In such a brief article, I have only been able to touch upon each character in order to suggest that they are not, as has so often been argued, mere eccentrics pursuing their own idiosyncratic philosophies, but are far more intimately connected. Originally, it is true, Philip had thought of the contrapuntal technique almost as a joke, Jones murdering his wife juxtaposed to Smith wheeling a perambulator, but in its maturer and more developed form, as it functions in the outer novel itself, it is infinitely more subtle. There, presented in a natural setting with various people apparently engaged in interweaving social, marital, and amorous activities, we are in fact provided with a spectrum of the various responses to one central problem, the shared predicament of the age.

When Huxley presents that dilemma himself, not mediated through one of the characters, it is then that music performs its most prominent role in the novel. The two passages on Bach at the beginning of the work are delightfully written—amusing, ironical, and presented with the panache of the true satirist. Yet as one might expect from a true satirist, beneath the surface humor lies a deeply disturbing question. After warning us how each player in the orchestra imagines that his is the only true statement and, as that truth slides away and is replaced by another, leaves us bewildered by the complexity and variety of such supposed truths, he begins to describe the Bach fugue. For him such music represents not only absolute beauty, but also the supreme proof to the soul that there *is* an ultimate harmony, order, and goodness in the universe. But as the Walter-like heart responds to the romantic message, a Philip-like intellect interrupts in parenthesis to remind us of the harsh, incontrovertible facts which nullify that affirmation of splendor. It is the perfect image of the mind countermanding the heart, each emotional point being cancelled by its objective counterpoint: "His is a slow and lovely meditation on the beauty (in spite of squalor and stupidity), the profound goodness (in spite of all the evil), the oneness (in spite of such bewildering diversity) of the world. It is a beauty, a goodness, a unity that no intellectual research can discover, that analysis dispels, but of whose reality the spirit is from time to time suddenly and overwhelmingly convinced" (32–33).

In that last sentence there is a somber reversal of expectation. The phrase "that no intellectual research can discover" leads us to anticipate by rhythmic repetition "and that no analysis can dispel" to prove the superiority of the soulful harmony to scientific interference; instead, however, comes the chilling admission that analysis does dispel the assurance of the heart. There is, it is true, the *certitude*, the author's conviction at such moments that beauty is supreme in a noble universe; but the passage concludes with the far more limited material facts that science can actually prove, that the violin bow, analyzed to its components, is being drawn across the string of the instrument: "A girl singing to herself under the clouds suffices to create the certitude. Even a fine morning is enough. Is it illusion or the revelation of profoundest truth? Who knows? Pongileoni blew, the fiddlers drew their rosined horsehair across the stretched intestines of lambs."

This theme is echoed throughout the novel in numerous variations to underscore its centrality. The noble sound of Bach, wafted upwards to arouse ecstasy in the heart of Lord Edward, becomes in scientific terms merely a series of vibrations agitating the hairy endings of the auditory nerve by means of the *malleus*, *incus*, and stirrup bones. So much for the physicist. A little later we are offered the chemist's version of such sublime music. A young composer eats a sheep's hind leg for dinner, which is broken down by his stomach acids and transformed into brain cells. The result—a sheep's leg creates the Jupiter symphony. And how does the concept of man created in the image of God fare in the face of biology?

> Six months from now her baby would be born. Something that had been a single cell, a cluster of cells, a little sac of tissue, a kind of worm, a potential fish with gills, stirred in her womb and would one day become a man—a grown man, suffering and enjoying, loving and hating, thinking, remembering, imagining. And what had been a blob of jelly within her body would invent a god and worship; what had been a kind of fish would create, and, having created, would become the battle-ground of disputing good and evil; what had blindly lived in her as a parasitic worm would look at the stars, would listen to music, would read poetry. (2)

Here is man seen, not metaphorically but literally, as a kind of worm or fish evolving it is true into a full-grown man but within the Darwinist evolutionary process now no more than a creature propagating like all the other insects and animals swarming on the surface of the earth. The one difference is that he has illusions of grandeur and of a godhead created in his own image—illusions which he must now abandon as baseless. Need one search any further to explain the prevalence in Huxley of zoological images applied to humans?[7] As lover, as social creature, as religious mystic he had become one with the barnyard fowl in a frighteningly new sense. The modern novelist, Philip notes, will need to write differently. He will have to be a professional zoologist, with his hero and heroine spending their honeymoon by a lake where the grebes and ducks will illustrate all the aspects of courtship and matrimony. Observing the "pecking order" prevailing among hens he will meditate on the Catholic hierarchy and Fascism; and the mass of intricately copulating snakes will remind the libertine of his orgies (438). It is an entertaining picture, yet at the same time infinitely degrading.

Spandrell is a further variation on Philip and Walter, and with the climax of his story, the novel returns to the theme of music. The coldly analytical mind of Philip is here combined with a fervor of the heart, but this time religiously oriented. Had he been born in an earlier age, he could have lived contentedly as a scholastic dwelling within a monastery; but born into the twentieth century he cannot simply accept the firm conviction of his heart. He must have tangible or visible proof of God's existence before he can believe. The intellect, once again, is at war with the heart in this specifically scientific setting. Despairing of any other proof, he deliberately embarks on a life of debauchery. One way of knowing God, he says, is to deny him. He is hoping, as it were, for a thunderbolt from heaven to strike him in punishment for his sins so that in that fraction of a second in which he sees it coming he will at last know beyond doubt that God does exist, that God is not dead as Nietzsche had claimed. Yet even the murder of the Nietzschean Webley produces no response from heaven. He is near despair, but there is one final possibility. Perhaps God does exist, but does not think him worthy of an answer, worthy of punishment, and so he turns for his final test to music. If the slow movement of the Beethoven A Minor Quartet cannot prove the existence of God, then nothing can, and he invites Rampion, one of the only men whose opinion he respects, to be the judge. "It proves all kinds of things—God, the soul, goodness—unescapably," he insists. "It's the only real proof that exists." The melody unfolds. Everything becomes clear and bright; no mists, no vague twilights (and here Huxley speaks, not Spandrell). "It was the calm of still and rapturous contemplation, not of drowsiness or sleep. It was the serenity of the convalescent who wakes from fever and finds himself born again into a realm of beauty. But the fever was 'the fever called living' and the rebirth was not into this world; the beauty was unearthly, the convalescent serenity was the peace of God" (595). Such is the proof. But Rampion, much as he admires the music, is not convinced; and Spandrell in final despair walks out of the room to his planned suicide. Here is the ultimate agony of the novel, as music, the symbol of the soul, is set against the intellectual's need for scientific proof—a need which Huxley himself seems to have recognized as valid. The heart yearns to believe in beauty and in the nobility of man, while the mind perceives the grotesqueness of his zoological or physiological state.

This is the theme which unifies the novel beneath the light banter, and once that theme has been perceived, the multiplicity of viewpoint emerges not as an entertaining trick but as an artistic tool for exploring the contradictory and diverse truths of the new era. To regard *Point Counter Point* as an aesthetic failure, as so many have, on the grounds that "the pattern promised by the title is never achieved,"[8] or even to argue that the dominant device is plot repetition with minor variations[9] is, I think, to miss the extraordinarily subtle relationship between the characters, which counterpoint each other as in a fugue, each producing its own variation on the central tragic theme.

Notes

1. David Daiches, *The Novel and the Modern World* (Chicago: University of Chicago Press, 1939).

2. Peter Firchow, *Aldous Huxley: Satirist and Novelist* (Minneapolis: University of Minnesota Press, 1972), p. 95.

3. Jerome Meckier, *Aldous Huxley: Satire and Structure* (London: Chatto & Windus, 1969), pp. 43, 132.

4. Peter Quennell, "A Critical Symposium on Aldous Huxley," *The London Magazine*, 2 (1955), 51–64.

5. Aldous Huxley, *Point Counter Point* (London: Chatto & Windus, 1928), p. 266. All subsequent quotations are from this edition.

6. The title of course contains a play on words. "Counterpoint" alone represents the world of music and harmony. The placing of the word "Point" before it changes the meaning to one of contradiction, of point being countered by a different point.

7. See Sanford E. Marovitz, "Aldous Huxley's Intellectual Zoo," *Philological Quarterly*, 48 (1969), 495–507. Marovitz views the zoological imagery as a device for displaying the idiosyncrasies of the characters or the bestiality of their behavior.

8. E. B. Burgum, *The Novel and the World's Dilemma* (New York: Oxford University Press, 1947), p. 152.

9. E. K. Brown, *Rhythm in the Novel* (Toronto: University of Toronto Press, 1950), p. 8. In *Aldous Huxley: A Study of the Major Novels* (London: Athlone Press, 1968), Peter Bowering provides a perceptive analysis of the passion-reason theme in the novel, but sees it primarily as an attack on intellectualism.

Mental Music: Huxley's *Point Counter Point* and Mann's *Magic Mountain* as Novels of Ideas

PETER FIRCHOW

Mais, vous savez, dans les romans, c'est toujours dangereux de présenter des intellectuels. Ils assomment le public; on ne parvient à leur faire dire que des âneries, et, à tout ce que les touche, ils communiquent un air abstrait.
—André Gide, *Les Faux-monnayeurs*

1

In the memorable late essay on sewage treatment and the history of sanitation, "Hyperion to a Satyr" (1956), Aldous Huxley gives a brief account of a walk that he and Thomas Mann took down a deserted Southern California beach a few months before the outbreak of the Second World War. It must have been, to use one of Huxley's favorite expressions, an extraordinary sight: here were two world-famous novelists, one a squat German walrus and the other a tall English carpenter, engrossed in talking of literary cabbages and bellicose dictators while their wives, like obedient oysters, trailed along behind. After some time, urged by their ostreaceous companions to examine their immediate surroundings, they were astonished to discover that they were treading upon a carpet of spent condoms, spewed forth from a nearby open sewage pipe and laid down by the ebb and flow of the sea.

Quite apart from any hygienic considerations, there is something profoundly symbolic about this scene. On the one hand, there is the eternal creative and destructive force of nature; on the other, man's feeble attempt to control that force within himself by technological means; and in-between, the ironic, spectatorial intellect. Finally, in the background, there is the rumble of ignorant armies about to clash by night, for while these two eminently peaceful men of letters were confronting the gruesomely comic

From *Studies in the Novel* 9 (Winter 1977): 518–36. Copyright © 1977 by North Texas State University. Reprinted by permission of the author and publisher.

genocide of the never-to-be-born in the new world, their respective nations were preparing to engage in a tragically gruesome attempt to annihilate the living in the old. In some disused corridor of Huxley's mind, one feels sure, there must have resounded the verses he had written as a young man nearly a quarter of a century earlier:

> A million million spermatozoa
> All of them alive
> Out of their cataclysm but one poor Noah
> Dare hope to survive.[1]

But in this case even poor Noah had been abandoned to the spermatocidal sea; here all potential Pickfords and DeMilles were doomed to remain forever mute and inglorious.

A graveyard of semen, a microbiological Noah—these were the sorts of things which appealed to Huxley's imagination, an imagination that mixed the latest scientific theories with sociological statistics and recondite literary allusions, in order to produce, by almost alchemistic means, a brilliant novelistic style and substance which were virtually unique in the literature of this century. Unique in Britain and America, that is, but not elsewhere, for the Huxleyan novel of ideas is a recognizably Continental phenomenon. It is not surprising, therefore, that Huxley's reputation still looms larger outside than within Anglo-Saxondom, and that the writers whom he seems most to resemble are neither English nor American, but French (especially Gide, but also Stendhal, France, and Proust), Russian (Dostoevsky), and German (Mann). Why this should be so, it is not easy to say, though it is probably connected with the traditional Anglo-Saxon suspicion of abstract intelligence and preference for concrete feeling. It was Stendhal—perhaps the greatest of all novelists of ideas and a favorite of both Huxley and Mann—who remarked that an idea immediately loses twenty-five percent of its value on crossing the English Channel. How much more it loses on crossing the North Atlantic, both Huxley and Mann had ample reason to learn from personal experience.

The excursion down the littered Southern California beach is not, however, mentioned anywhere in the published work or correspondence of Thomas Mann. What struck Huxley's imagination as one of life's not so little ironies, seems to have left Thomas Mann unmoved. It did not occur to him to raise a monument, either scatological or eschatological, on so slight a foundation. The difference is, I think, illuminating. For in Mann and in Huxley we have the two most notable novelists of the twentieth century who attempted to come to grips literarily—and were mentally and artistically equipped to do so—with the intellectual and scientific revolution overtaking Western civilization. Both men were fascinated by the characteristically modern magic of science and both believed that the Great War had left man in a state resembling that of the sorcerer's apprentice, with scientific technology bringing the world to the brink of disaster and with no master in sight to put a stop to it. Both saw in biology and psychology the leading sciences which threatened, as well as promised, the most for man's future development. And both therefore shared a kind of *odi-et-amo* attitude toward these sciences, wavering between the hope for a Prospero and the fear of a Faust.

In Mann's case, the result of this complex world-view was *The Magic Mountain*, a massively learned and searching fictional synthesis which, in its aims at any rate, bears comparison with *The Divine Comedy*. Here are symbolically ranged the major philosophical and scientific ideas of our time, like great magnets exercising their attractions (and repulsions) on the seemingly slight and unworthy figure of Hans Castorp, finally raising him to tragicomic proportions. Huxley was able to write this kind of novel as well, though perhaps not *quite* as well. *Point Counter Point* also pulls together the major philosophical and scientific strands of the age, also employs a musical analogy to give structure to the narrative (but using Bach and Beethoven as models, not Wagner), and also has extended conversational duels between "liberal" and "conservative" viewpoints. But for all these resemblances, important differences remain, and in the end perhaps outweigh the similarities. A chapter like "Snow" is simply beyond the Huxley of the late Twenties, not so much because he lacks the ability to envision it as because he lacks the faith to execute it. The equivalent in Huxley's novels to Castorp's allegorical musings at the top of the world is Cardan's despair at the bottom, in *Those Barren Leaves*—a statement of cynicism rather than of qualified faith. Not that Huxley fails to take the alien power of Nature, or the erratic nobility of human nature, seriously; he does, emphatically and eloquently, but he does not take them seriously enough to approximate Mann's level of "high seriousness," not until *Eyeless in Gaza* at any rate. Somewhere in the early Huxley, as he knew very well and admitted himself, there lurked a sneaking Thersites ready to scrawl graffiti on Venus's posterior. This is a weakness in Huxley; it is probably what keeps him just outside the pale of literary greatness. But it is also a strength. It makes him suspicious of all substances, literary and otherwise, which are too pure. Excessive purity, artistic or chemical, is not natural, as Huxley once wrote, and can be achieved only at the expense of sacrificing the whole truth. To a degree, of course, this is an insight to which Thomas Mann, as an ironist, would have subscribed as well—irony being by nature inimical to those claims to exclusive allegiance which all "pure" truths exercise. The ironic intelligence is inevitably skeptical, and, during the Twenties at least, there was no novelist more skeptical and ironic than Huxley, not even Thomas Mann.

2

Though there are, as we shall see, a number of striking resemblances, both in substance and form, between *Point Counter Point* and *The Magic Mountain*, I would like to have it understood at the outset that I shall not attempt to make a case for these resemblances being the result of any direct influence. Huxley did not meet Mann until the summer of 1933 in Sanary-sur-mer (France), and while by that date he had read some of Mann's work, it is not clear just what he had read and when. The earliest reference to Mann in Huxley's correspondence occurs on 6 January 1931, when Huxley tells Flora Strousse that if she wants "to read a *good* book, get *The Castle* by Kafka, translated by Edwin Muir: it makes the other German novelists, even Mann, look pretty thin and insubstantial."[2] From another letter, dated 19 June 1930, to Stephen Hudson [Schiff], it appears that Huxley actually read this novel by Kafka (and Hermann Hesse's *Steppenwolf* as well) sometime in early 1930 (perhaps in connection with his trip to Berlin later that year with J. W. N. Sullivan), and it may be that Huxley was brushing up on contemporary German fiction at this time.[3] Even so, the casual reference to Mann in the later letter, mentioning no specifics, suggests that Huxley was acquainted with Mann's work before that period, though there is no hard evidence to prove such a hypothesis. The only one of Mann's titles that Huxley ever names is "Mario und der Zauberer," to which he refers obliquely in the one letter he addressed directly to Mann, a note of congratulation on Mann's sixtieth birthday in April 1935. In that letter, in which he expresses his hope that Mann will return to Sanary "at least for the duration of a short story or even (would it be too much to hope?) for that of a whole novel," he refers to Mann himself as Mario the Magician, which if Huxley had actually read Mann's story, or at least had read it attentively, it is doubtful he would have done.[4] The magician, in that story, after all, is not Mario, but the evil Cipolla, whose speech and actions betray an unmistakable and intended resemblance to Mussolini. The source of Huxley's confusion is perhaps to be found in the fact that the magic of "Mario and the Magician" evoked for him the far greater and "whiter" magic of *The Magic Mountain*, as well as in the circumstance that Mann was habitually referred to by members of his immediate family as "Der Zauberer" ("The Magician"). Huxley was actually in much closer contact, both at Sanary and later in the United States, with Thomas Mann's eldest son, Klaus, than he was with Mann himself, and it is not inconceivable that he might have gathered this kind of information from him.[5] Be that as it may, it seems fairly safe to assume that Huxley had read some of Thomas Mann's fiction by the late 1920s, and probably at least part of *The Magic Mountain*, which had enjoyed great popularity in a variety of languages, including English, soon after its publication in 1924, and which was an essential contributing factor in the decision to award Thomas Mann the Nobel Prize in 1929.

Despite Huxley's homage to Mann on his birthday—and another, briefer message, together with Somerset Maugham, H. G. Wells, and others on the occasion of Mann's seventieth birthday—Huxley never appears to have considered "The Magician" a novelist of the first rank;[6] compared to Kafka, as we have seen, he found him "thin and insubstantial." And in the list of books which Huxley drew up in his sadly prophetic essay, "If My Library Burned Tonight" (1947), none of Mann's books is included, nor, for that matter, any German writers except Goethe, Schopenhauer, and Heine. Though Huxley had had a German governess as a boy and had gone to Marburg in his teens to study German, though he had visited Germany twice in the interwar period and was quite close to several Germans, including his eventual biographer Sybille Bedford, Huxley's knowledge of and sympathy for things German (with the notable exception of German music) were very limited. It is difficult to escape the conclusion that, if pressed, Huxley would have admitted sharing what D. J. Enright sees as the "commonest or most-commonly voiced English objection to German literature . . . that this literature is wordy, philosophical, humorless, highly abstract, and crammed with details. In brief, heavy-handed."[7] To be sure, he might have exempted Mann from the charge of being humorless, but he would probably have let the remainder of the indictment stand. And as far as Mann personally was concerned, it seems that Huxley was not specially fond of him either, despite occasional birthday greetings, or joint ocean-crossings—as in 1937, on the *Normandie*—or friendly strolls down surprising Southern California beaches. Writing to Dr. Felix Mann (no relation) in 1961, several years after Mann's death, Huxley thanks him for "your description of yourself," and goes on to say that "long acquaintance with your namesake, Thomas, has led me to visualize you as an eccentric German of about 65. It is very gratifying to find that I was mistaken!"[8] One eccentric German like Thomas Mann, in other words, was enough to last Huxley a lifetime.

Thomas Mann, on the other hand, took a far more positive view of Huxley. Writing in 1934 to Karl Kerenyi in response to the latter's request for his views on Huxley, Lawrence, and J. C. Powys, Mann says that "von den englischen Schriftstellern auf die Sie hinweisen, kenne ich zweie recht gut," that is, Huxley and Lawrence; and then praises Huxley, especially Huxley's essays, as "eine feinste Blüte west-europäischen Geistes. Ich ziehe ihn D. H. Lawrence vor, der zweifellos eine bedeutende und zeitkarakteristische Erscheinung ist, dessen hektische Sinnlichkeit mich aber wenig anmutet."[9] That this view was one which Mann held consistently is confirmed by other references elsewhere in his published work. In *Die Entstehung des Doktor Faustus* (1949), for instance, Mann recalls reading Huxley's *Time Must Have a Stop* shortly after it was published in 1944, and enjoying it hugely, calling it "eine kecke Spitzenleistung des heutigen Romans ohne Zweifel."[10] And in a brief survey of postwar fiction, "Wie steht es um die Nachkriegsdichtung?" (1949), Mann even goes so far as to suggest indirectly that he considers Huxley an approximate professional equal: "Brochs 'Vergil', meines Bruders Spät-Roman 'Der Atem', Hesse's [sic] 'Glasperlenspiel', manches von Aldous Huxley, selbst mein eigener 'Faustus'-Roman sind grösser und als Dokumente der Zeit ausgiebiger, als was die Jungen bisher hervorgebracht."[11] While these observations, it is true, have a certain sameness about them and do not reveal any particularly penetrating insight into Huxley's work, they unquestionably demonstrate Mann's continuing respect and admiration for that work, even to the point (as in the letter comparing Lawrence with Huxley) of implying a kind of kinship in the ideals underlying Huxley's and his own writing.

The case for influence, one way or the other, will not, let me repeat, be argued here; even if such influence could be shown to exist, it would be, I suspect, negligible. For while both writers share a number of important interests and descend from common intellectual origins, their ways of combining those interests and transforming those origins—their "styles," in short—are rather different. Nevertheless, it is worth noting how close, in many respects, they actually were. Both Mann and Huxley had unregenerately "encyclopedic" minds, and in practice they habitually disregarded Goethe's advice to the writer to read all the philosophers but keep them out of one's work. They read, if not all, at least most of the philosophers—and the scientists, sociologists, psychologists, and intellectual historians as well—and put them merrily into their stories, novellas, novels, essays, lectures, and, in Huxley's case, poems, plays, and scripts. They were both also extremely well read in French literature, to which they repeatedly acknowledged their debt, and—perhaps surprisingly so in Mann's case—in English literature, notably the humorous novelists of the eighteenth and nineteenth centuries. In the "Princeton Introduction" (1939) to The Magic Mountain, for instance, Mann explicitly refers to the "englisch-humoristisch ausladende Stil" in which he composed his novel[12]; and Huxley's admiration for English novelists beginning with Fielding (and for English poetry and drama in general) is well known. Both writers shared a strong interest in psychic and extrasensory phenomena, and both dealt with these subjects in fiction and nonfiction alike. Both were fascinated by the irrational, "demonic" aspects of human nature and at the same time distrusted these aspects profoundly, preferring instead the "world of light" to the dark human underworld which predecessors like Nietzsche and Dostoevsky, or contemporaneous psychologists like Freud and Jung, had revealed to them; and both accordingly explored that underworld cautiously and hypertactically, attempting to encompass as much of it as possible in an orderly, rational linguistic framework. Both, paradoxically, were at the same time convinced vitalists, rejecting any system which sought to explain the world by purely rational, positivistic, or "mechanistic" means. Both were practitioners, as Georg Lukács clearly recognized in Mann's case, of "bourgeois realism," conscious inheritors and preservers of the great tradition of the nineteenth-century European novel; and yet at the same time both partook of their own age's lust for literary experimentation, especially in terms of temporal distortion and the employment of musical analogies. Both were novelists who "used" the novel for ends which, from a purely formalistic point of view, were nonliterary: that is, for the promulgation of what they considered to be essential political, social, and religious truths; and both perceived themselves therefore, a little ironically perhaps, as noncongenital novelists: witness the remarks of Huxley's novelist-within-the-novel, Philip Quarles, in this respect; or Thomas Mann's words on the occasion of the death of the popular German novelist, Jacob Wassermann, in 1934: "Sein Werk hat mir wegen eines gewissen leeren Pompes und Feierlichen Geplappers oft ein Lächeln abgenötigt, obgleich ich wohl sah, dass er mehr echtes Erzählerblut hatte als ich."[13] Both would have been more than a little tempted to agree with Ortega y Gasset's observation, in *Notes on the Novel* (1925), that man's love for pure storytelling as such is an atavism left over from the childhood of the race; and that what really matters in a work of fiction is not the story, but the intellectual content and the intellectual implications of the way the story is told.

Not only in their spiritual and literary biographies are there numerous striking parallels, but in their personal lives as well. Both were members of distinguished families belonging to the prewar *haute bourgeoisie*, though in Mann's case intellectual distinction was achieved only in his and his brother's generation; both married women who were prepared to subordinate their own very genuine personalities to their husbands' talents, and who—as with Elinor Quarles in *Point Counter Point*—acted as emotional dragomen for their hyperintellectualized spouses. Both were and felt themselves to be "exiles" of a sort, almost from the very start of their literary careers: Mann because of the sense of alienation from the bourgeois North German Lübeck which drove him to the antithetical Bavarian and bohemian Munich of the turn of the century—as well as later, of course, his quite literal exile from Nazi Germany; Huxley, because of his revulsion against the intrigues of London literary life and his preference for Italy, France, and finally California, as well as his emotional inner exile brought on by the near-blindness that befell him as a teenager. Both were literary prodigies, establishing their reputations (even on an international scale) with breathtaking precocity: Mann at twenty-six with *Buddenbrooks* and Huxley at about the same age with *Limbo* and *Crome Yellow* and various collections of poems. And both, oddly enough, were attracted by the very same places in which to live or spend their holidays: Forte dei Marmi, where both Mann and Huxley spent summers vacationing in the Twenties; Sanary, where Huxley owned a house and where Mann lived during the first months of exile in 1933; and Los Angeles, where Huxley made his home from the late Thirties onwards and where Mann resided during most of the Forties.

With all these resemblances, it may seem surprising that more has not been made of the Mann-Huxley connection. Hitherto only one essay, Ernst Kohn-Bramstedt's "Intellectual as Ironist: Aldous Huxley and Thomas Mann" (1939), has been devoted specifically to comparing these two writers.[14] Inevitably, one is tempted to ask: why this paucity of critical comment? It is difficult to say for certain, though one reason surely is the relative lack of interest in the connection by Mann and Huxley themselves, who, despite their similarity of interests and frequent physical propinquity, are known to have exchanged only one letter during their entire lives, and that a very formal one. Another reason may be that Huxley's intimate links with French literature have kept students of his work away from any, necessarily more remote, German associations; just as Mann's intense and self-avowed "Germanness" may have intimidated those who would view him from a more Anglo-Saxon perspective.

3

The novel of ideas is, in a very fundamental sense, a misnomer. As anyone with literary training, or even with an intelligent acquaintance with a variety of novels, knows, there are no novels without ideas. Even the most notoriously non- or anti-intellectual novelists—even Mickey Spillane or Harold Robbins or Rudyard Kipling—have ideas: if only the ideas that might is right, or that the will to power is the basic human impulse, or that the British Empire is the summit of human achievement. Furthermore, every really successful serious novel (and often unserious ones as well) is, among other things, an intellectually sophisticated statement. Dickens's *Great Expectations*, for instance, has never, to the best of my knowledge, been classified as a novel of ideas; but it is undeniably a novel which raises, and attempts to answer, such vitally important intellectual questions as: what is man's relation to his society? what respect does he owe to his tradition and family? what is the nature of evil—inherent or environmental, or both? The same could be said of countless other novels, from Defoe's to Margaret Drabble's.

What this means in connection with the novel of ideas is, I think, that this type of fiction does not belong to a different genre, but is simply a species within the genre. The difference is in degree, not kind. Put another way, the novel of ideas cannot be expressed by the formula: novel + ideas = novel of ideas; the novel of ideas is first and foremost and finally a novel, but it is a novel in which the intellectual content is either more overt or more stressed, or both, than is the case with other species of the novel.

A failure to perceive the primary *artistic* essence of the novel of ideas leads to misunderstandings of the kind embodied in Eliot's famous remark about James, that "he had a mind so fine that no idea ever crossed it." To this sort of definition of ideas which makes them into utterly abstract and fleshless universals, the only proper reply is that of Erich Heller in *Enterbter Geist* (1954):

> Definiert man aber Denken auf solche Weise, dass das, was Shakespeare tat, als er die Reden Hamlets, Ulysses' oder Lears ersann, als Nicht-Denken erscheint, so ist es um das Denken auch schon geschehen. . . . Wenn ein Denken ohne die mitfühlende Phantasie und ein Fühlen ohne den mitdenkenden Gedanken zum Vorbild für Denken und Fühlen wird, dann ist die Leid-Stadt da, die fruchtlose Stätte der Trauer, oder das *Waste Land*, das Ödland, vor dem Nietzsche und Rilke und Eliot erschrecken, der Gedanke sowohl wie das Gedicht.

In a novel of ideas, the ideas are embodied, not left hanging in the void, and where they are not embodied, the result is not a novel of ideas, but a treatise, like Johnson's *Rasselas*, or a kind of Platonic dialogue, like W. J. Turner's *Aesthetes*. Or, as André Gide puts it, by way of reply to the criticism I have prefaced to this essay: "À cause des maladroits qui s'y sont fourvoyés, devons-nous condamner le roman d'idées? En guise de romans d'idées on ne nous a servi jusqu'à présent que d'éxecrables romans à thèses. Mais il ne s'agit pas de cela, vous pensez bien. Les idées . . . , les idées, je vous l'avoue, m'intéressent plus que les hommes; m'intéressent pardessus tout. Elles vivent; elles combattent; elles agonisent comme les hommes."[15]

Because the novel of ideas is inherently concerned with people who have, or think they have, ideas (as well as emotions and imaginations), because these ideas tend to figure prominently in this type of novel, its audience is usually more sophisticated and intellectual—and more limited—than that for most other sorts of novel. But this surely need not mean that the novel of ideas must for that reason be inferior in artistic quality to other kinds of novels; on the contrary, it may mean that the novel of ideas can be the vehicle for some of the greatest novels of all: as it is, say, in Stendhal's *Rouge et Noir*, Goethe's *Wahlverwandschaften*, Flaubert's *Bouvard et Pecuchet*, Dostoevsky's *Brothers Karamazov*, Gide's *Faux-monnayeurs*, and Nabokov's *Pale Fire*. Philip Quarles sums it all up nicely in one of his journal entries, in which he characteristically puts *this* idea within the framework of his own personality:

> Novel of ideas. The character of each personage must be implied, as far as possible, in the ideas of which he is the mouthpiece. In so far as theories are rationalizations of sentiments, instincts, dispositions of soul, this is feasible. The chief defect of the novel of ideas is that you must write about people who have ideas to express—which excludes all but about .01 per cent of the human race. Hence the real, the congenital novelists don't write such books. But then I never pretended to be a congenital novelist.[16]

The novel of ideas, in other words, is an elitist genre because, paradoxically, it takes, or seeks to take, the whole range of intellectual conceptions of reality into account, rather than being satisfied with a single such view, as "congenital" novels are.

Rather than draw up a list here of all the ideas expressed by all the characters in *Point Counter Point* and *The Magic Mountain*—a useful exercise, perhaps, but, as we have seen, not really pertinent to getting at what the novel of ideas is all about—I propose to focus on demonstrating (selectively) how both Huxley and Mann succeed in integrating ideas with character and narrative to produce a satisfying work of art, frequently by employing similar novelistic techniques.

One of the most important ideas in both novels is, ironically and paradoxically, the idea that the rational intellect is an inadequate means for probing the "whole truth." This is one of the chief reasons, I think, why Mann puts, and puts up with, the ambiguously "mediocre" and certainly quite unheroic Hans Castorp at the centre of his novel; and why he allows him to gain insights (in the "Snow" chapter, for instance) which are beyond the intellectually far more formidable Settembrini and Naptha. This is also the reason why the inarticulate and nonintellectual Mynheer Pieter Peeperkorn—who, in his ample proportions and vast relish for sensual pleasure, embodies, if it is possible to say so, the flesh—why this odd and surprising figure is able, on the one hand, to neutralize the conversational duels of Settembrini and Naptha, and on the other, by stopping their mouths, to bring them eventually and indirectly to the point of converting their unsublimated verbal energy into tragic action.

Aldous Huxley seeks to bring his reader to similar conclusions by contrasting the over-intellectualized novelist Philip Quarles with the "balanced" painter Mark Rampion: the former a man whose body is damaged, whose emotions are nearly atrophied, and whose excessively developed brain works so exclusively with abstractions that it is utterly lost in personal relations; in contrast, the latter is a fully integrated personality, willing to give equal attention to the claims of the body, the emotions, and the mind (but not, it is important to note, the soul). In this sense, Huxley's antiintellectual Rampion is a more subtle and credible creation than Mann's intellectual nonintellectual Castorp; we can believe in someone with Rampion's mental and artistic gifts superseding the purely cerebral point of view of a Philip Quarles, or the purely materialistic point of view of an Illidge. It is not so easy to accept the simple, plain, insignificant, mediocre ("simpel," "einfach," "unbedeutend," "Mittelmässig," as Mann repeatedly insists) Hans Castorp doing the same for the extremely sharp-witted and complex Settembrini and Naptha. Mann, of course, is fully aware of the problem; indeed, insofar as *The Magic Mountain* may be said to tell a story, its story is that of the transformation—the *magical* transformation—brought about in Hans Castorp by his quasi-Zarathustran stay on the mountain. Mann explicitly points to this aspect of Castorp in the "Princeton Introduction" when he isolates as a basic theme of the novel the "heightening" or "raising to a higher power" ("Steigerung") which he terms alchemistic: "Sie erinnern sich: der junge Hans Castorp ist ein simpler Held. In der fieberhaften Hermetik des Zauberbergs aber erfährt dieser schlichte Stoff eine Steigerung, die ihn zu moralischen, geistigen und sinnlichen Abenteuern fähig macht, von denen er sich in der Welt, die immer ironisch als das Flachland bezeichnet wird, nie hätte etwas träumen lassen" (I, xv). Mann makes much the same point in the antepenultimate paragraph of his novel: "Lebewohl, Hans Castorp, des Lebens treuherziges Sorgenkind! Deine Geschichte ist aus. Zu Ende haben wir sie erzählt; sie war weder kurzweilig noch langweilig, es war eine hermetische Geschichte. Wir haben sie erzählt um ihretwillen, nicht deinethalben, denn du warst simpel. Aber zuletzt war es deine Geschichte; da sie dir zustiess, musstest du's irgend wohl hinter den Ohren haben . . ." (II, 509). Here we have it again, the "simple" hero who is not so simple after all—a complicated simpleton, as it were. This paradoxical condition permits Mann to have his hero and mock him too, to be simultaneously tragic and ironic. It also permits him to introduce, by way of educating or "transforming" his hero, a great mass of intellectual material which would otherwise appear only marginally relevant or aesthetically monstrous; and, perhaps most important, it permits him to retain his distance from both his hero and the ideas which that hero either formulates for himself or comes into contact with. The reader is therefore kept continually guessing as to whether Mann (or the narrator) really "means" it or not, with the inevitable ironic result that the published criticism on *The Magic Mountain* is unable to make up its collective mind whether to be awestruck at Hans Castorp's profundity or smile at the "hoariness of his philosophical musings."[17]

In *Point Counter Point*, Huxley does not enjoy similar opportunities for turning dross into gold by means of this kind of philosopher's stonehead, but he is able to achieve aesthetic distance, to some degree at least, by opting for the next best alternative to the antihero, namely, to have no hero at all. Mark Rampion, to be sure, comes dangerously close at times to occupying the vacant position of hero, but, as I have argued elsewhere, he never really succeeds.[18] Mark Rampion's virile attempt to encompass, physically and mentally, the whole range of this-worldly existence is theoretically heroic, and is recognized as such by Philip Quarles, but it is by no means unequivocally endorsed by the events of the novel; Spandrell's "diabolist" or Augustinian otherworldly point of view receives at least equal attention and has the additional advantage of taking into account a number of phenomena which Rampion's ideas cannot cope with. Furthermore, by introducing excerpts from Philip Quarles's journal into the novel, Huxley is able to reflect naturally and effectively on the events and ideas in the novel, *without having to assume responsibility for these reflections*. Huxley, therefore, easily preserves a distance (intellectual and aesthetic) which Mann is only able to maintain by means of his complicated game of "does he or doesn't he" between Hans Castorp and the reader.

In both novels, it must however be admitted, this distance between the storyteller and his story occasionally breaks down, either partially or totally. In Mann, these breakdowns are sometimes carefully planned and "mannered" interruptions in what must have seemed to him the "English" style; so, for instance, the narrator pauses every now and then to speculate on the passage of time and to relate his (and his reader's) experience of narrative time to the time and/or times of Hans Castorp's "actual" experience. This kind of "Romantic irony"—as defined by Friedrich Schlegel—serves the double purpose of alerting the reader to the temporal aspects of the novel and of, paradoxically, reestablishing narrative distance by appearing to destroy it; that is, by transforming the narrator, as in a novel by Fielding or Thackeray, into another character of the novel, even if only momentarily. Hence the occasional pretense of the narrator to be unaware of the motives of certain actions, or even his apparent ignorance of such matters of fact as where Hans Castorp bought his scientific textbooks (I, 365).[19] More drastic, and from an aesthetic point of view, less justifiable are the narrator's more direct attempts to guide the reader's response to the characters and events of his story. Significantly, these attempts occur almost exclusively in the latter parts of the novel—a circumstance which suggests that Mann is either losing control of his vast and complex tale, or afraid that his reader may be. So, for instance, just before the crucially important chapter, "Snow," in which Castorp achieves a mystical, nonverbal understanding of the meaning of existence, Mann has his hero "see through" the futility of Settembrini's and Naptha's verbiage; but he is not content to leave it at that, he must underline Castorp's criticism with his own, more poetically ironic one: "Hans Castorp aber begab sich in seine Balkonloge, die Ohren voll vom Wirrwarr und Waffenlärm der beiden Heere, die, von Jerusalem und Babylon vorrück-end, unter den dos banderas zu konfusem Schlachtgetümmel zusammentra-fen" (II, 168). And just in case the hasty reader should have missed the point here, Mann repeats it for him in the chapter following "Snow," in which he denounces "jene Widersacher im Geiste" who carry on "ihre unauf-hörlichen Duelle, bei deren Vorführung wir irgendwelche Vollständigkeit nicht anstreben können, ohne uns ebenso ins Desperat-Unendliche zu ver-lieren, wie sie es täglich taten . . ." (II, 223).

In *Point Counter Point*, Aldous Huxley is, generally speaking, less guilty of this kind of *parti pris* for the sake of manipulating the reader's reaction, though there are rare occasions when he will not hesitate to provide a helpful push or shove. So, for instance, describing Philip Quarles's disastrous efforts to educate his son, efforts culminating in a frustrated fury which Philip is too "gentlemanly" to express, Huxley remarks: "Instead of healthily breaking out he made an effort of will and more than ever tightly shut himself in" (427). This breach of narrative distance may seem trivial compared to Mann's, but it is sufficient to indicate to the alert reader the response which he is intended by the author to have to this character. And to the reader who is not merely alert but also aware of Huxley's book of "Lawrentian" educational theory, *Proper Studies* (1927), this moral bias reveals by implication a whole system of ideas.[20] Even more problematic, in this connection, is the fact— quite obvious to many of Huxley's first readers and by now a commonplace in the critical literature—that Philip Quarles, and to a lesser degree Walter Bidlake, are fairly accurate portraits of facets of Huxley's own personality. Here is narrative interference with a vengeance, since any truly thorough reading of the novel must inevitably come to grips with the question about how (and how much) Philip Quarles's views and ideas reflect Aldous Huxley's—or, for that matter, Rampion's reflect D. H. Lawrence's, or Spandrell's Peter Warlock's, or Burlap's Middleton Murry's, or Lucy Tantamount's Nancy Cunard's, or John Bidlake's Augustus John's, and so on. The interpretation of Huxley's novel of ideas is greatly complicated by the circumstance of its also being a *roman à clef* in which the real-life originals hold ideas analogous to those expressed by their counterparts in the novel.

To some extent, Thomas Mann is guilty of this sort of thing in *The Magic Mountain* as well. Hans Castorp's experience, as recounted in the opening pages of the novel, is self-avowedly and recognizably Mann's own experience during his first visit to Davos in 1912; and other aspects of Castorp's character and origins bear an obvious resemblance to Mann's. The spiritualist seance, for example, is based on an actual experience of Mann's in 1922.[21] Hofrat Behrens is confessedly a portrait of the head of the Berghof sanatorium at the time Mann and his wife stayed there. Settembrini, if not in his person, then in his capacity of "Zivilisationsliterat" bears some resemblance to Mann's brother, Heinrich; Naptha's physique, though possibly little else, is derived, as is by now well known, from that of the Marxist critic and philosopher, Georg Lukács; and Mynheer Peeperkorn's inarticulate vitality is, of course, notoriously based on Gerhard Hauptmann's. It would seem, then, that there is little difference between Huxley's method of translating actual personalities and their ideas into fiction, and Mann's. But such a supposition would be incorrect. With the possible exception of Peeperkorn, whose intellectual value is in any event minimal—"Ja, dieser dumme alte Mann," as the narrator says, "dies herrscherliche Zero!" (II, 339)—none of the characters in *The Magic Mountain* bears a more than superficial resemblance to his original. Behrens may look like "Behrens," may talk like "Behrens," but his ideas and history are not those of "Behrens"; so too with Settembrini, Naptha, and Castorp. As a consequence, the intellectual debate between "liberal" Settembrini and "conservative" Naptha, while sharing close connections with actual contemporaneous discussion of the same issues, is not identifiable with any particular, real-life spokesmen. Heinrich Mann's ideas, in other words, cannot be simply substituted for Settembrini's and Georg Lukács's for Naptha's. The result is that the ideas are self-contained within the artistic framework of *The Magic Mountain*—

hermetically sealed, one is tempted to say—in a way they are not in *Point Counter Point*, where fictional and nonfictional exponents of ideas overlap.

This criticism, however, should not be taken to mean that Huxley's characters (or even Mann's) are mere "mouthpieces." This is, of course, one of the traditional attacks made on the novel of ideas generally, and so it should not be surprising that neither Huxley nor Mann have been exempt from it. By its very nature (this argument usually runs), the novel of ideas produces two-dimensional characters, lacking credibility and vitality, mere puppets voicing their author's favorite ideas. The published criticism on *Point Counter Point* teems with versions of this argument, especially with reference to Mark Rampion. Criticism on *The Magic Mountain* is not quite so much given over to attacks of this sort, but they do exist, e.g., Ernst Robert Curtius's remarks in "Thomas Manns 'Zauberberg' " (1925) that Settembrini and Naptha are "Puppen, sie sind nur dazu da, um während vieler hundert Seiten sich in geschliffener Dialektik zu bekämpfen und zu zersausen. Sie sind Ideensymbole, die nicht Fleisch geworden sind."[22]

Both Huxley and Mann were well aware that the "puppet" character was one of the chief dangers facing the novelist of ideas, and both sought to guard against this danger by integrating character and ideas. Philip Quarles, as we have seen, insists in his journal on the need for having the personality of the character implicit in his ideas, and sees this as attainable in terms of viewing ideas as "rationalizations of sentiments, instincts, dispositions of soul" (409). Mann is less explicit about the means of avoiding fictional "puppetry," but he is no less clear about his aims. In the "Princeton Introduction" he admits freely that his characters are "lauter Exponenten, Repräsentanten und Sendboten geistiger Bezirke, Prinzipien und Welten," and then goes on to say, "Ich hoffe, sie sind deswegen keine Schatten und wandelnde Allegorien. Im Gegenteil bin ich durch die Erfahrung beruhigt, dass der Leser diese Personen, Joachim, Clawdia Chauchat, Peeperkorn, Settembrini und wie sie heissen [!], als wirkliche Menschen erlebt, deren er sich wie wirklich gemachter Bekanntschaften erinnert" (I, xv). Both Mann and Huxley are not afraid, as we can see, to admit that their characters are "mouthpieces" or intellectual spokesmen and representatives, but both deny that their characters are for that reason lifeless. One of the chief reasons they are not lifeless, I think, is that Huxley and Mann succeed, in general, in preserving an aesthetic distance between themselves and their characters, so that the characters are "mouthpieces" for themselves and *not* for their authors. While it may be that eventually Hans Castorp prefers Settembrini to Naptha, and while we may have the strong impression that Mann shares that preference, nowhere is Settembrini given an easy victory over Naptha. On the contrary, though Naptha dies in the duel with Settembrini, it is by his own hand, in a gesture of defiant nobility. The same is true of Huxley's novel, where Spandrell's equally defiant suicide provides the counter point to Rampion's "liberalism." Another reason they are not lifeless is that they are both more and less than their ideas; in other words, their actions are not merely exemplifications of their ideas in a purely allegorical way, but are frequently, and ironically, contradictions thereof. Illidge, for instance, is not a communist on intellectual grounds, but for very personal reasons, having to do with his own ugliness and smallness of stature. Similarly, Spandrell's diabolism derives to a considerable degree from a prepubertal mother-fixation; and Philip Quarles's hyperintellectualism is partly the result of an accident which left him clubfooted. Huxley is at great pains to show the psychosomatic sources of ideas, so that in a way which is perhaps true of all novels of ideas, *Point Counter Point* is as much concerned with psychology as it is with ideas. Certainly this is the case with *The Magic Mountain* as well. Even without the mediation of Dr. Krokowski, it would be difficult to miss Mann's careful probing of the underlying causes of Hans Castorp's "development"; or Mann's suggestion that Castorp's "mountain-change" has psychosomatic origins involving links between love, disease, and artistic sensibility. Similarly Mann provides enough information about Settembrini and Naptha to enable us to draw analogous conclusions about the origins of their intellectual biases. Finally, it should be remembered that part of both Mann's and Huxley's intention is to demonstrate that an intellectual bias inevitably leads to narrow and limited interpretations of reality as a whole.

The most striking and innovative of all the methods of "humanizing" ideas in both novels, however, is the method which Philip Quarles calls "the musicalization of fiction." From one point of view, this is paradoxical, because music, while the most abstract, is also the least intellectual of arts. There may be humorous music, tragic music, heroic music, even program music, but there is no intellectual music, not even Beethoven's late quartets; ideas, as distinguished from emotions, may enter music only when music mixes with language, as it does in opera or oratorio or lieder. This very nonintellectuality of music, however, turns out to be an advantage for the novelist of ideas, for by making use of music as a means for structuring his action and incorporating his ideas, he can, as it were, relativize those ideas, can treat them as the means to art rather than as ends in themselves. "Der Roman war mir immer eine Symphonie," Mann writes in this connection, "ein Werk der Kontrapunktik, ein Themengewebe, worin die Ideen die Rolle musikalischer Motive spielen" (I, xv). It is for this reason that Mann calls *The Magic Mountain* "diese in zwölf-hundert Seiten ausgebreitete Gedankenkomposition."

Let me say at once that I do not propose here to read and explicate the vast score, as it were, of this mental music in Mann's and Huxley's novels, especially in view of the fact that careful discussions of the use of musical technique in both novels exist already. Suffice it to say that literary counterpoint, as practiced by Huxley, is almost wholly dissonant (hence the satire), and, as used by Mann, only momentarily harmonious (hence the irony). It is this intellectual, literary counterpoint which, in the final analysis, reveals how closely related *Point Counter Point* and *The Magic Mountain* really are: both contain full orchestras of characters, but with no conductor, except for the usually remote author; both make much of the different intellectual tonalities of their character-instruments; both use contrapuntal technique on a small and a vast scale, either by juxtaposing word and thought, or idea-complex; both focus on a limited number of universal themes—love, disease, death—and variously modulate these themes, from heroic (Webley, Ziemssen), to tragic (Spandrell, Naptha), to comic (Burlap, James Tienappel), to sublime ("Snow," the final chapter of *Point Counter Point*), to ridiculous (Quarles Sr., Frau Stöhr).

Both writers also introduce music directly into their narratives: Mann by having Castorp play a series of recordings, chiefly operatic and other vocal selections; Huxley by providing lengthy descriptions of pieces by Bach and Beethoven. In both cases, the music serves the dual purpose of (re)calling the reader's attention to the musical elements in the structure of the novel and of adding richness or resonance—to important themes. As T. J. Reed observes, Hans Castorp's favorite operatic arias all evoke his own situation, that of a lover "corrupted" by his love into betraying the moral aspects of his nature; and Schubert's "Lindenbaum" (the only German, nonoperatic piece) even proposes death as a means of escape from that situation.[23] In *Point Counter Point*, the music is even more important, especially the final description of Beethoven's "Heiliger Dankgesang eines Genesenen an die Gottheit," in which music—precisely because it is nonverbal and nonintellectual—is viewed by Spandrell, and very likely by Huxley himself, as a quasi-mystical way to God.

The Magic Mountain and *Point Counter Point* are, as we have seen, closely related in a number of respects, at times strikingly so. Both novels devote a great deal of time to contrasting "liberal" and "conservative" ideas; both arrange to have the chief spokesman for the conservative side commit an elaborately staged suicide in order to "prove his point." Both novels present characters embodying a nonintellectual life-force (Pieter Peeperkorn and John Bidlake) as possible alternatives to these points of view, though *Point Counter Point* rejects this "mindless" alternative decisively in a way *The Magic Mountain* does not. Both perceive in love a force which can simultaneously corrupt (Hans Castorp and Clawdia Chauchat; Walter Bidlake and Lucy Tantamount) and ennoble (Hans Castorp and Clawdia Chauchat; Mark and Mary Rampion). Both bring in theoretical science, as well as practical biology and medicine, in a way that is unparalleled in the other fiction of the Twenties. Both approximate, in their vastness of scope and multiplicity of character, that Hegelian totality of objects which is a precondition for the greatest works of art and which also makes of these two novels something like epics of their respective times and places. All these resemblances are the result, not of influence, but of the *Zeitgeist* and the profound affinity of Mann's and Huxley's minds. And their profoundest affinity—the one which makes them

comparable in a way no two other novelists of the period are comparable—
is their obsession with the mental music of ideas.

Notes

1. Aldous Huxley, "Fifth Philosopher's Song," in *Verses and a Comedy* (London: Chatto & Windus, 1946), p. 58.

2. Huxley, *Letters*, ed. Grover Smith (London: Chatto & Windus, 1969), p. 345.

3. Clementine Robert, ed., *Aldous Huxley, Exhumations: Correspondence inédite avec Sidney Schiff* (Paris: Didier, 1976), p. 68.

4. Huxley, *Letters*, p. 392.

5. Huxley, at Klaus Mann's urging, became one of the three sponsors (the others being Heinrich Mann and André Gide) of the German emigré review, *Die Sammlung*, which was published in Amsterdam and edited by Klaus Mann. For further information concerning Huxley's contacts with Klaus Mann, see the latter's *Der Wendepunkt: Ein Lebensbericht* (Frankfurt: Suhrkamp, 1963), esp. pp. 286–87.

6. There is a remote possibility that Huxley may have inherited this view from D. H. Lawrence, who, in a 1913 notice of Mann's work, called him "the last sick sufferer from the complaint of Flaubert." See Armin Arnold, "D. H. Lawrence and Thomas Mann," *Comparative Literature*, 13 (Winter 1961), 38. It is perhaps also worth noting that Huxley held a similarly dim view of the other great contemporaneous novelist of ideas, André Gide.

7. D. J. Enright, "Aimez-vous Goethe?" *Encounter*, 22 (April 1964), 93.

8. Huxley, *Letters*, p. 909.

9. *Thomas Mann—Karl Kerenyi: Gespräch in Briefen* (Zürich: Rhein Verlag, 1960), p. 41.

10. Thomas Mann, *Die Entstehung des Doktor Faustus: Roman eines Romans* (Frankfurt am Main: Suhrkamp, 1949), p. 87.

11. Thomas Mann, *Gesammelte Werke*, Band X, *Reden und Aufsätze* (Oldenburg: S. Fischer Verlag, 1960), p. 924.

12. Thomas Mann, *Der Zauberberg*, Band I (Berlin: Deutsche Buch-Gemeinschaft, 1958), p. xi. All further references to this work will be incorporated in the text, by page number preceded by a Roman numeral indicating the volume, all enclosed in parentheses.

13. Quoted in Roman Karst, *Thomas Mann oder der deutsche Zwiespalt* (Wien: Fritz Molden Verlag, 1970), p. 122.

14. Ernst Kohn-Bramstedt, "The Intellectual as Ironist: Aldous Huxley and Thomas Mann," *The Contemporary Review*, 55 (April 1939), 470–79. Kohn-Bramstedt tends to favor Mann at the expense of Huxley, arguing that Mann creates unforgettable characters, Huxley forgettable ones. The basic source of their irony, in his view, lies in their characteristic solipsism. Hence it is no "mere accident that the two greatest literary figures the twentieth century has hitherto produced in England and Germany should resemble one another so closely."

15. Erich Heller, *Enterbter Geist: Essays über modernes Dichten und Denken* (Frankfurt: Suhrkamp, 1954), p. 210; and André Gide, *Les Faux-Monnayeurs* (Paris: Gallimard, n.d.), p. 236.

16. Aldous Huxley, *Point Counter Point* (London: Chatto & Windus, 1928), pp. 409–10. All further references to this work will be incorporated in the text by page number enclosed in parentheses.

17. T. J. Reed, *Thomas Mann: The Uses of Tradition* (Oxford: The Clarendon Press, 1974), p. 249.

18.   Peter Firchow, *Aldous Huxley, Satirist and Novelist* (Minneapolis: University of Minnesota Press, 1972), pp. 109–11.

19.   On one occasion, however, the narrator (or, more likely, Mann himself) commits a downright blunder: at one point he describes Marusja, the girl Joachim Ziemssen is in love with, as having blue eyes (1,276); then, only eight pages later, he changes his mind and tells us they are brown. Even Mann nods, it would appear.

20.   To be quite fair, it should be said that this is also true of the close connections between the ideas expressed in *The Magic Mountain* and Mann's earlier *Betrachtungen eines Unpolitischen* (1918).

21.   See Mann's "Okkulte Erlebnisse," in *Gesammelte Werke*, Band X, pp. 135–71; and "Thomas Mann and the Occult: An Unpublished Letter," *Encounter*, 46 (April 1976), 21–24.

22.   In Heinz Saueressig, *Die Entstehung des Romans 'Der Zauberberg'* (Biberach: J. Fink Verlag, 1965), p. 52.

23.   Reed, *Mann*, pp. 266 ff.

The Manuscript Revisions of *Brave New World*

Donald Watt

For Aldous Huxley, the late spring and summer of 1931 was a period of challenging creative activity. On 18 May he wrote Mrs. Kethevan Roberts that he was composing a novel about the future, "on the horror of the Wellsian Utopia and a revolt against it." He confided that he was finding the task "very difficult," and he expressed concern over his ability to manage it: "I have hardly enough imagination to deal with such a subject."[1] Nine days later Huxley felt compelled to cancel a trip to Russia with his brother, Julian, because of problems with the composition of his book. Everything he had written in the past month, he lamented, had to be rewritten "in quite another way." He regarded the setback as a "literary catastrophe" which "throws me right back in my work" (*Letters*, 348–49). In a few weeks Huxley wrote Sidney Schiff (21 June 1931) about his deep involvement in his revisions: "I'm working very hard, re-writing large chunks of what I had thought definitively done and praying heaven that this time the revision may be final—while before me lie great deserts of the yet unwritten. So the Summer promises to be a well-occupied time."[2] Almost three months after his reluctant renunciation of the Russian venture with Julian, Huxley apologized to his father for a "shockingly long" hiatus in their correspondence: "My only excuse is that I have been harried with work—which I have at last, thank heaven, got rid of:—a comic, or at least satirical, novel about the Future." The sigh of relief in Huxley's letter is almost audible: "It has been a job writing the book and I'm glad it's done" (*Letters*, 351).

The cause of all the turmoil, and what occupied Huxley during those intervening three months, was of course the preparation of *Brave New World*.

Such labor in the composition of a novel was not unusual for Huxley. He told an interviewer toward the end of his life: "Generally, I write every-

From the *Journal of English and German Philology* 77 (1978): 367–82, © 1978 by the Board of Trustees of the University of Illinois. Used with permission of the author and the University of Illinois Press.

Previously unpublished materials from Huxley's manuscript are here printed with the kind permissions of Mrs. Laura Huxley and the Humanities Research Center, The University of Texas at Austin. I am grateful to the Research Foundation of the State University of New York for fellowship aid during Summer 1976 in support of the preparation of this article.

thing many times over. All my thoughts are second thoughts. And I correct each page a great deal, or rewrite it several times as I go along."[3] What is unusual is that, in the case of *Brave New World*, the manuscript of the novel is extant. A fire which in 1961 ruined Huxley's home in California also destroyed most of the manuscripts of his works, including *Antic Hay* and *Point Counter Point*.[4] It seems reasonable to conclude that the *Brave New World* script is probably the only surviving record of how Huxley composed his major fiction. The study of this script therefore yields some rare insights into the Huxleyan creative process in action.

A glance at the script confirms the impression of high challenge and laborious pursuit that Huxley gives in his correspondence on the composition of the novel. *Brave New World* was born amid a tangle of lined-out phrases, typed-over words, rearranged passages, and tireless autograph insertions. Huxley composed the novel on his typewriter and revised it by autograph emendations on successive versions of typed pages. The cover page of the extant script contains in Huxley's hand the notation that what follows is the "corrected typescript—the nearest approach to a manuscript version."[5] The sheets which follow, numbered sequentially 2–248, A1, B1–B9, and C1–C2, clearly attest to the struggle of which Huxley complains in his letters. The Park Lane Hospital scene, which occupies pages 189–99 in the script, is an anomaly inasmuch as it is in autograph and fills both sides of the sheets, which are accordingly numbered 189, 189^2, and so forth. I shall discuss later the probable significance of this manuscript insertion in light of what may have been for Huxley a moment of crisis in his work on the script.

Imperfections in the script, though, are important enough to require discussion before Huxley's revisions are considered in detail. For one thing, there is a distinct probability that substantial parts of the existing script are a conflation of an early worksheet version of the book with a later, more finished, but by no means final version. Periodic variations in the typeface strongly suggest this conflation. Sections of the script with the typeface bold and clear, containing relatively few and simple holograph revisions, alternate with sections with a much lighter, faded typeface in which Huxley's changes, both holograph and typed, are numerous and frequently involved. For another thing, there are some remarkable lacunae in the script. Most of the Solidarity Service in CW 94–99 is missing,[6] as are Dr. Shaw's explanation of *soma* to John at the beginning of Chapter XI, and the final scene of Chapter VIII (which includes Bernard's invitation to John to go to London, and the accompanying allusion to *The Tempest* from which the novel's title is derived). The imperfections suggest that what survives of the *Brave New World* script is a patchwork of Huxley's first draft and subsequent revisions before he put together fair copy for his publishers.

Despite these limitations, the extant script of *Brave New World* yields insights into Huxley's creative mind at almost every stage of the narrative's construction. The bulk of Huxley's revisions will be aired only when a variorum edition of the novel becomes available. The most that can be done within the limits of this essay is to describe representative examples of the types of changes, improvements, and, occasionally, problems that Huxley's script reveals. Accordingly, in order to give some shape to the welter of Huxley's revisions, I have organized the most important types of changes in his script into five groups: the sharpening of local details to achieve verisimilitude, the exercise of restraint and concision for narrative impact, the addition of authorial comments by the omniscient observer to create a satirical tone, the recasting of especially Bernard's and John's characters, and the apparent discovery, during a later stage of revision, of a dramatic structure for the book's climax.

Huxley sought persistently in his script to create a vivid, concrete picture of his brave new world. A major concern of his revisions was to filter out vague generalities and to replace them with life-evoking specific details comprehensible within the context of such a future society as he describes. At the opening of "Three Weeks in a Helicopter," for example, the gigantic black in Huxley's script at first embraces a mere "golden-haired young girl." In Huxley's revision she becomes "a golden-haired brachycephalic Beta plus female" (TS, 158/CW, 198). In describing "the famous British Museum Massacre" toward the close of Chapter III, Huxley originally had the unfortunate two thousand culture fans "squashed by tanks." In the revision it seemed more fitting to have them "gassed with dichlorethyl sulfide" (TS, 56/CW, 58). At the Amsterdam wrestling match in Chapter VI, Lenina in the script at first presses only *soma* upon Bernard. In a revision the *soma* turns into a "half-gramme raspberry sundae" (TS, 84/CW, 104). Lenina originally recalls Fanny's account of Bernard's unorthodoxy: "According to Fanny, Bernard was badly conditioned." This is given more point in the revision: " 'Alcohol in his blood surrogate,' was Fanny's explanation of every eccentricity" (TS, 83/CW, 102).

A short list of further autograph revisions which were incorporated into the novel's first edition will perhaps illustrate the direction of Huxley's efforts:

TS PAGE		CW PAGE	
27	"And when the babies were hatched . . ."	26	"And when the babies were decanted . . ."
33	one of the sex games	33	a game of Centrifugal Bumble-puppy
84	games were rather a waste of time	103	Electro-Magnetic Golf was rather a waste of time
85	tremulous voices	105	tremoloing falsettos
94	coffee	116	boiling caffeine solution

100	octaroon pilot	123	Gamma-green octaroon
133	"Perfectly" [safe]	166–67	"Safe as helicopters"
138	lessons in cleanliness, auto-erotism and class feeling, and many other such matters of vital importance	173	lessons in hygiene and sociability, in class-consciousness and the toddler's love-life
162	she had been too much upset	202	hers had been more than a one-gramme affliction
166	brushed away the crumbs	206	brushed from his purple viscose waistcoat
204	with a clanking of their anti-riot apparatus	253	goggle-eyed and swine-snouted in their gas-masks
230	the right to have disgusting diseases	283	the right to have syphilis and cancer

A special way in which Huxley sharpened the verisimilitude of his tale was by inserting and improving upon pieces of hypnopaedic wisdom. When Lenina tries in Chapter VI to calm Bernard, Huxley at first wrote: " 'Don't lose your temper,' she said, while repeating her nocturnal lessons; 'take *soma* instead.' " But Huxley later lined out the words following "she said" and inserted: " 'Remember, one cubic centimetre cures ten gloomy sentiments' " (TS, 85/CW, 104). The hynopaedic slogans are concrete emblems of the sense and the style of Huxley's Fordian future. One of Huxley's happiest changes in script, in fact, was the improvement of the flat "When a man feels, the state reels" to the melodic "When the individual feels the community reels" (TS, 88/CW, 109).

As conscientious as he was in working credible details into his presentation of the new world, Huxley knew he had to guard against excessiveness and tiresome exposition. For example, from Foster's account of the embryos' progress Huxley crossed out two-thirds of a script page dealing with bottle-labelling and the details of the Social Predestinators' tasks (TS, 10/CW, 10). A little later he cut out over half a page explaining the need for Epsilons as well as Alphas (TS, 16/CW, 15–16). Huxley must have realized his narrative could easily find itself bogged down in too much explicit description. Sufficient details were required for creating a sense of authenticity, but in many cases evocative, not explicit details were judged to be most effective. The children's games at the beginning of Chapter III, for instance, were introduced in the typescript quite literally: "The ball games were very elaborate, requiring They [*sic*] could only be played with the aid of a great deal of rather complicated apparatus." In Huxley's hand, though, this was deleted from the opening paragraph and replaced by a passage describing the setting: "The roses were in bloom, two nightingales soliloquized in the boskage, a cuckoo was just going out of tune among the lime trees. The air was drowsy with the murmur of bees and helicopters" (TS, 33/CW, 33). The unnatural union of those "bees and helicopters" does more for Huxley's narrative at this point than several pages of explanation. A second example of this sort of revision occurs later in Chapter III, where Huxley originally described the facilities of the Girls' Dressing-Room: "Eight scents and eau de cologne were laid on in every bathroom and there were flexible tubes from which, at a touch, a jet of warmed air would blow the finest talcum powder." Huxley scratched the passage out of this section of his script (the specific details would reappear later), and wrote instead: "Everyone was talking at the top of her voice. A Synthetic Music machine was warbling out a super-cornet solo" (TS, 41/CW, 40–41). Innuendo and concision, Huxley must have felt, were among the more effective ways of portraying the new world.

Huxley was usually vigilant in spying unwieldly materials, and he took care to avoid over-stating his case. In the script the Director in Chapter I asks Foster to take over the instruction because the Director is under the influence of *soma* (TS, 11, 19). As Huxley must have realized, the Director is more controlled, and therefore more commanding and sinister, without *soma*. His *soma* is accordingly revised out of Huxley's script. Again, Mond's citation of Ford's saying, "History is bunk," is followed in the script by Mond's explanation: "We have now given practical effect to what was, when our Ford first uttered it, a counsel of perfection. The Past, the stupid unnecessary Past, has been abolished" (TS, 38). Huxley at first emended and then deleted the explanation. His point is better conveyed by the list of specific names and historical places—for example, Odysseus, Gotama, King Lear, Thebes, Babylon—which, the reader is told, are whisked away as a logical extension of Ford's wisdom. Similarly, Huxley removed from his initial description of Helmholtz the sentence: "Looking at him, nobody could suggest that *he* had alcohol put into his blood surrogate" (TS, 69). The contrast with Bernard is explicit enough without this heavy-handed reminder. One last example of Huxley's striving for restraint occurs in his description of the Embryo Store and its workers in Chapter I. At first he had referred to the sealed-off room as an "enormous crypt," and he had endowed its workers with "horrible purple eyes." But he soon cut out the crypt reference entirely, he deleted the redundant "horrible" and, in a typed insertion, he added to the workers' faces "all the symptoms of lupus" (TS, 11/CW, 11). The result, a more controlled and evocative description, is perhaps an improvement consistent with the presiding style of *Brave New World*.

The script suggests that Huxley's initial chore was to conceive and to assemble the complex vision of the future he saw threatening to evolve out of the present. His letter to Mrs. Roberts expresses his reservations about his ability to accomplish the task. Simply to articulate that vision seems to have occupied the bulk of Huxley's attention as he wrote his first working draft. His attitude toward the new world, though, reflected through the satirical tone of the authorial voice, was the result of considerable pruning and shaping. Much of the book's irony was injected into Huxley's script during the process of revision.

There are a number of autograph insertions in the script that show Huxley in the act of adjusting the finer ironical tones of his narrative. For example, after the Solidarity Service of Chapter V has been consummated, Huxley at first described Fifi Bradlaugh's state of rapture as "the rich peace of balanced life, of energies at rest and in equilibrium." This was revised in hand to present Miss Bradlaugh's contentment as one "of balanced life, of energies at rest and in equilibrium. A rich and living peace" (TS, 82/ CW, 99). The change in emphasis is delicate, but the intensified irony of the added fragment is unmistakable. Similarly, when the Director begins his account of Bokanovsky's Process in Chapter I, Huxley wrote: "Making ninety-six human beings grow where only one grew before. [Illegible], for, paradoxically enough, the stimulus to do so is a negative stimulus." Huxley in a revision deleted the last sentence and inserted in hand the single damning word, "Progress" (TS, 5/CW, 5). Following are some other examples of autograph insertions which either clarify or intensify Huxley's ironic tone:

CONTEXT	ADDED MATERIALS
The Director's explanation of the male gametes (Ch. I)	"Rams wrapped in thermogene beget no lambs" (TS, 4/CW, 3)
The Director's rhetorical question about the use of dribbling out twins over a quarter of a century (Ch. I)	"Obviously, no use at all" (TS, 7/ CW, 7)
Foster's account of the embryos' progress to "daylight in the Decant-Room" (Ch. I)	"Independent existence—so called" (TS, 12/CW, 12)
The Director's account of the indissoluble wedding of flowers and electric shocks in the infant mind (Ch. II)	"What man has joined, nature is powerless to put asunder" (TS, 25/CW, 23)
The Director's explanation of the economic policy behind the electric shocks, and the student's reply, "I see" (Ch. II)	"and was silent, lost in admiration" (TS, 26/CW, 25)
The Director's remark that early investigators of hypnopaedia should have begun with moral education (Ch. II)	"'Moral education, which ought never, in any circumstances, to be rational'" (TS, 30/CW, 29)
The Controller's explanation that there is "No social stability without individual stability" (Ch. III)	"His voice was a trumpet. Listening, they felt larger, warmer" (TS, 46/ CW, 48)
The Controller's reassurance to the	"'Ford's in his flivver,' murmured

students that everything has been done to protect them from emotions (Ch. III)	the D. H. C., 'All's well with the world' " (TS, 49/CW, 50)
Linda drinking *mescal* and saying *The Complete Works of Shakespeare* "seemed to be full of nonsense" (Ch. VIII)	" 'Uncivilized' " (TS, 129/CW, 154)
Mond's defense of the Bokanovsky Groups to John (Ch. XVI)	"Mustapha Mond's oratory was almost up to synthetic standards" (TS, 211/CW, 261)

These insertions, I believe, contribute much to the ironical perspective Huxley uses implicitly to deplore the values celebrated by his brave new world. One wonders, in view of the care Huxley took internally to express his dismay with Fordian London, how so many of his book's early reviewers could have thought he was advocating its view of the future.[7]

Verisimilitude in the construction of details, concise and emphatic styling, and the creation of an ironic tone were refinements that Huxley in his vintage years as a novelist was well equipped to accomplish as he revised *Brave New World.* Characterization, on the other hand, was another question. In his *Paris Review* interview Huxley conceded: "I'm not very good at creating people; I don't have a very wide repertory of characters."[8] The revisions of *Brave New World* illustrate the sorts of problems Huxley encountered as he sought to give life to some of his main characters. Moreover, one can trace in Huxley's revisions of his three leading male characters the evolution of his novel's larger meaning. Huxley's script suggests that he thought first of making Bernard an orthodox rebel against his society, and then, instead, of making John a potentially redeeming noble savage hero brought into that society from the outside. But the progress of the revisions shows Huxley painstakingly rejecting both options to create the collapsing structural ironies to which he alludes in his 1946 Foreword to the book.[9]

The revisions dealing with the molding of Bernard Marx's character are among the most extensive in the script. Huxley's readily acknowledged difficulties in character creation are at once illustrated and complicated by the manuscript changes he makes in Bernard's role in the novel. That Huxley was not sure enough of his drawing of Bernard can be seen in revisions which show him inserting statements of what the narrative amply dramatizes. When he alluded to the practical jokes other Alpha men play upon Bernard owing to his substandard physique, Huxley felt obliged to elaborate in autograph: "The mockery made him feel an outsider; and feeling an outsider he behaved like one, which increased the prejudice against him and intensified the contempt and hostility aroused by his physical defects. Which in turn increased his sense of being alien and alone" (TS, 68/CW, 76). A page or two later, as Huxley developed the contrast between Bernard and Helmholtz, he inserted in hand: "What the two men shared was the knowledge that they were individuals" (TS, 70/CW, 79). Such additions are unnecessary, if not intrusive. The point is that in his uncertainty Huxley goes against the grain of his other revisions, which sustainedly guard against too much explicitness.

Huxley must have wrestled with the creation of Bernard's character all the way to the publisher. There are some pertinent materials missing from the extant typescript which nonetheless appear in the first edition, evidently as a result of last-minute revisions by Huxley. For example, the final two paragraphs of the middle section of Chapter VI, where Bernard gives Helmholtz a boastful and exaggerated report of his encounter with the Director, are not in the typescript. This is important, because without those two paragraphs Bernard leaves the Director, after receiving a reprimand for his unorthodoxy, on a modestly positive note: "Iceland was just a threat. A most stimulating and life-giving threat. Walking along the corridor, he actually whistled" (TS, 93/CW, 115). But the added paragraphs remove any trace of real assertiveness from Bernard and stress the hypocrisy of his character. Another late addition to Huxley's portrait of Bernard occurs in Chapter II, as Lenina explains to Fanny why she thinks Bernard's smallness is attractive: "One feels one would like to pet him. You know. Like a cat" (CW, 53). This remark is not in the extant typescript. Huxley must have wished in his last revisions to prepare his reader early in the story for Bernard's essential domestication.

Amid Huxley's struggles to flesh out Bernard's character, one can discern in the script the progress of his thoughts about what Bernard would mean in the book. Huxley's initial conception of Bernard's role changed significantly during the course of his revisions. Alterations in the script suggest Huxley at first thought of Bernard as the novel's hero, then switched to John as more fitting for the hero's role, and finally decided that Helmholtz, if anyone, should be the book's only authentically uplifting character.

Huxley flirted seriously with the prospect of making Bernard a more positive character. In a rejected version of the discussion between John and Bernard the morning after John's refusal to display himself at a party, John rallies Bernard, snatches *soma* from him, and urges: "Play the man, Bernard. Haven't you often said that you only wanted the opportunity? Well, here it is. Take it." Huxley continued: "Bernard looked at him for a few seconds in silence. Then, drawing a deep breath and squaring his shoulders, 'All right,' he said[.] I'll do it' " (TS, A1). In the rewritten version of the scene, Bernard is evasive, bitter, and unjust to John (TS, 169/CW, 211). When in Chapter VII Lenina looks for *soma* to compensate for the horrors of Malpais, Huxley originally had Bernard explain to her why his pockets were empty: "Why should I want to take a holiday from my holiday?" (TS, 105). But this is crossed out of the script, so that the published version makes it appear simply an oversight, not a deliberate act of courage, that Bernard is without his society's omnipresent escape from reality.

Bernard's affirmative character was short-lived in Huxley's composition. The script reveals several examples of Huxley's efforts to bring out first Bernard's negativity and, soon, his fundamental shallowness. When he went back over his script to the initial conversation Lenina and Fanny have about Bernard in Chapter III, Huxley elaborated in autograph upon Lenina's thoughts about Bernard's shyness: "Frightened almost—as though she were a World Controller and he a Gamma-Minus machine minder" (TS, 51/CW, 51). At Malpais, as Bernard and Lenina observe the disconcerting spectacle of nursing Indian mothers, Huxley added in his own hand: "Ashamed, now that the effects of the *soma* had worn off, of the weakness he had displayed that morning in the hotel, he went out of his way to show himself strong and unorthodox" (TS, 105/CW, 129). These revisions suggest Bernard's shyness is at heart a debilitating inferiority complex, his arrogance toward his society's conformism a hollow pretense.

Traces of genuine rebellion and integrity in Bernard turned, in Huxley's emergent characterization, to presumptuousness and egotism. Huxley stressed Bernard's pompous behavior, his inflated sense of self-importance, in Chapter IX as Bernard informs the New Mexico warden of his telephone conversation with Mond. Huxley in autograph expanded his description of Bernard from "His tone was weary, bored" to "His bored tone implied that he was in the habit of talking to his fordship every day of the week" (TS, 134/CW, 168). Bernard's report to Mond in Chapter XI originally ended with Bernard explaining John's belief in the soul. But Huxley typed in the two paragraphs showing Mond discovering Bernard's overweening advice to him (TS, 148–49/CW, 186–87). Similarly, Huxley revised into his script Bernard's flirtation with Miss Keate. Two paragraphs showing Bernard inviting Miss Keate to one of his parties displaying the Savage are inserted in hand in the margin of the typescript. Huxley further added in autograph, and then retyped, the sequence where Bernard makes advances to Miss Keate during the *Penitentes* film (TS, 152–54/CW, 190–92). Again, when Bernard goes to Helmholtz after the Savage party debacle, Huxley found it fitting to insert a remark on Bernard's humbled search for Helmholtz's friendship— "which, in his prosperity, he had not thought it worth while to preserve" (TS, 169/CW, 212). Significantly enough, in the script (TS, 179) John in Chapter XIII looks forward to confiding in Bernard, while in the first edition (CW, 222) the name was silently changed to Helmholtz.

Part of Huxley's motivation in making alterations upon Bernard was surely his wish to differentiate his characters one from another. But at the same time Huxley in the process of composition may have seen his story evolving along new lines. Revisions of John and Helmholtz suggest Huxley possibly shifted his attitude toward his book a considerable time after he first became immersed in it. His development of what he wanted to say in *Brave New World* must have taken definitive form just as he was discovering a dramatic arrangement for the book's climax.

Huxley at one point must have entertained a more heroic presentation of John's revolt against Fordian London. In a passage in the typescript which is absent from the first edition (at the close of Chapter XIV), after the khaki twin asks John if Linda is dead, Huxley wrote: "In the Savage's mind it was as though a sheet of opaque glass were suddenly and violently broken. There was light. He saw in an instant what he must do." But Huxley replaced this in the published novel with: "The Savage stared at them for a moment in silence" (TS, 199/CW, 245). Further, at the very end of the dialogue between John and Mustapha Mond in Chapter XVII, Huxley typed and then crossed out the following after Mond shrugs his shoulders: " 'You won't find many other claimants,' [he?] said. 'That's where I believe you're wrong,' said the Savage" (TS, 230). One is led to suspect that Huxley had a more crusading reading of John in mind at some stage in the writing.

The revisions, though, show Huxley deciding to stress that John's options are rather inhibited by the social and moral environment of his childhood. For instance, as he and Lenina leave the theatre after experiencing "Three Weeks in a Helicopter" in Chapter XI, Huxley added to John's suppressed desire his sense of unworthiness: "He was not worthy, not . . . [sic]." A few lines later, as John disengages his arm from Lenina's, Huxley again wrote in his script: "He was obscurely terrified lest she should cease to be something he could feel himself worthy of" (TS, 160/CW, 200). Half a page later, as they sit in the taxicopter, Huxley typed in the following to clarify John's inner turmoil: "Bound by strong vows that had never been pronounced, obedient to laws that had long since ceased to run" (TS, 160/CW, 200). This is conceivably another example of Huxley intruding to explain what the narrative ought fully to dramatize. But the point I want to make is that Huxley qualified to a noticeable extent his initial inclination to lionize John.

Of the three incipient rebels, the only one who escaped Huxley's sobering modifications as he revised his script was Helmholtz. Helmholtz's character is largely unrealized, surely neglected and underdeveloped. But Huxley did make a pair of autograph revisions of some significance for Helmholtz's role in the book. Huxley emphasized Helmholtz's natural kindness and his genuine personal quality by stressing the contrast between him and Bernard in Chapter XII, where Helmholtz generously overlooks Bernard's neglect and revives their friendship. Huxley added in hand to his script: "Touched, Bernard at the same time felt himself humiliated by the magnanimity, which was the more extraordinary and therefore the more humiliating for him in that it owed nothing to *soma*: it was the Helmholtz of daily life who forgave and forgot, not the Helmholtz of a half-gramme holiday" (TS, 171/CW, 212). A page later Huxley added a key paragraph concerning Helmholtz's creative instincts: "Helmholtz only laughed. 'I feel,' he said after a silence, 'as though I were beginning to have something to say. As though I were beginning to be able to use that power inside me—that extra latent power.

Something seems to be coming. . . .' In a strange way he seemed profoundly happy" (TS, 172). With minor emendations this would find its way into the published novel (CW, 214). It is perhaps instructive to note, too, that earlier in the script Bernard refers to "poor little Helmholtz Watson" (TS, 97), that the adjectives are subsequently deleted, and that, accordingly, the two characters may have reversed roles in Huxley's mind as he labored over his story. At the least, Huxley must have envisioned Helmholtz adopting a more positive role as the characters of Bernard and John were undergoing revision.

What all this means, I believe, is that as Huxley approached the climax of his book he was still working out the identities and relationships of his main characters. Evidence in the script suggests that Huxley also must have had important second thoughts about the novel's concluding chapters. At a comparatively late stage of the composition, Huxley rearranged his script to enliven what threatened to become a dull confrontation scene and to add greater clarity and force to his presentation of the Savage. Most important, Huxley interjected the Park Lane Hospital sequences (Chapters XIV–XV) between Lenina's abortive seduction of John and John's appearance before Mustapha Mond. The Park Lane Hospital additions bring Huxley's trio of rebels into open defiance of their society. By this significant move, Huxley discovered at once a means of adding substantial drama to his narrative's crisis point and a way of lending greater credibility to his final presentation of John's motivations. Huxley's revisions of his last chapters thereby show him fusing what he finally wished to say in the book with the most effective way of saying it.

The last five chapters of *Brave New World* include the Park Lane Hospital scene where John witnesses Linda's death (Chapter XIV), the rebellious efforts of John and Helmholtz to liberate Delta twins from their *soma* (Chapter XV), the interview with Mustapha Mond (Chapters XVI–XVII), and the sequence with John at the lighthouse (Chapter XVIII). There is reason to believe, though, that Huxley initially thought of bringing the Savage face to face with Mond immediately after Lenina's misunderstanding with John in Chapter XIII. In some of the supplementary pages (B1–B9) added to the main body of the typescript, there is a shorter and evidently earlier version of the exchange between Mond and John. This alternate version finds Mond and John together without Bernard and Helmholtz. No allusions are made in this version to Linda's death or to the riotous disorder over the *soma* distribution. At the opening (B1) of this version Mond sends Bernard instructions to have John come to him for an interview which is to be a routine part of John's grand tour of civilization. As this sequence continues (B4–B5), John's expression to Mond of his dislike of the new world derives only from his horrified response to the massed twins in the factories. There is no mention here of "those human maggots swarming round Linda's bed of death," or of "the endlessly repeated face of his assailants," or, indeed, of

John's bandaged left hand (which he injures in the *soma* distribution riot). These would all appear in that version of the scene in the main body of the script and, ultimately, in the first edition (CW, 261). But these revisions would be accompanied by major additions designed to adjust the emphasis of Huxley's book.

The conflation to which I have referred in my description of the script's imperfections offers substantial assistance in reconstructing the progress of Huxley's composition in its later stages. The entire B1–B9 sequence is in light, faded type and is in worksheet condition, as is all of Chapter XIII (Lenina's flirtation with John) in the main body of the script (TS, 177–88). But after the handwritten Chapter XIV, the condition of the remaining typescript (not counting the supplementary materials, A1–C2) is as follows:

Ch. XV   John and Helmholtz's efforts to liberate the Deltas from *soma* (TS, 200–207/CW, 246–55): dark type and relatively clear copy; this was evidently added to the script to give the rebels an active, if ineffectual, way of expressing their dissatisfaction.

Ch. XVI   the Mond interview (TS, 208–11/CW, 256–61): dark type and relatively clear copy; this is probably a revision to incorporate Bernard and Helmholtz into this initial stage of the Savage's confrontation with Mond.

Ch. XVI   the Mond interview (TS, 212–14/CW, 262–65): light and faded worksheet version with only John and Mond included in the conversation—Huxley apparently saw no need to change this part of the dialogue.

Ch. XVI   the Mond interview (TS, 215–18/CW, 265–70): dark type and relatively clear copy; probably a revision with Bernard and Helmholtz worked in so Huxley could break up the monotony of the dialogue by showing Bernard's abject collapse into hysteria.

Ch. XVII   the Mond interview (TS, 219–30/CW, 271–83): light and faded worksheet version with only John and Mond included in the dialogue; as this part of the confrontation most starkly pits the two systems of values against each other, Huxley wisely left it unaltered.

Ch. XVIII   John at the lighthouse (TS, 231–48/CW, 284–306): dark type and relatively clear copy; probably added during the time Huxley wrote Chapter XV and revised Chapter XVI.

Of course, the new materials could have been part of Huxley's larger revision from worksheet to cleaner copy for the entire script, but this possibility does not alter what we can learn from his modifications.[10]

The evolution of these later chapters from the shorter B1–B9 fragment to what would become the expanded, finished version gives one a rare insight into Huxley's creative instincts. Sometime after he completed the B1–B9 version of the Mond interview, Huxley must have arrived at the final, substantially more dramatic construction of the book's climax. He added the riot of Chapter XV as an effective way to illustrate vividly the spirit of John and Helmholtz (and the inertia of Bernard) and to bring all three of his rebels together before Mond. He also went back over the Mond interview to work into the scene the presence of Bernard and Helmholtz. Thus in a few strokes Huxley injected tension and variety into what promised to lapse into a protracted and monotonous dialogue. Bernard's hysteria at the close of Chapter XVI, as well as Mond's personal confidences—probably a way of encouraging Helmholtz—was worked into the main script. Huxley then wrote the final chapter of the book; also, at some time difficult to determine during this reordering of the story, he wrote in autograph the Park Lane Hospital chapter.

Now the Park Lane Hospital sequence could have been composed either before or after the last four chapters. While the evidence is not conclusive, two substantial autograph revisions suggest that Huxley wrote the hospital scene, recounting Linda's death, after he had written Chapters XV–XVIII. At the beginning of Chapter XV, as John shoulders his way through the hordes of Deltas assembled in the hospital's vestibule, Huxley in his script originally described John's revulsion: "The reality to which he had woken was the bad dream that had haunted him through all the period of his sojourn in the civilized world. The dream of a great crowd with only a single face, a single shrill or raucous laugh, a single expression, stature, colour, sex, to every hundred of its constituent individuals." But Huxley in autograph removed this and entered instead: "Twins, twins. . . . [sic] Like maggots, they had swarmed defilingly over the mystery of Linda's death. Maggots again, but larger, full grown, they now crawled across his grief and repentance" (TS, 200/CW, 247). Later, in Chapter XVIII, as John stares in horror at the swarms of uninvited visitors stepping out of helicopters around the lighthouse, Huxley typed, and then crossed out by hand, this passage: "Luckily, as well for his sanity as their safety, his visitors were all of the higher castes. The faces at which he so wildly stared were not identical; each of them belonged to only one owner. A sudden invasion of twins might have made him lose his reason; and, mad, what fearful execution he could have done with bow and hatchet! As it was, however, the nightmare was supportable. After the first shock his staggering reason recovered its balance" (TS 243/CW 301). Since these two changes occur in materials (Chs. XV and XVIII) which were evidently added in the later stages of composition, it is possible that Huxley may have felt these revisions were necessary as a result of inserting Chapter XIV by hand into his then finished script.

In any case, the point at which Huxley inserted Chapter XIV into his script is considerably less important than the effect which that insertion has on his novel. The main significance of that hospital chapter, as these late revisions demonstrate, is that the reasons for John's revolt and subsequent suicide shift from his outrage over the massed twins to which humanity has been reduced to his sense of loss and guilt over his mother's death.[11] Accordingly, some revisions inside the manuscript Chapter XIV are instructive. A crossed-out passage shows that Huxley at one point thought of having John's summons to the nurse save Linda's life: "The injection acted at once & almost miraculously. She breathed—faintly, Linda lay still, unconscious; but breathing" (TS, 197[2]). Then, in another passage deleted from the script, Huxley had the nurse indifferently console John: " 'It's all that *soma*,' she said. 'It always gets the respiratory centre in the end. That & the heart. The smallest shock. . . . [*sic*]' " (TS, 198). In the published version, of course, John's only consolation is the nurse's reprimand for his indecent behavior (CW, 243–44). Huxley's final account of John in this scene shifts the emphasis of his book to a remarkable degree. John is much less of a hero than an unsettled and misguided fanatic who comes to embody an untenable alternative to the brave new world.

Besides diversifying his characters and dramatizing the action, Huxley in his revisions was in the act of discovering what he really wanted to say in *Brave New World*. The old world of noble savagery from which Huxley's friend, D. H. Lawrence, derived meaning was, Huxley was now coming to see, dead.[12] The impulse which caused Huxley at first to think of John as his hero was perhaps one of the last effects of Lawrence's influence upon him. On the other hand, the new world of H. G. Wells was not at all powerless to be born. It is significant that Huxley's revisions of Bernard show him not as an authentic rebel against dystopia, but as one whose discontent derives mainly from his desire to be accepted in such a society. Huxley in the early 1930s was beginning to believe that man's hope for any authentic existence lay beyond these two worlds. Huxley's few revisions sketching the latent mysticism of Helmholtz possibly represent an instinctive foretelling of the much fuller conversion which would be the heart of his next novel, *Eyeless in Gaza* (1936). That *Brave New World* was revised up to the moment of its submission to the publisher suggests that the turmoil Huxley experienced in the summer of 1931 was far from over when he expressed his relief in that tardy letter to his father. The manuscript revisions of *Brave New World* give us some rare glimpses into Huxley's creative imagination hard at work. They also form a record in themselves of the conception and the incipient coalescence of his later vision as he was approaching the crossroads of his writing career.

Notes

1. *Letters of Aldous Huxley*, ed. Grover Smith (London: Chatto and Windus, 1969), p. 348. Hereafter cited in text as *Letters*. Huxley said his novel "started out as a parody of H. G. Wells's *Men Like Gods*, but gradually it got out of hand and turned into something quite different from what I'd originally intended." See *Writers at Work: The "Paris Review" Interviews*, Second Series (New York: Viking, 1963), p. 198.

2. Clementine Robert, *Aldous Huxley, Exhumations: Correspondance inédite avec Sydney Schiff (1925–1937)* (Paris: Didier, 1976), p. 73.

3. *Writers at Work*, p. 197.

4. Sybille Bedford, *Aldous Huxley: A Biography*, *Volume Two: 1939–1963* (London: Chatto and Windus, 1974), pp. 278–79.

5. The script consists of 8½″ × 11″ typing paper with various watermarks: EX-CELSIOR, F. Guerimand & Co., VOIRON; PERFECT (with abstract device); ARGENTINE TYPE-WRITER; EXTRA STRONG (with bird-like emblem). Most of the sheets are of the first two types, some are completely plain. The sheets are loose in a folding case with cover for manuscript and case. The Humanities Research Center acquired the script in 1958 as part of the T. E. Hanley Collection from Bradford, Pennsylvania.

6. CW refers to the Chatto and Windus first edition of *Brave New World* published in London in 1932; TS refers to the typescript.

7. See *Aldous Huxley: The Critical Heritage*, ed. Donald Watt (London: Routledge and Kegan Paul, 1975), pp. 197–222. Two recent source studies by Peter Firchow are of considerable help in understanding the complex influences Huxley brought to his novel: "Science and Conscience in Huxley's *Brave New World*," *Contemporary Literature*, 16 (Summer 1975), 301–16; and "Wells and Lawrence in Huxley's *Brave New World*," *Journal of Modern Literature*, 5 (April 1976), 260–78.

8. *Writers at Work*, p. 206.

9. "At the time the book was written this idea, that human beings are given free will in order to choose between insanity on the one hand and lunacy on the other, was one that I found amusing and regarded as quite possibly true." "Foreword," *Brave New World* (New York: Modern Library, 1946), p. [vi].

10. Some of the earlier scenes in the cleaner typescript copy, especially those modifying the main characters, also could have been in themselves late additions to the body of the script: e.g., the Director's threat to exile Bernard in Chapter VI, John's stabbing of Popé in Chapter VIII, and the exchanges between John and Helmholtz in Chapter XII.

11. Keith May, in his chapter on *Brave New World*, recognized the appropriateness of the Park Lane sequence: "Artistically and as a means of best illustrating the theme the scenes at the hospital are in their proper place. As comedy they provide the hectic culmination of many preceding absurdities, and thematically they present the crux of the whole matter of the book." *Aldous Huxley* (London: Paul Elek, 1972), p. 113.

12. See Jerome Meckier, "Huxley's Lawrencian Interlude: The 'Latin Compromise' That Failed," *Aldous Huxley: Satire and Structure* (London: Chatto and Windus, 1969), pp. 78–123.

Brave New World and the Rationalization of Industry

JAMES SEXTON

Rationalization: "the methods of technique and of organisation designed to secure the minimum waste of either effort or material. They include the scientific organisation of labour, standardisation of both materials and products, simplification of processes, and improvements in the system of transport and marketing. . . . [T]he judicious and constant application of . . . rationalisation is calculated to secure . . . to the community greater stability and a higher standard of life."
    —World Economic Conference, Geneva, sponsored by the League of Nations, 1927, defined in L. Urwick, *The Meaning of Rationalisation*, 1929.

Near the passage which Huxley took as an epigraph to *Brave New World*, Nicolas Berdyaev speaks of socialist Russia as a satanocracy where the individual is subordinated to the collectivity. He asserts that human and spiritual values are being sacrificed to the false god of materialism, that life's centre of gravity has shifted to economics, and that man has been converted to a mere economic category.[1]

Much of Berdyaev's thought is a footnote to the Grand Inquisitor chapter of Dostoevski's *Brothers Karamazov*, which sets in opposition two views of human nature: wholly materialistic man (*homo oeconomicus*) versus "soul-encumbered" man. But interestingly the Grand Inquisitor's materialist vision of man is congruent with that of Henry Ford, whose *My Life and Work* is the bible of *Brave New World*. There Ford states, "The average worker . . . wants a job in which he does not have to put forth much physical exertion—above all, he wants a job in which he does not have to think."[2] He then goes on to say that the minority of creative thinkers, those few who would be appalled by repetitive, routine work, should look for a more vital pastime than mere music or painting:

[H]igher laws than those of sound, or line, or colour; [apply in the field] of industrial relationship. We want masters in industrial method—both from

Reprinted from *English Studies in Canada* 12 (1986): 424–36, with the permission of the author and publisher.

the standpoint of the producer and the product. We want those who can mould the political, social, industrial, and moral mass into a sound and shapely whole. We have limited the creative faculty . . . for too trivial ends. We want men who can create the working design for all that is right and good and desirable in our life. . . . It is possible to increase the well-being of the workingman . . . by aiding him to do more. . . . If he is the happier for using a machine to less than its capacity, is he happier for producing less than he might and consequently getting less than his share of the world's goods in exchange?[3]

Huxley saw that the common denominator between Fordism and socialism was uncritical veneration of rationalization. Mark Rampion in *Point Counter Point* (1928) points to the sameness of Bolshevik and Capitalist goals, and incidentally, he uses the same infernal imagery as does Berdyaev. The squabbling between Bolshevists and Fascists, Radicals and Conservatives was really a fight

to decide whether we shall go to hell by communist express train or capitalist racing motor car, by individualist 'bus or collectivist tram running on the rails of state control. The destination's the same in every case. . . . They all believe in industrialism in one form or another, they all believe in Americanization. Think of the Bolshevist ideal. America but much more so. America with government departments taking the place of trusts and state officials instead of rich men. And then the ideal of the rest of Europe. The same thing, only with the rich men preserved. Machinery and government officials there. Machinery and Alfred Mond or Henry Ford here. . . . They're all equally in a hurry. In the name of science, progress and human happiness![4]

In the years 1928 and 1929 Huxley reveals the probable source and a later confirmation of Rampion's views, for two books influenced him enough to base three *Vanity Fair* essays on them. I refer to "The Cold-Blooded Romantics," "Machinery, Psychology and Politics," and "This Community Business." The first essay refers lengthily to René Fülöp-Miller's *The Mind and Face of Bolshevism* (which is a rich source for *Brave New World*, including the orgy-porgy scene); the last two deal extensively with Alphonse Séché's *La morale de la machine* (1929), a book which Huxley says made his flesh creep.[5]

Both books discuss the Bolsheviks' and the capitalists' fascination with rationalization and mechanization, and both discuss the materialist legacy left by F. W. Taylor and Ford: a legacy of scientific management and rationalization.

Summarizing the thesis of Fülöp-Miller's book, Huxley says that the communist revolution aimed to transform the individual into a component cell of the great Collective Man:

that single mechanical monster who, in the Bolshevik millenium, is to take the place of the unregimented hordes of "soul-encumbered" individuals who now inhabit the earth. . . . Individuals must be organized out of existence; the communist state requires, not men, but cogs and ratchets in the huge "collective mechanism." To the Bolshevik idealist, Utopia is indistinguishable from one of Mr. Henry Ford's factories. . . . The condition of their entry into the Bolshevik's Earthly Paradise is that they shall have become like machines.[6]

The problem with Taylor's time and motion efficiency schemes and Ford's rational and efficient systematizing is that Ford and Taylor approached the organization mechanistically, seeing the organization member as a mere instrument of production to be handled as easily as any other tool, and failing to consider the individual's emotions or aspirations.

Ford states that the net result of the application of his principles of assembly is "the reduction of the necessity for thought on the part of the worker and the reduction of his movements to a minimum. He does as nearly as possible only one thing with only one movement."[7] For Ford and Taylor, man has become a machine for whom any other end than increasing productivity is irrelevant. Ford boasts that his foundry worker "must be skilled in exactly one operation which the most stupid man can learn within two days."[8] But it is in his description of "man-high" work that Ford sets the stage for Huxley's parody of the Laputan abuse of science in chapter II of *Brave New World*:

In the early part of 1914 we elevated the assembly line . . . we had one line twenty-six and three quarter inches and another twenty-four and one half inches from the floor—to suit squads of different heights. The waist-high arrangement and a further subdivision of work so that each man had fewer movements cut down the labour time per chassis to one hour thirty-three minutes. . . . Our machines are placed very close together—every foot of floor space . . . carries the same overhead charge. . . . We measure on each job the exact amount of room that a man needs. . . . [I]f he and his machine occupy more space than is required, that . . . is waste. This brings our machines closer together than in probably any other factory in the world. To a stranger they may seem piled right on top of one another, but they are scientifically arranged, not only in the sequence of operations, but to give every man and every machine every square inch that he requires and, if possible, not a square inch, and certainly not a square foot, more than he requires.[9]

By a *reductio ad absurdum*, Huxley satirizes this aspect of rationalization—the elimination of waste time and motion—literally not a centimetre of waste space being permitted in Huxley's helicopter lighting sets factory. Human tools are manufactured to fit snugly together over the conveyer belt: "forty-seven blond heads were confronted by forty-seven brown ones. Forty-seven snubs by forty-seven hooks; forty-seven receding by forty-seven progna-thous chins."[10] In Huxley's Laputan factory, man is deliberately moulded to fit the machine: "eighty-three almost noseless black brachycephalic Deltas were cold-pressing. . . . One hundred and seven heat-conditioned Epsilon Senegalese were working in the foundry. Thirty-three Delta females, long-headed . . . with narrow pelvises, and all within 20 millimetres of 1 metre 69 centimetres tall, were cutting screws" (188).

But Huxley had also been reading *La morale de la machine* (The Machine Ethic) shortly before working on *Brave New World* in the French Mediterra-nean village of Sanary. Séché makes the same point that Ford made above (and which Huxley makes often), that "[o]nce started the machine demands (under threat of economic ruin) that it shall never be unnecessarily stopped, never thrown out of its stride. Production and yet more production—that is the fundamental law of the machine's being. The necessary corollary to this law is consumption and yet more consumption."[11] (This is Mustapha Mond's main point in his justification of the rationalized world which he helps control.)

Séché's book is written from a right-wing perspective, and dedicated to certain heads of industry such as Ford, Citroën, Michelin, J. P. Morgan, as well as to Benito Mussolini "and to the unknown young men who tomor-row will have to take their responsibilities in a new world,"[12] where the imperatives of mechanization will dictate the eclipse of the individual by the collectivity.[13]

Huxley gleans the same message from this work: the ineluctable tri-umph of the machine over human individualism. With the triumph of the machine ethic, man is reduced to a mere aspect of the productive process: his importance lies only in his relationship to increased productivity. Séché points approvingly to an American technique to increase productivity, which becomes a cornerstone of the Fordian Brave New World: making free films available at noon to the factory workers, "for management has calculated that the worker produces more when he is happy."[14] Thus the worker's emotional state is simply a function of his productive capacity, to be manipu-lated by the paternalistic offerings of celluloid diversion. In *Brave New World*, the feelies serve a parallel function, only they are not provided free at lunch hour.

Oddly, Séché also dedicates *La morale de la machine* to Berdyaev, for Séché is not being ironic in his championing of the machine ethic. He speaks of two civilizations: one defending its sentimental ideal of individualism and the other fighting for its ideal mechanistic order of collective discipline—the order of the factory, the collective of the machine.[15] He later reveals his penchant for the closed society when he ringingly affirms that the disorder of democracy necessitates a return to authority. Thus we see Mark Rampion's words borne out by the Bolshevik and Fascist-leaning mentalities. In both, the community—especially in its industrial role—takes precedence over the individual. And Séché's warm description of the unique spirit of emulation in the rationalized American factories, with their constant reference to production records, takes us to the threshold of Huxley's Central London Hatchery. He speaks approvingly of the American manager's mastery of technique: "Management has thought of everything: height of seats, orientation and price of lighting, selection of employees according to principles of natural aptitude (acuity of vision, selection by length of fingers, body mass, etc.)."[16] Séché comments, "There one measures man as one calibrates a piston so that it may slide in the cylinder."[17]

In this context, one thinks of Henry Foster, the brainy organization man who devotes his working life to trying to match or even better the record yields of Bokanovsky babies from one ovary: sixteen thousand and twelve in Central London Hatchery; sixteen thousand five hundred in Singapore, and nearly seventeen thousand in Mombassa. " 'Nothing like oxygen shortage for keeping an embryo below par.' Again he rubbed his hands. . . . 'The lower the caste . . . the shorter the oxygen.' The first organ affected was the brain. After that the skeleton. At seventy per cent of normal oxygen you got dwarfs. At less than seventy, eyeless monsters" (15). Foster, this artist of industrial relations, then concludes, "Who are no use at all" (15). Huxley translates Séché:

> The morality of the machine . . . is the most imperious of moralities, because it is more than a merely materialistic morality; it is . . . a morality of cogs and wheels, of driving belts and cranks and moving pistons, a morality subjected automatically to the will to power of organized mechanical force. . . . The modern man does not work for himself, does not live for himself; he works for society (the mechanized society whose watchword is production) . . . he lives to insure the movement, the equilibrium, the . . . prosperity of the . . . community.[18]

Thus one has a right to existence only insofar as one helps keep the assembly line moving smoothly.

In November 1929, Huxley states that *La morale de la machine* is the best account of the effects of mechanization on politics and the behaviour of the individual. Huxley continues:

> The ethic of the machine, as M. Séché points out, is an ethic of discipline, of regimentation, of the total sacrifice of individual interests to the interests of the mechanized community. . . . The modern industrialized State, according to M. Séché, should be organized (and in Italy already is organized) like a very efficient factory, or group of factories, with hierarchically graded experts in charge of every department and a single Henry Ford at the head to co-ordinate their activities and dictate the policy of the whole concern.[19]

It is no accident that Huxley alludes to the figure of Alfred Mond as the single Henry Ford at the head of Western Europe. Huxley's description of Mustapha Mond is consistent with that of Sir Alfred Mond. His voice is described as deep and resonant, and he is said to be "of middle height . . . with a hooked nose, full red lips, eyes very piercing and dark" (36). Such a description jibes perfectly with the portrait of Mond set out in the biography by Hector Bolitho: "He had rich, dark eyes, flaming with the power within him"[20] and a "harsh" voice; while in contemporary caricatures the hooked nose is evident.

Yet surprisingly, despite the Rampion reference to Mond quoted above, critics have been silent about the richly symbolic name Mustapha Mond, which Huxley gave to the world controller of the Brave New World. The name is probably a pun on French "monde"—world, although such a pun is avoided by the French translator of *Brave New World* (French translation: *Le meilleur des mondes*), who assigns the name Mustapha Menier to the world controller. To do so, however, is to ignore an allusion to the eminent industrialist-politician Sir Alfred Mond, Lord Melchett. Moreover, to be unaware that Huxley alludes to Alfred Mond is to miss an important aspect of the satire on the rationalization of industry. For Alfred Mond was so closely associated with the modish concept of rationalization in the late nineteen-twenties that the editor of *Nuttall's Standard Dictionary* asked Mond to define the concept for a new edition of the work in May 1929.

Mond obliged, and Nuttall printed his definition of rationalization: "The application of scientific organization to industry, by the unification of the processes of production and distribution with the object of approximating supply to demand."[21]

Even the concepts within Mond's rather limited definition of rationalization are specifically satirized. For example, by employing electronic advances such as the loudspeaker and the hypnopaedic methods developed in psychological experimentation, the operatives of *Brave New World* follow one of the basic tenets of rationalization as defined by Alfred Mond: "In the nurseries, the Elementary Class Consciousness lesson was over, the voices were *adapting future demand to future industrial supply* . . . [emphasis mine]. 'I do love flying, I do love having new clothes' . . . 'the conscription of consumption'. . . . 'Every man, woman, and child compelled to consume so much a year. In the interests of industry' " (56–57).

Then too, another related goal of rationalization, the invention of new wants which the business will be in a good position to supply,[22] is parodied in the dictate that no new game can be officially approved unless it can be shown to require "at least as much apparatus as the most complicated of existing games" (34).

Further, as Leslie Hannah points out in *The Rise of the Corporate Economy*, post–World War I Britain experienced a brief inflationary boom followed by a fierce slump:

Economic depression was, then, a central fact of the interwar experience: to the labourer it meant the dole, to the employer it meant overcapacity; for both it provoked a further re-evaluation of their political, social and economic beliefs and of the economic institutions they sustained . . . [and] nothing [appeared] between the wars to reduce the tenacity of the belief that the market economy was failing, and that it was the process of rationalization . . . that offered the way out of the predicament which this posed.[23]

No one in the inter-war period in England was more convinced of the value of rationalization than Alfred Mond. Indeed in the years from 1925 until his death in 1930, Mond campaigned for his program of rationalization. He elaborates on his program of rationalization in two books: *Industry and Politics* (1927) and *Imperial Economic Unity* (1930), as well as in numerous speeches. To Mond the solution to the failing market system was a growing rationalization of economic units—he hoped to see a kind of economic League of Nations, where industrialists could effectively and co-operatively shape the economic destiny of most of the world. With Beaverbrook he championed the idea of a kind of common market within the British Empire, a potentially larger market than the rest of Europe combined, and larger than the market which he envied, the United States.

He personally pushed through the amalgamation of the British chemical industries into one massive, multi-national corporation: Imperial Chemical Industries Limited (ICI), in 1926, and was a staunch advocate of increased scientific research for industry.

Indeed, a form of state capitalism is present in *Brave New World*. Although Huxley is rather silent as to the exact form the Fordian economy takes, it is clear that the world controllers are representatives of a world economy based upon rationalized, amalgamated economic units.

In *The Art of Being Ruled* (1926), Wyndham Lewis, not unlike Mark Rampion, describes such a possible scenario: "Giant Trusts and Cartels everywhere, at the present time, as they coalesce, approach the economic pattern of the socialist state. Whether the trust-king is a highly salaried servant (as Lenin said he should be, if proved to be the most efficient organizer), or a capitalist magnate (when these chiefs become fewer and fewer, as they do every day), does not particularly matter."[24]

Mond's blueprint would have been consistent with an economy that blurred the demarcation line between Capitalism and Bolshevism, though doubtless as an arch–anti-communist, Mond would have preferred the post-liberal, centralized, and rationalized economy to remain safe for corporate rationalizers. There is an amusing cartoon in the *Glasgow Evening Times* (19 September 1927),[25] entitled "Peeps into the Wonderful Future," which no doubt reflects a typical public response to Mond. The caption, "Mond Amalgamates Everything in Sight," runs below the depiction of a futuristic City of London with airships called Mond Meteors bound for Paris, Moscow,

Tokyo; skyscrapers festooned with signs advertising Palmondolive Soap, *The Mondy Wail*—World's greatest newspaper, the Mond United Church, the Mondworth Sixpence Store, Mond Stout, Mond Soap, Paramond Pictures. Between two of the skyscrapers runs the Mond Electric Railway and at a less dizzying height, a tree-lined road—the *Champs du Monde*. From another skyscraper above the whole spectacle in an elevated theatre box sits Alfred Mond. Clearly the amalgamation of ICI and Mond's speeches on rationalization made not only Huxley view Mond as a forerunner of economic world controllers.

Séché, like Mond, saw the First World War as a deathblow to liberal capitalism.

> Only the Machine won something from the war . . . her adversary, individualist, bourgeois democracy is ruined. As well, war gives a formidable push to industry, which constructs admirable factories and modernizes its equipment. Besides, war permits the Machine to demonstrate the superiority of the collective organization of her factories over individual anarchy. Finally, from the war arose the League of Nations, which although now only a debating society, constitutes, nevertheless, the primary base of a world society which will follow the laws and ethos of the Machine. . . . Already the League has created an international economic cooperation.[26]

Remember that Huxley looked upon Séché's scenario as inevitable. In this context, Mond's speech of March 1927 resembles an implicit attitude of Wellsian "open conspiracy," that is, make government an enterprise run by experts. He states that international leaders of industry, "those who had to deal practically with the great affairs of daily life were more likely to help finally to the solution of international difficulties."[27] He applauds the growing trend towards combination or grouping of industries in all countries— which, among other advantages, enabled the larger questions of industrial policy to be discussed by relatively few people and solved in a measurable distance of time. Moreover, Mond saw that with increased rationalization industrialists could speak with one voice through direct discussions of industrial chiefs.[28] Mond ended the speech by expressing the hope that he would see an economic arm of the League of Nations as powerful and authoritative as the League was in political affairs. Like Séché, Mond speaks in evolutionary terms about the inevitability of international consolidation of industry: "the amalgamation of units—the creation of enterprises of a greater size . . . of a coordinated character—was an absolute part of the evolution of modern industry and was entirely unavoidable."[29]

But it is in "Research and the Future," a chapter from *Industry and Politics* where Alfred Mond so closely resembles his Fordian namesake. Indeed the speech amounts to the same thesis that Mustapha Mond outlines in chapter 3 of *Brave New World*: the inevitable choice between world control or chaos:

We are entering on an economic and . . . coldly scientific war, which will
lead to the extinction of the less strong and efficient industries, and perhaps
even nations. The most effective methods of promoting scientific research and
the application of scientific discoveries are the only things that can carry this
country through. . . . Muddling through is fatal in these days of highly
efficient research and highly specialized industries . . . ; we must cut our way
through by a definite predetermined path to the final fully utilized triumph.

The welfare of the whole nation depends on this complete application of
science to industry. The welfare . . . of the human race depends on the
efficiency of its . . . scientists in every field. The amazing . . . progress made
in recent years must not induce . . . complacency. We are not living on the
apex of time . . . or civilisation. Rather are we at the foot of great ascent,
which will take us to higher forms of civilisation than any that even we
moderns can predict. . . . [The] final triumph is by no means certain. The
welter of the Great War taught us that there are dangers inherent in our
highly advanced . . . complex civilisation, and taught us . . . that a relapse
into chaos is by no means an impossibility. There is only one possible policy.
Rightly or wrongly, we must pin our faith to the scientists of this and of
future generations. On their work and their discoveries the race must stand
or fall. Research and more and more research must clear the only feasible path
for the forward progress of mankind.[30]

Alfred Mond thus aligned himself in 1927 with the attitude of Séché
and Huxley: namely, that there is "no arguing with the machine; either you
do not set the thing going, or else, if you do, you adapt yourself to its
rhythm and obey the literally iron laws which it imposes. . . . [E]fficiency
has become absolutely necessary. . . . [E]ven the owner class has now become
subject to the ethic of the machine. . . . The result of this state of affairs
is that the doctrines of political democracy . . . are rapidly falling into
discredit."[31]

Significantly, Alfred Mond, to use Huxley's phrase, was an apostle of
"progress, production and efficiency."[32] He was also an admirer of Mussolini—he owned an Italian villa—and, according to his biographer, was
remembered by Mussolini as "not a democrat."[33]

Alfred Mond's utopian embracing of scientific research and rationalization as a safeguard against chaos, however, went far beyond mere lofty
generalization. Indeed, I believe that at least three utopian scientific research
schemes with which Alfred Mond was publicly associated are specifically
alluded to in Brave New World: the elimination of world hunger through
nitrogen fixation, the elimination of old age through the use of hormones,
and the elimination of certain tropical diseases.

One notes that Mustapha Mond tells John Savage that the biologist of
Brave New World had arrived at the point of synthesizing all the food needs
of the world (265). Here the fictional Mond responds to one of his namesake's
utopian hopes. In a story reporting Mond's 1928 speech to the United World

Chemical Societies, Mond refers to Lord Salisbury's query why the air could not simply furnish all nitrogen required for fertilizers instead of going to Chile for it. Mond claimed that "[i]n another 50 years synthetically-produced food might make the use of soil manures unnecessary. . . . [T]hey might be able to synthesize all the foodstuffs that they needed, so that in case of war there would be no necessity to starve . . . but only to put up a few more factories."[34]

Another idea with which Mond was publicly associated is an important part of the satire in *Brave New World*: the utopian advocacy of hormones as the possible elixir of youth. In July 1926, Mond presided over a chemical congress which, as reported in the *Times*, dealt with the means by which the human body resisted the attacks of old age through the influence of hormones.[35] Mond opened the section and praised British pharmacologists' work with three most important hormones: adrenalin, pituitary, and insulin; praising at the same time the spirit of co-operation between lab and industry, saying that a "new trinity had been formed consisting of the physiologist, biochemist, and the manufacturer, and upon their joint efforts depended . . . the future progress of medical knowledge and the alleviation of human suffering."[36] At Mond's session the "papers presented dealt with the experimental study and use of hormones, the chemistry of the pituitary gland and of insulin, and the commercial production of hormones"[37]; and claims were made that hormones could prolong human life and youthful vigour. One thinks here of Linda's jingle, "A, B, C, vitamin D," Benito Hoover's sex hormone chewing gum, the compulsory "Violent Passion Surrogate"—compulsory flooding of the whole system with adrenalin once a month as a condition of perfect health, compulsory pregnancy substitutes, pituitary doses, and the subsidy of two thousand pharmacologists and biochemists in A.F. 178.

Yet another link between Sir Alfred Mond and the Brave New World was Mond's close association with research in tropical medicine. As Minister of Health in the Lloyd George government, Mond was chairman of the Board of Management of the London School of Hygiene and Tropical Medicine— to which two million pounds had been offered by the Rockefeller Foundation. According to the report in the *Times*, the building was destined to house the greatest centre in the world for research into tropical medicine.[38] The importance of research in tropical medicine for the Brave New World economy (and for that of the British Empire) is evident when one remembers the loss to sleeping sickness of the promising young Alpha-Minus administrator at Mwanza-Mwanza (in then-Tanganyika). One also thinks of Henry Foster's references to the hatcheries at Mombassa and the routine injection of embryos with typhoid and sleeping sickness organisms at the Central London Hatchery. ("We immunize the fish against the future man's diseases"[18].) Obviously the tropical centres represent a prodigious investment in production.

Perhaps yet another reason why Huxley considered Alfred Mond such a fitting prototype of the world controller of the rationalized society of *Brave New World* is that he was so publicly associated with the allied ideas of paternalism, industrial co-operation, team spirit, loyalty, and tractability of the worker. Mond was a highly visible delegate to a conference devoted to rationalization in December 1927. There, Sir Arthur Balfour pointed out that post-war conditions made rationalization more necessary, stating also that "by means of co-ordination boys and girls and men of no skill could be transformed into useful units of production."[39] There is a disturbing similarity between Balfour's utterance, the Human Element Manager's declaration that he hardly ever has any trouble with his workers (129), and Mond's speech, "Commerce," in which he said that British workers were "the most easily handled of any people he knew."[40]

Another parody of extreme rationalization takes on further ironic overtones in connection with Mond's career in industry. Huxley mordantly parodies a key element of rationalization—the scientific elimination of waste in industry—as Henry Foster praises the wonders of the phosphorus recovery plant at the Slough Crematorium: "On their way up the chimney the gases go through four separate treatments. P_2O_5 used to go right out of circulation every time they cremated some one. Now they recover over ninety-eight percent. of it. More than a kilo and a half per adult corpse. Which makes the best part of four hundred tons of phosphorus every year from England alone. . . . Fine to think we can go on being socially useful even after we're dead. Making plants grow" (85–86). This is rationalization with a vengeance. Significantly, the Mond name was associated with the sulphur-recovery process. Moreover, in 1929, shortly after Mond realized the merger of the four chemical giants in Britain, his newly-formed Imperial Chemicals Industries pressed ahead with a grandiose and fully-reported scheme—building a huge fertilizer plant at Billingham. It was hoped that with this plant "ICI would be able to supply all the nitrogenous fertiliser needed by farmers, not merely in the United Kingdom, but everywhere in the British Empire."[41]

Benito Mussolini twice called Mond "a great man" in an interview with Mond's biographer.[42] No doubt Mond's autocratic, rational approach to economic problems appealed to Mussolini, for Mond too was impatient with labour strife and offered a blueprint for industrial harmony based on industrial co-operation.

It was typical of Alfred Mond, Fellow of the Royal Society, the "grand dreamer,"[43] the Utopian, that he should hold the first meeting of the Melchett-Turner conferences in the rooms of the Royal Society at Burlington House. Bolitho notes the Utopian quality of Mond's goals, saying, however, that "the Utopia was not easily born."[44] Mond, however, was able partly to overcome opposition there to rationalization, which the Trades Union Council saw as the science of the big combines of America,[45] so that Mond, reflecting on the accomplishments of the Melchett-Turner conference, was able to state: "on the subject of rationalization. . . . The conference determined that this tendency should be welcomed and encouraged insofar as it leads to improvements in the efficiency of industrial production, services and distribution, and to the raising of the standard of . . . living of the people. . . . The new industrial revolution, upon the threshold of which we already are, will be the age of the machinery of organisation. Machinery has already been organised."[46]

Mond's career justifies to some extent Huxley's view of Mond as the embodiment of what he called "consumptionists," "prosperity-mongers" and believers in "Progress."[47] He says, however, that political reform

> and industrial rationalization are necessary and valuable. But do not let us make the mistake of supposing that they automatically create happiness. The only people who derive happiness directly from them are the reformers and rationalizers themselves. Absorbed as they are in occupations which are felt to be valuable, they lose themselves in their work and consequently are happy. But the people for whom they work do not share this happiness. All that reform and rationalization can do for them is to provide . . . an environment propitious to the kind of working and living that brings self-forgetful happiness.
>
> One admires the wisdom of the Russian revolutionary leaders who so organized society that a large proportion of the population came to be actively engaged in the work of reform and rationalization.[48]

Obviously he groups Mond in the school that sees the "Ideal Man" as "a kind of deindividualized worker-bee, whose sole duty is towards society," not the school that sees him as "an improved and more gentlemanly version of the Free Individual of the Renaissance."[49]

The germ of *Brave New World* is contained in Mark Rampion's dialogue with Philip Quarles in *Point Counter Point* (1928) where he positively identifies Mond as a proponent of the hypothetical world *Brave New World* will later flesh out. The satanocracy would be endorsed by Mond, Wells, and also Lenin, Mussolini, MacDonald, and Baldwin—that is, by Bolsheviks, Fascists, social democrats, and Tories, "All equally anxious to take us to hell and only squabbling about the means of taking us" (*Point Counter Point*, 415).

By late 1929 Huxley had the economic, esthetic blueprint for *Brave New World* filed for future reference. All the *bêtes noires* are being assembled and placed ready for toppling: H. G. Wells, Alfred Mond, progress, consumerism, cubism, rationalization.

Philip Quarles says that neo-Luddism would be impossible, that "given our existing world, you can't go back, you can't scrap the machine . . . unless you're prepared to kill off about half the human race. Industrialism made possible the doubling of the world's population in a hundred years" (*PCP*, 416).

Rampion then states that the next war will make [the slaughter of half the world's population] "only too practical," and goes on to speculate on the inevitability of war, since industrial progress means "over-production . . . [and] the need for getting new markets . . . international rivalry . . . war" (PCP, 416).

So far, Rampion anticipates Mond's history lesson in Brave New World. "And mechanical progress means more specialization and standardization of work . . . more ready-made and unindividual amusements . . . diminution of initiative and creativeness . . . means finally a kind of individual madness that can only result in social revolution. . . . Wars and revolutions are inevitable, if things are allowed to go on as they are at present" (PCP, 416–17).

And Quarles and Rampion take us speculatively to the threshold of Brave New World, when they agree, "So the problem will solve itself. Only by destroying itself" (PCP, 417). Then with an unconscious irony, Rampion provides the solution—not for amelioration as he thought, but for the entry into Brave New World: "The root of the evil's in the individual psychology; so it's there . . . you'd have to begin. The first step would be to make people live dualistically, in two compartments. In one compartment as industrialized workers, in the other as human beings. As idiots and machines for eight hours out of every twenty-four and real human beings for the rest" (PCP, 417).

This is close to the utopian solution of Island. But the Brave New World will take the easier path by tripling the duration of idiotic-machinelike existence, from eight hours to twenty-four hours per day. The starting point for the Brave New World is a war caused by the imperatives of laisser-faire industrialism, and a permanent solution to all future wars is the same industrialism—only rationalized. The individual psychology is made consistent with a rationalized world system with the individual scientifically engineered to serve production and consumption—in short, to serve the ethic of the machine. Rampion's fear that the "industrialists who purvey standardized . . . amusements to the masses . . . to make you as much of a mechanical imbecile in your leisure as in your hours of work . . . standardizing and specializing every trace of genuine manhood or womanhood out of the human race" (PCP, 418–19) comes to fruition in the rationalized Brave New World.

Notes

1. Nicolas Berdyaev, The End of Our Time, trans. Donald Atwater (London: Sheed and Ward, 1933). French edition published 1927.

2. Henry Ford, My Life and Work (London: Heinemann, 1922), p. 103. Peter Firchow's interesting study, Brave New World, The End of Utopia (1984), came to my attention after this essay had been accepted. He, too, quotes extensively from Ford's biography and also refers to Fülöp-Miller's The Mind and Face of Bolshevism.

3. Ford, pp. 104–05.

4. Aldous Huxley, *Point Counter Point* (London: Chatto and Windus, 1928), pp. 414–15. Subsequent references to the first edition are included in the text by page numbers in parentheses.

5. Aldous Huxley, "This Community Business," *Vanity Fair*, New York, 33 (December 1929), 62.

6. Aldous Huxley, "The Cold-Blooded Romantics," *Vanity Fair*, New York, 30 (March 1929), 64.

7. Ford, p. 80.

8. Ford, p. 87.

9. Ford, pp. 82, 113.

10. Aldous Huxley, *Brave New World* (London: Chatto and Windus, 1932), p. 188. Subsequent references to the first edition are included in the text by page numbers in parentheses.

11. Huxley, "This Community Business," p. 62.

12. Alphonse Séché, *La morale de la machine* (Paris: Grasset, 1929), p. iii. Except where Huxley translates a passage from Séché in his review article, "This Community Business" (see n. 18), the translations from Séché are mine. The book has never been translated into English.

13. Séché, p. 71.

14. Séché, p. 32.

15. Séché, p. 69.

16. Séché, p. 34.

17. Séché.

18. Huxley, "This Community Business," p. 62.

19. Aldous Huxley, "Machinery, Psychology and Politics," *The Spectator*, 143 (23 November 1929), 749.

20. Hector Bolitho, *Alfred Mond, First Lord Melchett* (London: Secker, 1933), p. 71.

21. Bolitho, p. 290.

22. Lyndall Urwick, *The Meaning of Rationalisation* (London: Nisbet, 1929), p. 108.

23. Leslie Hannah, *The Rise of the Corporate Economy*, second edition (London: Methuen, 1983), pp. 31–32.

24. P. Wyndham Lewis, *The Art of Being Ruled* (New York: Harper, 1926), p. 111.

25. W. J. Reader, *Imperial Chemical Industries: A History* (London: Oxford University Press, 1970), plate 38.

26. Séché, pp. 79, 80.

27. Alfred Mond, quoted in *Times*, "International Aspect of Industry," 9 March 1927, 11d.

28. *Times*, "International."

29. *Times*, "U.S. Finance and the Empire. Sir Alfred Mond on Cooperation," 18 April 1928, 11c.

30. Alfred Mond, *Industry and Politics* (London: Macmillan, 1927), pp. 169–70.

31. Huxley, paraphrasing Séché, "Machinery, Psychology and Politics," p. 750.

32. Huxley, "Machinery."

33. Bolitho, p. 306.

34. Mond, quoted in *Times*, "Synthetic Foods of the Future. Sir Alfred Mond's prediction," 23 March 1928, 9e.

35. *Times*, "Chemical Congress. Sir A. Mond and Supply of Insulin," 21 July 1926, 11e.

36. *Times*, "Chemical."

37. *Times*, "Chemical."

38. *Times*, "London School of Hygiene," 8 July 1926, 18d.

39.   *Times*, "Trade Barriers," 15 December 1927, 11c.

40.   *Times*, "Britain's Advantages. Sir A. Mond on Outlook for Industry," 18 April 1928, 18e.

41.   Reader, "Personality, Strategy and Structure: Some Consequences of Strong Minds," in Leslie Hannah, *Management Strategy and Business Development: An Historical and Comparative Study* (London: Macmillan, 1976), p. 122.

42.   Bolitho, p. 381.

43.   Bolitho, quoting Lord Beaverbrook, p. 378.

44.   Bolitho, p. 315.

45.   Bolitho, p. 311.

46.   Mond, in Bolitho, p. 317.

47.   Huxley, "The Problem of Faith," *Harper's*, 166 (January 1933), p. 213.

48.   Huxley, "Problem," p. 214.

49.   Huxley, "Problem," p. 215.

Technology and Gender in Aldous Huxley's Alternative (?) Worlds

JUNE DEERY

Technology is old, older than science, yet there has been greater technological advance this century than in all of previously recorded history. According to Aldous Huxley, this phenomenon is remarkable also for its lack of impact on twentieth-century literature. Some of his own works are exceptions, particularly the utopian *Brave New World* (1932)—now a byword for nightmarish technocracy—and the other alternative worlds of *Ape and Essence* (1949) and *Island* (1962). But just how alternative are these worlds? In order to determine this, I shall examine Huxley's portrayal, not only of the impact of technology on the social body as a whole, but also its impact on the female citizen in particular in each of these texts.

To utopianize is to clear a space, to examine fundamentals, and, in making a selection of what is most vital in an autonomously constructed society, what the author omits is often as interesting as what is included; so it is with Huxley on female status. Technology, on the other hand, has been an important part of the utopian tradition since Francis Bacon. Yet Huxley was not one who thought technology alone would usher in the New Jerusalem, and one of the reasons he wrote *Brave New World* was to respond to the high-tech, steel paradises associated with H. G. Wells.[1]

In *Brave New World*, which began as a parody of Wells's *Men Like Gods* (Plimpton, 198), Huxley has a good deal of fun with technological innovations and anticipates several trends. Here technology underpins the whole of society and is worshiped in the name of Ford.[2] In detailing its various manifestations, Huxley approaches the technological fetishism of science fiction, yet there is not enough hard science for his accuracy to be tested. Fortunately, he has a happy knack for coining convincing terminology and at once giving it an air of familiarity.

In this novel, the notion of mass production is applied with a vengeance, being extended to consumers as well as consumer items. The entire society is organized along Fordian (or Taylorian) lines: so vital is Ford, in fact, that

From *Extrapolation* 33 (1992): 35–59. Reprinted with permission of the author and The Kent State University Press.

the calender dates from his first model-T car. Practically everything is not only disposable but synthetic: the highest praise accorded to any product is that it is "real . . .-surrogate" (52). Citizens are happiest in a neon-lit, artificial environment where nature is as far as possible ignored (76), their entertainment being provided by that new art form born of technology: the cinema. The helicopters the upper-class characters commonly use for private transport were, it is worth remembering, only at an experimental stage when this text was being written, and the effect of rapid transport on people's lives, the fast pace and the regimentation, was also just beginning to be felt. Huxley's characters remark if a transatlantic rocket-plane is but a few minutes late. " 'There's the Red Rocket,' said Henry, 'just come in from New York.' Looking at his watch. 'Seven minutes behind time,' he added, and shook his head. 'These Atlantic services—they're really scandalously unpunctual' " (61). Leaving aside this early portrayal of rocket technology, perhaps we forget that even the technology for standardizing World Time had been developed only twenty years earlier in 1912.[3] In other areas, Huxley anticipates everything from cloning, which only began with animals in the 1950s, to so-called test-tube babies, first successful in 1978, years after Huxley's death. The fact that Huxley's brother Julian and family friends such as the Haldanes were top biologists made Huxley privy to many current and anticipated developments.[4] In turn, *Brave New World* spurred on research in certain fields, according to the testimony of some biologists (McLaughlin, 62). But the really big revolution, Huxley predicts, is not only in bio- but also psycho-technology, and here again he was ahead of his time.

The scientific attitude in the new world is rigidly Baconian. Fordian researchers view themselves as conquistadors who, in an ecstasy of quantification, are out to put nature in its place. They delight because they have graduated from "the realm of mere slavish imitation of nature into the much more interesting world of human invention" (12). All of this is of course regarded as appallingly hubristic by the author. Note how the process of growing the human fetus is described as dependent on "massive doses of hog's stomach extract and foetal foal's liver" (11). And the idea of deliberately disabling a future human being, which is common practice on this production line, is surely repugnant, as is the sadistic postnatal conditioning with electric shocks (20), all in the Procrustian determination to fit the individual human being to the State's requirements.

But to what ends exactly? This is the question Huxley would have us append to every discussion of technological means. In this case the aim is simply to keep the machinery turning and maintain all citizens, male and female, in a state of calm though superficial contentment. Each has a limited and specialized function in the great mechanism of the State, the whole being lubricated by synthetic drugs. Any one individual knows very little about anything beyond his or her own specialized task. For example, Linda used to inject chemicals into test tubes, but when her son asks where chemicals come from she can only reply: "Well, I don't know. You get them out of bottles. And when the bottles are empty, you send up to the Chemical Store for more" (132). Interestingly, in *Brave New World* even science has been replaced by technology. "Pure" research has been muzzled to create a permanent state of normal science (Kuhn, 181) where technologists deal only with immediate problems and none risk theoretical or metaphysical upsets (*BNW*, 231–32). In accordance with Fordism, truth and beauty have been replaced by comfort and one brand of "happiness" for all, a happiness which to Huxley signals humanity's quiet and irreversible self-destruction.

But how does technology impact on female experience in particular? In answering this, one uncovers a gender bias in Huxley's technocracy, though such a bias is nowhere explicitly stated as a founding principle. We quickly learn that classes are rigidly defined, but there is nothing to suggest that within each class women are to be regarded as inferior to men. In practice, however, after the 200 meter mark when sex is discovered (11), citizens appear to be treated differently according to gender, and the difference often means inequality, with women being assigned the lower status. In some instances, Huxley both recognizes the bias in the system and explicitly condemns it, but in other instances it is a function of his own perspective and he is oblivious to the inequalities his illustration introduces.

Interestingly, it is possible to argue that in some areas, despite its being a dystopia, *Brave New World* offers women a better deal than the contemporary British society of the 1930s. There is no housework, no wifely subjugation, no need to balance children and a career. And if women do not appear to have the vote (which in Britain they had gained only six years earlier), then neither do the men, for all are equally disfranchised in this society.[5] Yet, for all this, if we compare their position to that of men in *Brave New World*, women are less well off. A dystopia is, of course, a negative picture, but this does not imply a simple reversal, when what appears to be approved is really condemned and vice versa. If women appear to have achieved a modicum of freedom, this is not frowned upon by the author, but then the disadvantages that they in particular face are not necessarily condemned either. The picture is much more complex. In fact, Huxley has often confused his readers because not everything in *Brave New World* is viewed as unpalatable. The point here being that one of the things Huxley does not always portray as objectionable is woman's relatively inferior role.

On occasion, he does recognize and explicitly criticize women's treatment in this society. This is most evident in his portrayal of sexual interplay. At first, the general promiscuity is seen as amusingly novel, and there is no serious discussion of what is revealed about a woman's position relative to men. The anonymous narrator is not explicitly gendered. Indeed, Huxley's desire to create a sense of lifeless uniformity means the language he employs is often less gendered than one might expect in a text of this period. Yet our first view of a woman is undoubtedly through male eyes, and the first comment is on her sexual attractiveness (15), or, from T. S. Eliot, her "pneumatic" appeal (44).[6] We subsequently learn that the correct etiquette is for a man to pat a woman on the behind and murmur "charming" while she returns a deferential smile (15). This sort of behavior rapidly becomes less amusing when it is pointed out that in this society women are seen, and regard themselves, as "meat," and (as in our society) meat which must be lean, not fat. While chewing their sex-hormone gum (we don't see women using these stimulants), men compare different women as sexual partners and seem to strengthen their own bonding by recommending previous lovers. " 'Yes, I really do advise you to try her,' Henry Foster was saying. . . . 'But, my dear chap, you're welcome, I assure you' " (46). According to Huxley's description, men tend to ask women out on dates, and it is they who drive the helicopters (this, I think, is crucial). All of this may be because upper-class men appear to date lower-class women, a class difference which en-genders another hierarchy. But as to why this is so or how common it is, we are given no clue. What we do witness is that this pattern makes it difficult for the female to refuse her body to her higher-caste sexual partner. (For women, it seems, "free love" means always having to say yes). Thus Lenina, in love with someone else, has to dope herself before having sex with a highly-placed male (181), but we don't see a man prostituting himself in this fashion. Bernard, the misfit, finds this attitude towards women repugnant and expresses his distaste at the men's locker room conversation: "Talking about her as though she were a bit of meat. Bernard ground his teeth. Have her here, have her there. Like mutton. Degrading her to so much mutton" (45). It is an attitude that is reinforced in the world of entertainment, if the film Huxley chooses to describe is anything to go by. This latest movie, or "feely," depicts a Beta blonde who, after being abducted by a lower-class black male, is rescued by a trio of upper-class white males and, in gratitude, becomes the mistress of all three of them (171), thus preserving both a gender and, it seems, racial hierarchy. Off the screen too, we note that the popularly admired type is the athletic, powerful, sociable "he-man" who always gets his girl (66–67). And it *is* always "he" and who gets his "girl" in this hermetically heterosexual society.[7]

It may be that Huxley is deliberately using the movie to highlight these biases, and it may be that he generally depicts a higher-class male soliciting a lower-class female in order to disclose a gender inequality. Certainly there is some distaste for the view of women as sexual "meat," but it may also be, and I think this is more likely, that men propositioning women and men driving helicopters is merely an unthinking mirroring of Huxley's own society. There are occasions when one cannot be sure that Huxley recognizes or would have us recognize instances of sexual discrimination which appear embedded in the system; for example, as opposed to the "Girls' Dressing-Room" (35), the men emerge from the upper-class "Alpha Changing Rooms" (57). This might be interpreted as a revelation that this society regards men not only as superior but also as the norm. However, none of this reading is actually underscored in the text, and so we are at a loss to decide whether the bias is the dystopians' or Huxley's.

There are other instances of simple neglect. Thus, we can assume that numerous upper-class females exist somewhere in this society—there is nothing which precludes this—but in Huxley's account we get only a brief glance of one of them—the headmistress at Eton. Even here we encounter her when she is in a position of need relative to the Alpha-Plus male who approaches her (164), and we note that her superior is a male Provost (163). The name of this upper-class female is, incidentally, "Miss" Keate, surely an anachronistic form of address in a society where there is no marriage. Perhaps Huxley has forgotten this in his desire to recreate the stereotype of the spinsterish headmistress, the woman who achieves position only by forfeiting her "true femininity."

In other cases it is even clearer that the gender bias is not, in fact, part of the dystopian system but is a function of Huxley's subsequent and unmindful portrayal of certain details once the society's basic principles have been established. Obviously there can be no denunciation where there isn't even a recognition of injustice. Rather, what we find is an automatic importation of the sexist norms of Huxley's own society into the imagined world. It is not a question of deliberately portraying the dystopia, "the bad place," as objectionable because, among other things, it treats women unfairly relative to men. Instead, the unequal treatment is frequently attributable to Huxley's own viewpoint. Rarely is the citizen in any dystopia in an enviable situation, but Huxley's portrayal goes further by placing women in an even lower position than men, *and* by not making a point of it. In short, there are many unattractive features of this society, but women's lack of position is not foregrounded as one of them.

Though there is nothing we know of in the dystopian constitution to bar them, Huxley simply fails to offer examples of women in power. The World Controller, the Director of Hatcheries and Conditioning, the Arch-Community Songster—all are men. There is even a male Assistant Director of Predestination (!), with the male gods of Ford and Freud hovering above. All of the women we encounter are slight characters, more objects than subjects, who are not able to break through the constraints of their society, much less Huxley's two-dimensional characterization, as some of the men begin to do. Although Kumar suggests that Lenina's falling in love might be the only door to overturning the present regime (287), it is such a static, one might almost say apolitical, society that it is difficult to see any possibility of upsetting the status quo to benefit either men or women.

Again, take the position, an important one in this society, of the technologist. The senior figures we encounter are invariably male. It is hardly surprising that, as recent studies have shown, there is a masculinist bias at the roots of modern science, both as an enterprise and worldview[8]; what

Brave New World does is simply reflect and perpetuate this tradition. We note that the novel opens with knowledge being handed on from senior males to younger male students. The association of technology with masculinity is reinforced by the fact that the sign for males in this society happens to be identical to the divine symbol of Fordian technology, the T. However, this identification is never explicitly remarked upon in the text and it is not clear if Huxley makes the association knowingly. Fertile women, on the other hand, are represented by a circle, which, apart form its obvious genital associations, suggests zero, nothingness, hollow space, and passivity (11). Moreover, if we see it as our own symbol of women (♀ Venus) minus the Christian cross, then, as men have gained divinity, women have had it taken from them. Other women who have been sterilized are designated by a question mark, as though suspicious or doubtful, and certainly something to snigger at. These "freemartins" do not constitute a third gender. They are still heterosexual and feminine, though, incidentally, since the latter comes from the root "to suckle," none of these childless women are in fact strictly "feminine." In any case, it is not clear if Huxley acknowledges a bias in the labeling of any of these categories (nor have I seen it outlined in any other critical works).

When it is a question of possessing knowledge or having an education, once again it is the men who appear to be in a superior position. In Huxley's account, women merely enter as narrative feeders, asking them for explanations. " 'Why do the smoke-stacks have those things like balconies around them?' enquired Lenina. 'Phosphorous recovery,' explained Henry telegraphically" (73), and he then goes on to lecture her at some length on this and other matters. Such interactions can again be explained by the fact that Huxley chooses to portray upper-class males addressing lower-class females. Instead of being scientists and leaders, the women we encounter perform auxiliary, service roles in nursing,[9] teaching, secretarial and factory work— the sort of jobs their contemporaries were in fact given in Huxley's society. These women therefore don't do science; they have science done to them. One area where technology has fundamentally altered female experience is motherhood, or, to use the industrial metaphor, "reproduction." In *Brave New World*, complete ectogenesis, not just in vitro fertilization, is the norm, which means that the site of reproduction is no longer the female body.

Again, why is this done? The ostensible reason, as Huxley presents it, is that ectogenesis facilitates conditioning and the efficient production of future citizens. This much is true. But could it also be attributed to a deeper masculine envy or fear, to the fulfillment of that ancient desire to create independently of the female, as in the Jewish Golem, the Christian "only-begotten" son, or Shelley's modern fantasy, *Frankenstein?* Despite the indisputable fact of the child emerging from the woman's body, for millennia male commentators have been quite ingenious at minimizing her role, for example, claiming that man is the active creator and woman only a passive container. Only in the 1870s, in fact, was it recognized that the woman's egg participated equally in fertilization.[10] But *Brave New World* takes us back to Aristotle, for now men (as scientists) can inform or design the fetus from mere feminine materiality. The biological mother is displaced and her awesome ability to create new life is safely curtailed. Male physicians or "pharmacrats" (Corea, 2) were already beginning to monopolize childbirth in the West by the 1930s, but in Huxley's future society they have entirely appropriated the maternal function, reducing the female role to Lenina mechanically injecting fetuses in test tubes. In fact, motherhood is made taboo. The worst thing that can happen to a woman in this society is for her to become pregnant and carry a child to term (120, 153), and there is some evidence that Huxley was in sympathy with his dystopians on this point. The artificiality of the alternative procedure is meant to be shocking, but Huxley also found the intimacy of natural motherhood to be repugnant and even dangerous, especially for the child. Elsewhere in *Brave New World*, the traditional nuclear family is pictured as an unhealthy trap in which mothers are suffocating, domineering, and even sadistic (38, 41–42). Perhaps the fact that women lose some of this control through ectogenesis is not so regrettable in Huxley's view, though again female disempowerment is not his explicit focus.

Ectogenesis is possible because women who are fertile sell their ovaries to the State (3), a transaction that is not very different from prostitutes in our society who also sell parts of their bodies and is something that perhaps anticipates the commercial "stables" of surrogate mothers that have gone into business in recent years. When the women in *Brave New World* feel a void because they can never bear children themselves, they go to the male Dr. Wells (a glance back at H. G. Wells perhaps?) who cheerfully prescribes a chemical "Pregnancy Substitute" (37). But it is not clear that this hormonal treatment is, in fact, an adequate compensation. Without known offspring, these citizens obviously have no close relatives, and sex is generally separated not only from reproduction but also from love. Despite the hectic socializing, each citizen is totally alone.

Of course, one might argue that only release from motherhood allows a woman to achieve true equality and avoid the biological essentialism that ties the female identity to her reproductive capacities.[11] But this does not appear to be the case here. Separating sex and reproduction has not freed or empowered these women. Huxley rightly anticipated the profound social impact of the oral birth control pill, and he also assumed, again correctly, as it turned out, that women would bear the burden of contraception. In *Brave New World* 70 percent of females are sterilized and the remaining 30 percent are drilled on how to use the pill; yet men's natural processes are not modified in any way, an imbalance which is not remarked upon in the text. Neither the lot of men nor of women is meant to appear particularly attractive in this, as in any other, dystopia; but what this study has shown is that women are generally worse off than men and only in some instances is this a deliberate portrayal of something which earns Huxley's disapprobation.

Ape and Essence, Huxley's second alternative world, is not so much a technological as a post-technological society. Published four years after the first detonation of an atomic bomb, this novel cum screenplay depicts the aftermath of a nuclear World War III and highlights the great irrationality of twentieth-century technology, that all our sophisticated "advances" are aimed at our destruction, that "the much touted technology, while it raises our standard of living, increases the probability of our violently dying" (40). Thanks to uncontrolled technological development to support idiocies like nationalism, the survivors of a nuclear holocaust have reverted back to horrible savagery. Generations later, there is long-term genetic damage, and it is with some sarcasm that Huxley introduces us to "a characteristic product of progressive technology—a hare-lipped Mongolian idiot" (80). Looking back, the narrator claims we should have foreseen that "men would be made so overwhelmingly bumptious by the miracles of their own technology that they would soon lose all sense of reality" (90). Now they are paying for it.

After the war, both technological products and know-how have largely been lost but not the desire to do exactly the same thing all over again. When the Botanist, Poole, arrives in neosavage California from a New Zealand which escaped most of the nuclear fallout, he is asked to explain his profession to the natives:

> "A botanist is a man who knows about plants."
> "War plants?" the Chief asks hopefully.
> "No, no, just plants. Things with leaves and stalks and flowers. . . ."

and so great is their disappointment that they propose to bury him alive on the spot (54). This is typical of the grim humor of the piece, but Huxley's serious point remains, that so long as technological knowledge is confined to a small caste of highly specialized experts then the knowledge base of our civilization is extremely fragile and can be shattered overnight. More generally, he is pointing to the gap between technological and ethical development,[12] to the sophistication of the means and the imbecility of the ends which are "ape-chosen" (35).

The Californians live in a pseudodemocracy that is actually a brutal hierarchy headed by what seems to be an all-male caste of administrators and eunuch priests, though again we learn of no explicit ruling which specifies that only men are to occupy superior positions. Here women *are* defined, or confined, by childbearing. Men capitalize on this function to punish them for giving birth to infants with genetic defects. Children are conceived during a short mating season of indiscriminate and casual sexual activity, after which biological fathers are not traced or held at all responsible. Male scientists such as Einstein, Faraday, Pasteur, and their military bosses, are named as ultimately responsible for the fallout that causes birth defects; nevertheless, women are used as scapegoats. As in *Brave New World*, motherhood is degrading, a curse. There is open hostility to women this time: it is part of the social structure and is condemned as such by Huxley. If, for example, a man finds a woman sexually attractive, she is blamed for bewitching him (an old idea in both Eastern and Western cultures) and it is she who is flogged (70). The violence against women is even more sadistic when young mothers are given just sufficient time to grow attached to their deformed infants before having to watch them be impaled on a butcher's knife in a public ritual (84). Catching the antifeminist strain of the Christian or Pauline Church, one character repeats the new catechism: "What is the nature of Woman? Answer: Woman is the vessel of the Unholy Spirit, the source of all deformity, the enemy of the race . . ." (55). Indeed, women are commonly referred to as "Unholy Vessels," that is, passive receptacles or perhaps tools for man the technologist. Needless to say, none of this is seen as attractive by the narrator.

As in *Brave New World*, gender differences are preserved, even exaggerated, both in neosavage America and among the "civilized" New Zealanders, and again it works against females, though this is not the narrator's major concern, nor is it always explicit and decried. The scientist Poole, for example, is first seen as an unfortunately effeminate man crushed by a domineering mother, while his female colleague, Miss Hook, is another caricature of the spinsterish career woman, complete with horn-rimmed glasses and tweeds (38). Though she and other females are scientists in New Zealand, we note that Huxley assigns them the "softer" fields of botany and anthropology. The "hard" sciences are still a male preserve and the women passively look on as male scientists bullishly stake a claim for the role of their particular field in the disaster of the previous war (38). "Miss Hook" is simply out to catch her man, the reluctant Poole, but this is fixed when he meets an ultrafeminine—that is, helpless—junior and takes on a dominant, protective role. This provides for a happy ending when the conventional heterosexual roles are reinstated and he leads her into a new life. The narrator appears to approve of this, although Poole is playing a role not very different from that scoffed at earlier when one character fantasizes that he is "Flash the perpetual knight-errant to girls, not as they lamentably are, but as the idealists of the brassiere industry proclaim that they ought to be" (21).

Island, Huxley's final Utopia, shows how things could be if there was as much effort put into moral and spiritual, as into technological, advance. *Brave New World* represents the peak of technological application and the human dependency it creates, and *Ape and Essence* represents the aftermath when this is suddenly wiped out; but in *Island* the Palanese keep firmly in mind that, as Huxley puts it, technology is made for man, not vice versa (*Island*, 164). They make a point of getting away from Fordian specialization and piecemeal, conveyor-belt work. In fact, on this matter Huxley would pit Darwin against Ford, pointing out that human survival has depended precisely upon our lack of specialization. The islanders, therefore, live a varied life, and as part of their work they focus on the life sciences, on nurturing plants (living plants this time) and human life, rather than stimulating consumerism with technological luxuries (156). They also avoid heavy industry, which in Huxley's eyes is always associated with the twin horrors of militarization and centralization (169). As opposed to what I would call the "cold" science of *Brave New World*, science here is "warm." "Cold" science is cut off from, and even hostile to, nature; in *Brave New World* this means aggression, competition, and triumph over natural processes. The talk may be of fertility rates, but the society as a whole is sterile. Notice the opening description of the technologists at work in *Brave New World*: "Wintriness responded to wintriness. The overalls of the workers were white, their hands gloved with a pale corpse-coloured rubber. The light was frozen, dead, a ghost" (1). The "warm" science of *Island*, on the other hand, aims to work with nature, and the result is accommodation rather than exploitation. This reflects Huxley's lifelong advocacy of a more ecological approach, long before this became fashionable. He drew on ancient ideas, Greek notions of hubris and nemesis as well as Eastern mysticism, to illustrate the universal importance of harmony and balance (*Island*, 248–49). Some lessons, he felt, had already been learned in physics and chemistry, but he wanted to see these applied in other fields. For example, biology was now passing from an earlier passive phase of categorization into more active manipulation—as in genetic engineering—and Huxley felt it imperative to prevent this from going too "cold." He also advocated supplementing Western, material technology with the ancient psychological "technologies" of the East and working towards inner as well as external progress (*Island*, 150–51).

But what of the progress of women's rights? Have these advanced? Huxley clearly found the outright hostility to women in the society of *Ape and Essence* distasteful, but in his eutopia Huxley still seems unable to portray any scenario that radically departs from his own society's attitudes. In *Island* we encounter more important female characters, but the main narrative role for women, here as previously, is to induct the male outsider into the alternative society: here Susila inducts Will, before Lenina inducted John, and Loola inducted Poole. We know that the present social system in Pala was designed by two men, and men still appear to hold senior positions (as much as these can be determined), both political and religious. This time women *can* drive but are seen to do so only when men are physically unable (265). As in *Brave New World*, women are more often in assistant and nurturing roles. It is assumed that all nurses are female (77) and, though we see female teachers, the Under-Secretary for Education is a man (234). Once again Huxley is slipping into the stereotypes of his own society. The nearest we come to a woman in power, the Rani or Queen mother, is a heavily mocked and destructive figure. Due to patrilineal descent, she possesses no actual power and holds her position only as the widow of the previous ruler and mother of the next, but she is nevertheless seen as manipulative and threatening. Among the rest of the populace, monogamous marriages, in which the woman evidently takes her husband's name, appear to be the norm, but no details are given of how women balance outside careers and childrearing, though it appears they take on both. Huxley does not regard this as sufficiently important to discuss in any detail.

For the first time in his alternative worlds, homosexuality is accommodated. But meanwhile, heterosexual gender roles are still clearly differentiated, however much differences are now also seen as positive and complementary. "On top of being two hundred per cent male," the ideal man is now "almost fifty per cent sensitive-feminine" (229) which means that Huxley accepts gender stereotypes ("feminine" sensitivity) but now recommends some blending. With one couple, it is the wife's "brain" which is matched by her husband's "brawn" (220), but in two different generations we see the pattern of a marriage between an absorbed, intellectual male and a less intelligent, awestruck wife (40–41, 83). At best, while he is straightforwardly intelligent, she is "intelligently simple" (206). As another wife explains to her husband, "I was always on tiptoes, always straining up towards the place where you were doing your work and your thinking and your reading" (40–41).

Again, the big change in female experience is in motherhood, which is at last seen as both positive and powerful. Huxley can now regard breastfeeding without flinching (218), and his hero, Will, learns to leave aside past associations of the womb and death (9) and embrace woman the life-giver. The romantic heroine we notice is a (widowed) mother and, through Susila, Will learns to reconcile the love and sexuality he previously divided between his wife and his mistress. Despite a phallic and powerful name, Will is actually emasculated and seeking a mother-figure-as-savior; this Susila is ready to provide along with her psychological first aid.

Now Huxley's focus is specifically on female as well as male happiness. In Will's previous experience—that is, our world—women are pictured as either angels, whores, or as passive, long-suffering wives and mothers. But on the island, we are assured that all women are much happier. Perhaps, for one thing, this is due to their greater say in matters of reproduction, a development that is regarded as beneficial for women and for society. State-issued contraceptives for both men and women presumably allow women some say on whether or not to have a child in the first place, though apparently only within marriage (92). Artificial insemination with donor sperm (A.I.D.) also enables them, no doubt in consultation with their husbands, to select the genetic makeup of their offspring. In such cases, donor sperm comes from a bank and the process involves no sexual impregnation, which means that there is still sexual, if not biological, fidelity between husband and wife. Nevertheless, this procedure does displace the husband as biological father and thereby undermines direct patriarchal descent. Apparently the Palanese men don't have any objections to this but happily stand aside so their wives' children can have a good genetic inheritance (220–21), whereas it is worth remembering that in our society, as late as 1963, A.I.D. was regarded as adulterous and grounds for divorce (Corea, 40). It may be that women are happier in *Island* also because Huxley has not neglected the female orgasm. The "yoga of love," which is part of Palanese religious practice, is apparently very satisfying for the female partner, giving her both sexual and spiritual equal opportunity (98)! Evidently, women have gained some ground in this eutopia, but there is still no direct indication that this greater control is paralleled in Pala's formal politics.

And what of the scientific sphere? Is the "warm" science I referred to earlier seen as more feminine than the scientific attitude found in *Brave New World*? The Palanese appear to have modified the West's seventeenth-century mechanization of nature, realigning themselves with an older, also Eastern, attitude which sees nature as vital and organic, a worldview that has indeed been associated with the feminine.[13] They are also more interested in the "soft" than the traditionally masculinist, "hard" sciences, and their methodology is more holistic and nurturing than destructive, again qualities conventionally associated with the feminine. However, there is no evidence that Huxley makes these associations or that he invokes the gendered polarity of nature (feminine) and science/culture (masculine) in any of these works.

What we have seen in each of these societies is that technology often radically affects women's experience but appears to be controlled by men and that, whatever their society, men and women appear to enjoy equal political status in principle; but this is not what emerges from Huxley's portrayal. Even when attempting to better the female lot, he repeatedly adopts the sexist norms of his own society without even being aware of it. It is not a question of realism, for one of the obvious features of utopias is that they need not reflect anything of the current status quo; indeed, their agenda is generally to radically alter it. Nevertheless, though *Island* does show some improvement of the female position compared to the two previous dystopias and compared to Huxley's own society, it is not as alternative a world as one might expect. This reflects the lack of serious attention to the position of women in the mainstream (or male-stream) utopian tradition. Even authors who in theory advocate equal opportunity for women don't appear to take the issue seriously enough to follow through and portray this in practice. In fictional utopias it is, quite legitimately, enactment which counts. This is no mere detail—rather, mere details are significant, for what is depicted, what is worked out in detail, is what most impresses the reader. One thinks of Edward Bellamy's hugely influential *Looking Backward* (1888) where women have theoretical opportunities that are simply not convincingly realized in practice. Bellamy's women supposedly have full-time careers outside the home; yet in practice, the heroine, Miss Leete, appears to be very little different from her Victorian ancestors, being occupied with nothing more than occasional shopping trips or flower arranging at the breakfast table. At least William Morris was more consistent when, writing in response to Bellamy a few years later, he came right out and said that women prefer these domestic tasks and should continue to perform them (234).

In Huxley's works, women have as much opportunity relative to men—at least in theory—in the dystopia *Brave New World* as in the eutopia *Island*; one social arrangement may in its entirety be obviously preferable to the other, but a woman's relative position does not greatly alter. In other words, it is clear that the fate of women alone does not define these societies as eutopian or dystopian, and it is not something to which Huxley pays a great deal of attention. Only on a few occasions does he suggest that women in *Brave New World* are treated differently or more unfairly than the male citizen. In the area of female rights, one might say that Huxley sins more by omission than intention. Perhaps this makes it the more damning; for all his ability to think differently on the technological front, in the underlying sexual politics the more things change, the more they stay the same.

Notes

1. Actually, it would be unfair, though common, to label Wells a facile or die-hard optimist. Nevertheless, he was very offended by *Brave New World*, seeing it as a betrayal both of science and the future. See Gerald Heard, 57.

2. Although Huxley found some solace in reading Henry Ford's *My Life and Work* after viewing the poverty of India (*Jesting Pilate*, 213–14), he generally loathed Ford and all he stood for. See, for example, *Music at Night*, 127–28.

3. This was established at the International Conference on Time in Paris. For the sociopolitical ramifications of this and other technological innovations, see Kern.

4. Huxley stayed with the Haldanes while at Oxford and no doubt got many of his ideas for *Brave New World* from J. B. S. Haldane's *Daedalus: Or Science and the Future*. For confirmation of this, see *Proper Studies*, 278.

5. In Britain women aged thirty and over got the vote in 1918 and were accorded equal voting rights with men (aged twenty-one and over) in 1928.

6. "Uncorseted, her friendly bust / Gives promise of pneumatic bliss." T. S. Eliot, "Whispers of Immortality."

7. This does not necessarily reflect Huxley's own views. Indeed, it is thought that Huxley's wife Maria was a lesbian. See Dunaway, 70.

8. For an introduction to feminist studies of science, see Ruth Bleier, Donna Haraway, Sandra Harding, Evelyn Fox Keller, Carolyn Merchant, and Nancy Tuana.

9. Interestingly, even when Huxley avoids assigning a gender to the nurses he mentions, in my experience students tend to assume they have been designated as female.

10. For an account of male trivialization of the female's role in reproduction, see Nancy Tuana, "The Weaker Seed: The Sexist Bias of Reproductive Theory," 147–71.

11. For example, Firestone sets the "freeing of women from the tyranny of their reproductive biology" as a primary aim in any feminist revolution (223).

12. See also *Literature and Science*, 92–93; *Letters*, 578–79; *Time Must Have a Stop*, 274, 78–79.

13. For an account of the seventeenth-century replacement of a more feminine worldview with masculinist modern science, see Keller and Merchant.

Works Cited

Bellamy, Edward. *Looking Backward: 2000–1887*. Ed. Cecelia Tichi. 1888. New York: Penguin, 1982.

Bleier, Ruth, ed. *Feminist Approaches to Science*. New York: Pergamon, 1986.

Corea, Gena. *The Mother Machine: Reproductive Technologies from Artificial Insemination to Artificial Wombs*. New York: Harper, 1985.

Dunaway, David King. *Huxley in Hollywood*. New York: Harper, 1989.

Eliot, T. S. "Whispers of Immortality." *Collected Poems 1909–1935*. New York: Harcourt, 1936.

Firestone, Shulamith. *The Dialectic of Sex*. New York: Morrow, 1970.

Ford, Henry, and Samuel Crowther. *My Life and Work*. New York: Doubleday, 1922.

Haldane, J. B. S. *Daedalus: Or Science and the Future*. London: Paul, 1924.

Haraway, Donna. *Primate Visions: Gender, Race and Nature in the World of Modern Science*. New York: Routledge, 1989.

Harding, Sandra. *The Science Question in Feminism*. Ithaca: Cornell University Press, 1986.

Heard, Gerald. "The Poignant Prophet." *Kenyon Review* 27 (Winter 1965): 49–70.

Huxley, Aldous. *Ape and Essence: A Novel*. 1949. London: Chatto and Windus, 1966.

———. *Brave New World*. 1932. New York: Harper, 1969.

———. *Island: A Novel*. London: Chatto and Windus, 1962.

———. *Jesting Pilate*. 1926. London: Chatto and Windus, 1948.

———. *Letters*. Ed. Grover Smith. London: Chatto and Windus, 1969.

———. *Literature and Science*. London: Chatto and Windus, 1963.

———. *Music at Night*. 1931. London: Chatto and Windus, 1970.

———. *Proper Studies*. 1927. London: Chatto and Windus, 1957.

———. *Time Must Have a Stop*. London: Chatto and Windus, 1945.

Keller, Evelyn Fox. *Reflections on Gender and Science*. New Haven: Yale University Press, 1985.

Kern, Stephen. *The Culture of Time and Space 1880–1918*. Cambridge: Harvard University Press, 1983.

Kuhn, Thomas S. *The Structure of Scientific Revolutions*. 1962. Chicago: University of Chicago Press, 1970.

Kumar, Krishan. *Utopia and Anti-Utopia in Modern Times*. Oxford: Basil Blackwell, 1987.

McLaughlin, Loretta. *The Pill, John Rock, and the Church: The Biography of a Revolution*. Boston: Little, Brown, 1982.

Merchant, Carolyn. *The Death of Nature : Women, Ecology, and the Scientific Revolution*. San Francisco: Harper, 1980.

Morris, William. *News from Nowhere and Selected Writings and Designs*. 1891. New York: Penguin, 1984.

Plimpton, George, ed. *Writers at Work*: *The Paris Review Interviews*. 2nd series. New York: Viking, 1963.

Shelley, Mary. *Frankenstein*: *Or the Modern Prometheus*. Ed. Maurice Hindle. 1818. New York: Penguin, 1985.

Tuana, Nancy, ed. *Feminism and Science*. Bloomington: Indiana University Press, 1989.

Wells, H. G. *Men Like Gods*. New York: Macmillan, 1923.

Literary Criticism in the Modern Novel: Huxley's Response to Joyce

BERNFRIED NUGEL

The centenary of Aldous Huxley's birth in 1994 may at long last induce critics to reconsider his place among modern novelists in a way that combines greater fairness with a new theoretical perspective. For to compare Huxley with Joyce has long been deemed an unrewarding, if not downright pointless undertaking. The prevailing taste among literary historians is nicely reflected in statements such as R. C. Churchill's: "Huxley and Orwell were to the generations of the twenties, thirties, and forties what Shaw, Wells, and Chesterton were to the pre-1914 public; comparison with a James is as irrelevant as comparison with a Joyce."[1] But surely such judgments simply depend on the set of criteria chosen and the purposes pursued by a critic, that is, on his basic assumptions about literature; in short, his literary theory. If he sticks to a fairly rigid system which allows him to define, for instance, the 'true' modern novel, or 'true' psychological realism, exclusionist judgments are inevitable. If, on the contrary, he is open to different frameworks of literature as reflected in different literary models in a continuous process of tradition and innovation, he will attempt to consider all the potentialities of literature in their own right and according to different presuppositions. He will thus compare writers, not primarily to evaluate but to elucidate their individual positions. R. S. Crane's dictum concerning basic assumptions about poetry appears to be as valid in our present postmodernist context as some 40 years ago: "There is a . . . strict relativity, in criticism, not only of questions and statements to frameworks but of frameworks to ends, that is, to the different kinds of knowledge about poetry we may happen, at one time or another or for one or another reason, to want."[2]

The kind of knowledge I happen to want as a literary theorist lies beyond the criteria of most established critics of the modern novel. I would like to find out what literary models the authors themselves had in mind at the time of writing and to what extent they took into account the propositions of their fellow writers. If one could determine, though only in part, the

Expanded and translated into English by the author, this essay is reprinted with the publisher's permission from M. Pfister, ed., *Anglistentag 1984: Passau* (Hoffmann Verlag: Giessen, 1985), 371–82.

literary-critical position, as I would call it, of an author, one might hope not only to obtain a greater insight into the relationship between intention and execution in his oeuvre, but also to gauge the degree of innovation that his position carries within the tradition of literary models.

An author's literary-critical position can be determined in several ways. The easiest seems to be to look for external evidence, that is, for any critical remarks an author has passed on himself or other writers in essays, reviews, letters, conversation, and so on. More often than not, however, these are isolated remarks which allow only tentative conclusions. In November 1918, for instance, Aldous Huxley wrote to his brother Julian that, besides the admired French writers Flaubert, Stendhal, and Balzac, he was reading parts of the still unfinished *Ulysses*: "Among the quite moderns I sip the brilliant *Ulysses* of James Joyce; it has, to be sure, a slight flavour of excrements, but is none the worse for that. For heavier reading I have been perusing an admirable book by one Arthur MacDowell, called *Realism*—a critical study of the phenomenon of realism in art and thought; very interesting."[3] Here Huxley acknowledges Joyce's artistic ability and his tendency to cope with taboos, but surprisingly reckons him among "lighter reading." At the same time his interest in realism as an artistic and philosophical concept is obvious. However, what exactly all these aspects consist in and how they are interconnected, is left open as the object of an intelligent guess. The difficulty of inferring details of the author's literary-critical position from such scattered remarks is enhanced by seemingly contradictory statements, as when we find Huxley calling *Ulysses* "obstreperously gross and blasphemous"[4] three years after its publication. Does this reflect a total change of attitude or does Huxley criticize only an excess of a basically acceptable literary procedure? In any case, we need a larger and more coherent context, as is, incidentally, also true of Joyce's own remark on Huxley, recollected and handed down from 1929 by Nino Frank, a writer and journalist acquainted with Joyce:

> When I once spoke to him about T. S. Eliot, he grimaced. The same thing happened when, learning that D. H. Lawrence was in Paris, I hurried to consult Joyce.
> "That man writes really too poorly," he said. "Ask his friend Aldous Huxley for something instead; at least he dresses decently."[5]

Joyce seems to accept Huxley as a stylist and a decent writer, possibly implying a jibe at Lawrence's alleged pornography. But surely such a comment contains no more than a hint at the author's literary-critical position.

Whenever external evidence does not provide sufficient clues, as in the case of Huxley and Joyce, one may start looking for internal evidence, that is, for literary criticism within the fiction of the author under consideration. This may be present in two forms, either as an explicit or an implicit manifestation. The texture and structure of any literary work will implicitly reflect literary-critical decisions on the author's part in favour of or against established narrative conventions, as, for instance, in the choice of the novel's title, its main themes, its narrative perspective and techniques, the number and length of narrative units, and its stylistic devices. Titles such as *Ulysses* or *Point Counter Point* invite the reader to draw analogies, but how far the analogies to the *Odyssey* or musical counterpoint really carry, can be derived only indirectly. Similarly, we may assume that Huxley had a decisive reason why he did not use the interior monologue technique, but again this is left to the critical reader to clarify. The consequences are well known: the more the literary-critical positions of the readers differ, the larger will the scale of interpretations be, as can easily be seen in the field of the modern novel, where critics rely chiefly on implicit manifestations of the literary-critical positions of writers such as Joyce, Huxley, Lawrence, or Virginia Woolf.

On the other hand, modern novels in particular contain a considerable amount of explicit statements about literature in the form of utterances either from the angle of a character or from the vantagepoint of an overall narrator. Provided we pay heed to any limitations imposed by specific narrative techniques, such explicit statements may allow us to reconstruct a framework, if not a system, of literary-critical notions, within which the author acts as narrator and which he often incorporates in the main themes of his novel. It ought to be the task of literary scholarship to analyze explicit statements about literature within their context and then to classify them according to various fields of literary theory, such as terminology and methodology, definitions of literature, criticism of individual works, literary genres, the artistic process, the reception of literature by the public, and the tradition of literary models or the canons of literature.[6] Now while a scholarly consensus seems feasible with regard to this formal distinction of fields and categories, one should beware of fixing their contents prematurely, in order to be able to do justice to the conceptual variety and innovativeness of the modern novel.[7]

Why should one choose Huxley and Joyce as a test case? In the field of the modern novel Joyce is widely accepted as an author who, more than most other contemporary writers, developed "an almost complete aesthetic system, a comprehensive formulation of his intentions and his critical standpoint," as the German critic Horst W. Drescher states in unison with many other Joyce critics.[8] In this manner, a great amount of research has been devoted to explaining Joyce's *Portrait*—beside his early critical writings—as a largely explicit statement of his system, which he may have modified in *Ulysses* and *Finnegans Wake* but never questioned in principle. On the other hand, critics such as Hugh Kenner, Richard Ellmann, and Wolfgang Wicht[9] argue for a reconsideration of Joyce's critical notions and contend that as early as *Portrait*, Joyce distanced himself from Stephen's explicit statements about literature and art. They concentrate on questions relating to the definition of literature, the poetic process, and the formation of literary canons. Equally important, in my view, is the attempt to qualify the halo of uniqueness that Joyce critics have predicated of his conception of literature, that is, to see Joyce's literary-critical position in perspective and place it within the tradition of literary models. As a first step in this direction a comparison between Joyce and his fellow writers seems appropriate; and here Huxley is an interesting special case because several times in his novels he alludes to Joyce's notions of literature, thereby revealing his own literary-critical position.

One of the key passages reflecting Huxley's view of Joyce is to be found in chapter 11 of *Eyeless in Gaza* (1936). Anthony Beavis, the central character, sociologist by profession, is writing chapter 11 of his *Elements of Sociology* on the concept of personality. The obvious correspondence between the eleventh chapters of both works at once poses the question of how far the positions of Beavis as character and of Huxley as authorial narrator coincide. For our purposes, a summary answer may suffice: in so far as Beavis criticizes conventional notions of personality, the authorial narrator seems to agree with him; but in so far as Beavis thereby tries to justify his particular way of life culminating in cynical irresponsibility, he is presented in an ironic light. Now Beavis's theory of personality springs from his insight that the conventional view of personality is based on a rigorous reduction of human life: "My 'personality', in the present conventional sense of the word, is what I think and feel—or, rather, what I confess to thinking and feeling. *Caco, eructo, futuo*—I never admit that the first person singular of such verbs is really *me*. Only when, for any reason they palpably affect my feelings and thinking do the processes they stand for come within the bounds of my 'personality.' (This censorship makes ultimate nonsense of all literature. Plays and novels just aren't true.)"[10] Here we can see straight from the beginning of the argument that, in Beavis's view, literature plays an important, if often bad role in the distribution of models of personality. In contrast to the conventional limited view of personality Beavis then postulates an atomism of the psyche by analogy with the atomism of matter: ". . . human experience is analogous to matter. Analyse it—and you find yourself in the presence of psychological atoms. A lot of these atoms constitute normal experience, and a selection from normal experience constitutes 'personality'" (140). In the course of the argument, Beavis, with increasing clarity and emphasis, distinguishes between "total experience" as the sum of all "psychological atom[s] or instant[s]" on the one hand and "experience in the lump and by the hour" or "feeling and thought" on the other (146). At the same time he admits that the techniques of psychological analysis have been refined up to the twentieth century and that literature has had its share in this process: "Thanks to the novelists and professional psychologists, we can think of our experience in terms of atoms and instants as well as in terms of lumps and hours" (141).

Shakespeare, by the way, is alleged to have attempted something similar in his time, and Huxley allows Beavis to make a few thought-provoking remarks about the character of Hamlet. Beavis even discovers a whole tradition of psychological atomism from Blake to Proust and Lawrence, which possibly tends toward a new ideal of personality: ". . . is it the beginning of a new kind of personality? That of the total man, unbowdlerized, unselected, uncanalized, to change the metaphor, down any one particular drainpipe of *Weltanschauung*—of the man, in a word, who actually is what he may be" (145). Because this reflection is put in brackets and is placed "quite outside the domain of sociology," the reader is bound to doubt whether such a new model of personality based on psychological atomism might be desirable, even more so because, in the concluding part of his argument, Beavis mentions only the psyche's connection with the body as the fundamental principle of coherence between the psychological atoms: "Each man a succession of states enclosed in the flesh of his own side. And if any other principle of coherence were needed, there was always some absorbing and delightful intellectual interest, like sociology, for example, to supplement the persisting body" (150).

The same irony on the part of the authorial narrator can be grasped even earlier in the argument when Beavis speaks of the models of personality cherished by modern novelists. To give a vivid impression, Huxley has Beavis use metaphors from the world of fashion. Starting with the observation, "There are fashions in personality" (142), Beavis surveys the change of fashions and then presents the personality models of modern writers like a fashion show:

> In our world, what are the ruling fashions? There are, of course, the ordinary clerical and commercial modes—turned out by the little dressmakers round the corner. And then *la haute couture. Ravissante person{n}alité d'intérieur de chez Proust. Maison Nietzsche et Kipling: person{n}alité de sport. Person{n}alité de nuit, création de Lawrence. Person{n}alité de bain, par Joyce.* Note the interesting fact that, of these, the *person{n}alité de sport* is the only one that can really count as a personality in the accepted sense of the word. The others are to a greater or less extent impersonal, because to a greater or less extent atomic. And this brings us back to Shakespeare and Ben Jonson. A pragmatist would have us say that Jonson's psychology was "truer" than Shakespeare's. Most of his contemporaries did in fact perceive themselves and were perceived as Humours. It took Shakespeare to see what a lot there was outside the boundaries of the Humour, behind the conventional mask. But Shakespeare was in a minority of one—or, if you set Montaigne beside him, of two. Humours "worked"; the complex, partially atomized personalities of Shakespeare didn't. (143)

Though, in Beavis's view, these writers—incidentally, including Shakespeare—are, in contrast to their contemporaries, on the right way, that is, on the way to psychological atomism, they still end up with limited models of personality. Neither the personality of the interior nor the personality of

night or the bathroom personality can be claimed to represent "total experience" or "total man." As for the pointed names of the several personality
models, Proust and Joyce are particularly prominent as representatives of
the modern novel of consciousness.

The leading position that Proust's *personnalité d'intérieur* holds in Beavis's
fashion show corresponds to the general evaluation that Proust is subjected
to elsewhere in *Eyeless in Gaza* or even earlier in *Point Counter Point*. He is
considered the most important representative of the modern novel and is
often presented as a subject of superficial talk or as the target of critical
remarks by the main characters of both novels. In the present passage, the
phrase "de chez Proust" alludes to the title of the first part of Proust's seven-
novel cycle *A la Recherche du Temps Perdu*, viz. *Du Côté de chez Swann*, which
Beavis refers to explicitly in a later passage of the same chapter 11 of *Eyeless
in Gaza*.[11] Moreover, the phrase *personnalité d'intérieur* carries at least two
connotations. On the one hand, it directly points to the fact that Proust
spent the last years of his life almost continuously in a sickroom and thus,
in his representation of human life, depended on the limited experience
possible in the interior of a building. On the other hand, it emphasizes
Proust's fundamental and nearly exclusive concentration on the depiction of
his characters' interiors. The attribute "ravissante," that is, "ravishing,"
appears to be particularly appropriate, inasmuch as it alludes to Proust's
admiration for involuntary memory, the so-called *souvenir involontaire*, which
is explained by Gerd Rohmann in the following way: "From the deepest
unconscious, the 'souvenir involontaire' brings to the surface what has long
been considered forgotten. In a sudden ecstasy, the past is experienced a
second time, but now in absolute purity. It is only chance that determines
the moment at which an immediate sense impression sets free a bundle of
associations, by which the 'souvenir involontaire' shakes up the whole interior
life with great force and so irresistibly draws it towards an experience that
this is lived through in all its depth as absolute truth."[12] If such ravishment,
according to Proust, seizes the self at the moment of an involuntary reminiscence, it may equally well carry away the reader (French *ravir* is an active
verb). Thus Huxley's phrase *ravissante personnalité d'intérieur* may also aim at
the emotional effect intended by Proust, which, in Rohmann's opinion,
ultimately ends up with some kind of mysticism of art. Judged by the
criterion of "total experience," however, this "ravishing" tendency proves
to involve a limitation of the scope of experience.

Something similar seems to be intended for Joyce. *La personnalité de
bain* suggests an area even more intimate and secluded from human relationships than Proust's sickroom. The bathroom, after all, is the place where
the human body may present itself in its elementary needs and its nakedness,
in a word, as what it really is, and it is well known that Joyce, more than
any other contemporary writer, treated this taboo subject in a naturalistic
manner. Moreover, the bathroom personality specifically evokes the "Lotus

Eaters" episode of *Ulysses*, in which Bloom imagines himself taking a bath and observing his naked body in the bath water:

> Enjoy a bath now: clean trough of water, cool enamel, the gentle tepid stream. This is my body.
> He foresaw his pale body reclined in it at full, naked, in a womb of warmth, oiled by scented melting soap, softly laved. He saw his trunk and limbs riprippled over and sustained, buoyed lightly upward, lemonyellow: his navel, bud of flesh: and saw the dark tangled curls of his bush floating, floating hair of the stream around the limp father of thousands, a languid floating flower. [13]

Judged by the moral conventions of Joyce's time, this in itself rather consider-ate visualization of a bathroom scene amounted to nothing less than the breaking of a taboo and came to be reckoned among the allegedly indecent passages of *Ulysses*. In Huxley's more sympathetic view, Joyce appears as a specialist in the representation of the most private bodily functions, quite in the same way as Proust is credited with the subtle rendering of emotional life. On the basis of psychological atomism, both approaches can be justified to a certain extent, but they still remain one-sided phenomena, [14] even if they are to be counted among *la haute couture* or high fashion. Furthermore, this last qualification carries another hint. *Haute couture* means exclusiveness with regard to the average customer, means esoteric standards or even eccen-tricity, and thus adequately characterizes the remoteness of the novel of consciousness from the common reading public.

What could not be surpassed in this respect, would be a combination of Proust and Joyce, and no less than this seems aimed at by Huxley in a different passage of *Eyeless in Gaza*. Nearly seven years after his draft of the *Elements of Sociology*, Beavis's attitude toward Proust has become even more critical. [15] As an adherent of psychological atomism in the extreme, Beavis wishes to suppress all memories and with them all responsibility for his past actions. Although the authorial narrator presents Beavis's philosophy ironically, he still appears to share Beavis's criticism of Proust, if so for a different reason: it is not Proust's preoccupation with the past as such that is satirized but his consequent inactivity and lack of responsibility. In the following passage, this Proustian attitude is exaggerated and reduced to absurdity in the manner of the bathroom personality attributed to Joyce:

> . . . Then, in a tone of disgust, "All this burden of past experience one trails about with one!" he added. "There ought to be some way of getting rid of one's superfluous memories. How I hate old Proust! Really detest him." And with a richly comic eloquence he proceeded to evoke the vision of that asthmatic seeker of lost time squatting, horribly white and flabby, with breasts almost female but fledged with long black hairs, for ever squatting in the tepid bath of his remembered past. And all the stale soapsuds of countless previous washings floated around him, all the accumulated dirt of years lay

crusty on the sides of the tub or hung in dark suspension in the water. And there he sat, a pale repellent invalid, taking up spongefuls of his own thick soup and squeezing it over his face, scooping up cupfuls of it and appreciatively rolling the grey and gritty liquor round his mouth, gargling, rinsing his nostrils with it, like a pious Hindu in the Ganges. . . . (8)[16]

At this stage, an intermediate summary seems appropriate. From Beavis's remarks and from the perspective of the overall narrator we may abstract central notions of Huxley's literary-critical position with regard to the novel of consciousness:

1.   Its main representatives, Proust and Joyce, orientate their depiction of human life, or more exactly, of human consciousness, towards personality models which cannot fully claim to represent total experience, though they may penetrate into taboo areas of human behaviour.

2.   Their technique of rendering consciousness, the so-called psychological atomism, as compared with that of their predecessors, means a real step forward in so far as subtlety and depth of analysis are concerned but ought not to be regarded as the absolute purpose and ultimate goal of narration.

3.   Their esoteric remoteness, their being high fashion, decisively limits their reception by and consequently their impact on the reading public.

In contrast to the prevailing opinion of literary historians, we cannot but draw the astonishing conclusion that, in Huxley's view, the novel of consciousness does not achieve enough, or in other words, that farther-reaching techniques and goals are conceivable. In what direction we may look for such ideas, can be seen, for instance, from the structure of *Eyeless in Gaza*: it is no discontinued artist novel such as the Stephen-oriented units of *Ulysses* but a modern Bildungsroman leading the protagonist to self-recognition and a sense of responsibility.

Considered formally, the foregoing conclusions belong to three important categories of literary theory. Within the field concerned with the definition of literature two categories apply, viz. "scope and subject of representation" and "manner of representation." The third category, "impact on the reading public," is to be subsumed under the reception of literature. This general framework of literary-critical notions can easily accommodate various other explicit remarks on literature in Huxley's novels. Some examples for each category from *Point Counter Point* and *Eyeless in Gaza* must suffice here.

SUBJECT OF REPRESENTATION   Traditional literature is often criticized for its limited scope of subject. As early as in the first chapter of

Point Counter Point, Huxley has his fictitious author Philip Quarles refer to Shelley's *Epipsychidion* in order to make the following statement about poetry:

> "It's apt to be too true. Unadulterated, like distilled water. When truth is nothing but the truth, it's unnatural, it's an abstraction that resembles nothing in the real world. In nature there are always so many other irrelevant things mixed up with the essential truth. That's why art moves you—precisely because it's unadulterated with all the irrelevancies of real life. Real orgies are never so exciting as pornographic books. In a volume by Pierre Louys all the girls are young and their figures perfect; there's no hiccoughing or bad breath, no fatigue or boredom, no sudden recollections of unpaid bills or business letters unanswered, to interrupt the raptures. Art gives you the sensation, the thought, the feeling quite pure—chemically pure, I mean," he added with a laugh, "not morally."[17]

In chapter 46 of *Eyeless in Gaza*, Mark Staithes, a minor character, argues in a similar way, and his remarks are explicitly approved of by Anthony Beavis. Now the novel of consciousness certainly attempts to compensate for this deficit of traditional literature: it treats relevancies side by side with "irrelevancies of real life."

MANNER OF REPRESENTATION   New methods of how to expand

the scope of subject are presented by Huxley in a general as well as in a special form through Philip Quarles, who is given the status of an experimenting novelist. In chapter 14 of *Point Counter Point* Quarles speaks of "a new way of looking at things that I want to experiment with" (265) and explains it as follows: ". . . the essence of the new way of looking is multiplicity. Multiplicity of eyes and multiplicity of aspects seen. For instance, one person interprets events in terms of bishops; another in terms of the price of flannel camisoles; . . . . And then there's the biologist, the chemist, the physicist, the historian. Each sees, professionally, a different aspect of the event, a different layer of reality. What I want to do is to look with all those eyes at once. With religious eyes, scientific eyes, economic eyes, *homme moyen sensuel* eyes . . ." (266). This a multiplicity of perspectives that is perhaps approximately achieved in Joyce's *Ulysses*,[18] and indeed Quarles's affinity with the modern novel à la Joyce becomes particularly clear when he describes how he would represent reality in his proposed novel: "However queer the picture is, it can never be half so odd as the original reality. We take it all for granted; but the moment you start thinking, it becomes queer. And the more you think, the queerer it grows. That's what I want to get in this book—the astonishingness of the most obvious things. Really any plot or situation would do. Because everything's implicit in anything. The whole book could be written about a walk from Piccadilly Circus to Charing Cross" (266). Incidentally, one of Quarles's favourite "way[s] of looking at things" is the analogy between music and literature, which he calls "musicalization of fiction" (ch. 22, 408) and wants to use as a principle of novel writing. Here again, parallels with Proust, Joyce, and other modern writers come to mind. What seems important for Huxley, is the insight that none of the many perspectives ought to be pursued absolutely; all of them, on the contrary, must be taken into account if a novelist is to render reality as completely as possible. Into this framework of methods we may also incorporate well-known concepts like the "novel of ideas" or "the novelist within the novel" mentioned in chapter 22 of *Point Counter Point*.[19]

IMPACT ON THE READER   How difficult, in Huxley's view, it is for the reading public to accept and digest the modern novel à la Joyce, is revealed by a passage that is almost entirely neglected in Huxley criticism. In chapter 33 of *Point Counter Point* Philip Quarles is depicted as engaged in an extraordinary reading process:

> Philip was dining alone. In front of his plate half a bottle of claret and the water-jug propped up an open volume. He read between the mouthfuls, as he masticated. The book was Bastian's *On the Brain*. Not very up to date, perhaps, but the best he could find in his father's library to keep him amused in the train. Halfway through the fish, he came upon the case of the Irish gentleman who had suffered from paraphasia, and was so much struck by it that he pushed aside his plate and, taking out his pocket-book, made a note of it at once. The physician had asked the patient to read aloud a paragraph from the statutes of Trinity College, Dublin. "It shall be in the power of the College to examine or not examine every Licentiate previous to his admission to a fellowship, as they shall think fit." What the patient actually read was: "An the bee-what in the tee-mother of the trothodoodoo, to majoram or that emidrate, eni eni krastrei, mestreit to ketra totombreidei, to ra from treido as that kekritest." Marvellous! Philip said to himself as he copied down the last word. What style! The richness and sonority of the opening phrase! "An the bee-what in the tee-mother of the trothodoodoo." He repeated it to himself. "I shall print it on the title-page of my next novel," he wrote in his notebook. "The epigraph the text of the whole sermon." Shakespeare only talked about tales told by an idiot. But here was the idiot actually speaking— Shakespeareanly, what was more. "The final word about life," he added in pencil. (545)

On the same evening, Quarles attends a concert at the Queen's Hall with compositions by Erik Satie and Ludwig van Beethoven. Satie was known in the 1920s as an *enfant terrible* of modern music. His eccentric tendency to give his works funny or even silly titles is parodied by Huxley inasmuch as he ascribes to him a fictitious piece called *Borborygmes Symphoniques* (literally: "symphonic rumbling of the bowels").[20] Well suited to the task in hand, the conductor Tolley, to boot, is shown parading his modern taste and omnicompetence. But compared with Beethoven, that is, with "real music," both Satie's and Tolley's deficiencies become clear. Satie is hissed, and Tolley cannot properly conduct "old man Ludwig's portentosities," as an acquaintance of Quarles expresses it in the interval. This is the occasion for Quarles to comment on Tolley as follows:

> "He's almost as modern as the Irish genius whose works I discovered this evening." Philip took out his pocket-book and, after a word of explanation, read aloud. "An the bee-what in the tee-mother of the trothodoodoo. . . ." At the foot of the page were his own comments of an hour before. "The text of the whole sermon. The final word about life." He did not read them out. He happened to be thinking quite differently now. "The difference between portentosity and Satie-cum-Tolleyism," he said, "is the same as the difference between the statutes of Trinity College, Dublin, and this bee-what in the tee-mother of the trothodoodoo."
>
> He was blankly contradicting himself. But, after all, why not?

Having actually experienced the musical avant-garde, or "Satie-cum-Tolleyism," Quarles now shrinks back from his initial enthusiasm for the quasi-Shakespearean sound sequence of the speech-impeded Irishman. What had impressed him as a grand literary revelation ("What style!"—"The final word about life"), is now unmasked as nothing but a specious specimen of the literary avantgarde.

Is it too farfetched a connotation to think of Joyce when one hears the phrase "almost as modern as the Irish genius whose works I discovered this evening"? Just in 1927, when *Point Counter Point* was being composed, the Parisian journal *transition*, from April onward, published the first instalments of Joyce's "Work in Progress," *Finnegans Wake*. In *transition* No. 1, the beginning of this work was presented as "Opening Pages of a Work in Progress." Is it only by coincidence that Philip Quarles is first of all impressed by "the richness and sonority of the opening phrase"? Unfortunately, a close textual comparison between the words of the Irish gentleman and the beginning of *Finnegans Wake* cannot reveal any more allusions, since Huxley strictly adheres to the sound sequence actually given in Bastian's book *The Brain as an Organ of the Human Mind* (1880).[21] As further clues there remain only the affinity with Shakespeare and the cryptic phrases "The epigraph the text of the whole sermon" and "The final word about life." But they are too general to have to be specifically linked with Joyce, however well they might suit his literary aspirations. The answer probably depends on how definitely the phrase "Irish genius" in connection with "paraphasia" referred to Joyce and nobody else in the view of the contemporary reading public. Whoever still cannot recognize an allusion to Joyce in this chapter, will at least have to read it as a harsh criticism of the treatment of language at the hands of the literary avantgarde and its resulting unintelligibility, as it was for instance practised and cultivated by Dadaist writers. We remember the world of *la haute couture* in *Eyeless in Gaza*: Too great a fascination with linguistic effects, as Quarles's process of thought has shown, necessarily leads to eccentricity and difficulties of communication. From a medium meant to convey sense, language threatens to be turned into a purpose for its own sake supported by an attitude of *l'art pour l'art*, thereby detracting a great deal from the impact of a literary work.

So much for a first tentative investigation of literary criticism in the modern novel. Huxley's response to Joyce reveals an astonishing similarity of their literary-critical positions with regard to the scope of subject and manner of representation, while implying a considerable divergence in respect of the reception of the literary work by the reading public. Moreover, this preliminary result supports the premise that, in principle, even seemingly different authors may have important notions in common. Thus literary criticism in the modern novel does not only reflect the self-consciousness of individual writers but also the often hidden connection between literary models within the continuous process of tradition and innovation.

Most of Huxley's later remarks on Joyce focus on his strangeness or even idiosyncrasy, as can be seen from the reminiscences and interviews collected by Richard Ellmann, Sybille Bedford, and George Wickes.[22] And in his lecture series at the University of California at Santa Barbara, held in 1959, Huxley once again mentions Joyce as a representative of psychological atomism.[23] But what are those isolated remarks and comments compared to his literary response? There was only one occasion when Huxley felt obliged to formulate a coherent critical statement concerning Joyce. In 1952 he collaborated with Stuart Gilbert in a curious enterprise entitled *Joyce the Artificer* and issued for private circulation,[24] which set out to comment upon, and illustrate by corrected proofs, Joyce's technique of continuous revision. But characteristically, Huxley evades his task by writing half a page on various authors and their habits of revision and then concluding with just one paragraph on Joyce, in which he uses the literary device of an extended metaphor to convey his view, quite in the fashion of his response to Joyce in his earlier fiction:

> James Joyce was a man of afterthoughts. His inspirations, as we can see from these much-corrected proofs of *ULYSSES*, were successive. The first was a key, as it were, to a second, and the second to a third. His discovery of what he wished to say was like the conquest of Mexico. It began with the islands, touched the mainland, climbed to an astounding vision of pyramids and feathered warriors, and ended in the triumphant capture of Tenochtitlan. Shakespeare would have landed on the roof of Montezuma's palace by helicopter. Joyce had to take the longer, harder road. However, he got there in the end. And that, after all, is the only thing that matters.
> —Aldous Huxley

Notes

1. "The Comedy of Ideas: Cross-currents in the Fiction and Drama of the Twentieth Century," *The Modern Age*, The Pelican Guide to English Literature, VII, ed. B. Ford (3rd ed., Harmondsworth: Penguin, 1973), 243.

2. *The Languages of Criticism and the Structure of Poetry*, (Toronto: University of Toronto Press, 1953), 27.

3. Letter No. 149, Grover Smith, ed., *Letters of Aldous Huxley* (London: Chatto & Windus, 1969), 170.

4. "What, Exactly, Is Modern?", *Vanity Fair*, 24 (May 1925), 94; cited by P. Firchow, *Aldous Huxley: Satirist and Novelist* (Minneapolis: University of Minnesota Press, 1972), 39.

5. W. Potts, ed., *Portraits of the Artist in Exile: Recollections of James Joyce by Europeans* (Seattle and London: University of Washington Press, 1979), 87; see also R. Ellmann, *James Joyce* (Oxford: Oxford University Press, 1982), 615.

6. Also labelled *intertextuality*. Another important field is analogizing, that is, thinking about literature in terms of other disciplines, such as the age-old topos of the sister arts poetry and painting. For such formal subdivisions see, for instance, R. Wellek and A. Warren, *Theory of Literature* (Harmondsworth: Penguin, 1963); R. Wellek, *A History of Modern Criticism* (8 vols., New Haven and London: Yale University Press, 1955–92); J. Strelka, *Methodologie der Literaturwissenschaft* (Tübingen, 1978); B. Nugel, *Englische Literaturtheorie von Sidney bis Johnson* (Darmstadt, 1984), 1–14.

7. Of course, literary criticism is not only to be found in the modern novel but also earlier in the tradition; see, for instance, R. Alter, *Partial Magic: The Novel as a Self-Conscious Genre* (Berkeley: University of California Press, 1975).

8. "James Joyce und Virginia Woolf: Ästhetik, Funktion und Form des modernen Romans," *Englische und amerikanische Literaturtheorie: Studien zu ihrer historischen Entwicklung*, ed. R. Ahrens and E. Wolff, II (Heidelberg, 1979), 344 (my translation).

9. See H. Kenner, *Dublin's Joyce* (London: Chatto & Windus, 1955); R. Ellmann, *The Consciousness of James Joyce* (London: Oxford University Press, 1977); W. Wicht, *Virginia Woolf, James Joyce, T. S. Eliot: Kunstkonzeptionen und Künstlergestalten* (Berlin, 1981); J. F. Carens, "*A Portrait of the Artist as a Young Man*," *A Companion to Joyce Studies*, ed. Z. Bowen and J. F. Carens (Westport and London: Greenwood Press, 1984), 344–349. The latest poststructuralist discussion of Joyce's literary theories in *Portrait* is to be found in J. W. Rademacher, *'James Joyce's Own Image': Über die allmähliche Verfertigung der Begriffe 'Image' und 'Imagination' beim Schreiben in "A Portrait" und "Ulysses"* (Münster, 1993).

10. *Eyeless in Gaza* (London: Chatto & Windus, 1950), 141; subsequent page references in brackets.

11. See p. 150: "He sighed. In spite of *Hamlet*, in spite of *The Prophetic Books*, in spite of *Du côté de chez Swann* and *Women in Love*, the world was still full of Jonsonian Humours."

12. *Aldous Huxley und die französische Literatur* (Marburg, 1968), 149–150 (my translation).

13. *Ulysses*, ed. H. W. Gabler (New York and London: Random House, 1984), I, 175.

14. For a similar comment see J. Meckier, *Aldous Huxley: Satire and Structure* (London: Chatto & Windus, 1969), 116.

15. Because of the nonchronological arrangement of chapters, this passage is to be found at the beginning of the novel (ch. 1).

16. Stylistic parallels to Joyce result not so much from exact verbal correspondences, such as "tepid," "pale," and "float" in the "Lotus Eaters," but from conspicuous devices such

as alliteration, repetition, and frequent participle constructions as well as from the distinctly naturalistic concentration on conventionally disgusting details.

17. *Point Counter Point* (London: Chatto & Windus, 1974), 10; subsequent page references in brackets.

18. See, for instance, the elaborate but often forced categories of the so-called Linati Schema, reprinted by R. Ellmann, *Ulysses on the Liffey* (London: Oxford University Press, 1977), between 188 and 189.

19. See, for instance, F. J. Hoffman, "Aldous Huxley and the Novel of Ideas," *College English* 8 (1946), 129–37; P. Bowering, *Aldous Huxley: A Study of the Major Novels* (London: Athlone Press, 1968); J. Meckier, above; L. Fietz, *Menschenbild und Romanstruktur in Aldous Huxleys Ideenromanen* (Tübingen, 1969); P. Firchow, above; K. M. May, *Aldous Huxley* (London: Paul Elek, 1972).

20. See R. H. Myers, *Erik Satie* (London, 1948); similar to Huxley's fictitious title is Satie's "*Socrate*, a 'drame symphonique' in three parts . . . Satie's masterpiece . . ." (55).

21. See H. C. Bastian, *The Brain as an Organ of the Human Mind* (London, 1880), 668: "*An the bewhat in the temother of the trothotodoo, to majorum or that emidrate, eni enikrastrai mestreit to ketra totombreidei to ra fromtreido as that kekritest*" (italics in original).

22. See R. Ellmann, *James Joyce* (Oxford: Oxford University Press, 1982), 361, 615, 622, 622n; S. Bedford, *Aldous Huxley: A Biography* (New York: Alfred A. Knopf/Harper & Row, 1974), 197, 216; G. Wickes and R. Frazer, *Writers at Work: The "Paris Review" Interviews. Second Series* (New York: Viking Press, 1963).

23. See *The Human Situation*, ed. Picro Ferrucci (London: Chatto & Windus, 1978), 187.

24. *Joyce the Artificer: Two Studies of Joyce's method by Aldous Huxley & Stuart Gilbert; with five Collotype reproductions from the Proofs of "Ulysses" and "Tales of Shem and Shaun", together with a letter and notes thereon by J. Schwartz* (London: Chiswick Press, 1952). Huxley's contribution (unpaginated) is to be found on the first page after the title-page.

Huxley's Either/Or: The Case for *Eyeless in Gaza*

JERRY WASSERMAN

"Huxley's finest novel" was David Garnett's verdict, reviewing *Eyeless in Gaza* in 1936; but, he added, "on the whole the plan of popping about in time is a mistake. If the chronological method had been followed, I should have stopped reading at page 500 and have missed almost all the boring parts of the book." More recently, George Woodcock has recalled how "the radical young" who had grown up under the liberating influence of Huxley's earlier work "were disturbed and disappointed at what seemed a retreat into obscurantism on the part of one of the writers we most admired."[1] The issues that perplexed the novel's first readers—the obscure chronology and Anthony Beavis's conversion to pacifism and mysticism—have since received a good deal of critical explanation. But they are worth examining again, for this is a richer and more carefully conceived novel than the explanations have led us to believe.

Anthony's commitments, we now know, are those which Huxley himself made in 1935–36 and continued to pursue until his death. With his entire literary output before us, it is easy to detect the desire for spiritual wholeness and *engagement* latent in the cynicism of Gumbril Jr. (*Antic Hay*), Calamy (*Those Barren Leaves*), and Philip Quarles (*Point Counter Point*), who lead as naturally to the achieved transformation of Anthony Beavis as Huxley's disappointing later work follows from it. So *Eyeless in Gaza* has come to mark the end of the vital and much admired novelist of the 1920s and early 1930s, and the beginning of the social prophet *cum* publicist of the late 1930s and beyond.[2]

We also understand now the mimetic function of the novel's structural dislocations. They reflect not only the chaos and discontinuity of Anthony's early world-view, but also the sense of order and unity which underlie the fragmentary surface of reality.[3] Under the tutelage of Dr. Miller, Anthony learns to see (in the primary metaphor of the novel) the patterns to which he has previously blinded himself. Simultaneously, the reader learns to per-

From NOVEL: *A Forum on Fiction* 13, no. 2 (Winter 1980): 188–203. Copyright NOVEL Corp. ©
Reprinted with the permission of the journal and the author.

ceive the *Gestalt* coherence attained by the interactions of past and present, parts and whole. "One in division; united and yet separate," Anthony concludes.[4] As he meditates himself into divine Oneness in the last chapter, he sees his life *sub specie aeternitatis*, from the Spinozan perspective that Huxley had attacked in an essay seven years earlier.[5] Anthony's recantation, it appears, is Huxley's too.

But Spinoza is not the major influence upon this novel; rather, Kierkegaard's *Either/Or* provided Huxley with the specific philosophical and structural framework for *Eyeless in Gaza*. The intertextual relationship between the two works throws revealing light on the internal dialectics of the novel. Looking first at some of the novel's central themes and its structural methodology, and then at its relationship with *Either/Or*, we are forced to reassess Huxley's narrative attitude towards his protagonist and to re-examine the common critical assumption that Huxley's own "sincere" conversion meant his wholehearted approval of Anthony's. Finally, we see how the complexities of *Either/Or* allowed Huxley appropriate structural latitude for his own complex and highly ambivalent fiction.

1

> We live in a world of *non sequiturs*. . . . Our life is spent first in one watertight compartment of existence and then in another.
> —Huxley, *Music at Night* (1931)

The problem of "discontinuity" was often at the forefront of Huxley's writing in the decade preceding *Eyeless in Gaza*. It encompassed for him a variety of related phenomena: the discontinuity of the self in time, the schisms dividing various elements of the self, the gap between self and world. In "Personality and the Discontinuity of the Mind" (1927), Huxley argues: "The man who would face the world with a complete and consistently effective personality cannot resign himself to his discontinuity. . . . It is indispensable for him to have some unifying principle that shall preserve him identical with himself through all the changes in the outward and inward environment of his mind" (*Proper Studies*, 246–48).

Yet Huxley's fictional characters often see virtue in the implication that discontinuity is our natural and unavoidable condition. In an extraordinary passage in *Point Counter Point*, the novelist Philip Quarles—himself suffering from "not knowing among the multiplicity of his roles who was the actor"— comes upon the case of a paraphasiac who is asked to read aloud a simple sentence and responds with a string of nonsense syllables.

> Marvellous! Philip said to himself as he copied down the last word. What style! what majestic beauty! . . . "An the bee-what in the tee-mother of the

trothodoodoo." He repeated it to himself. "I shall print it on the title-page of my next novel," he wrote in his notebook. "The epigraph the text of the whole sermon." Shakespeare only talked about tales told by an idiot. But here was the idiot actually speaking—Shakespeareanly, what was more. "The final word about life," he added in pencil. (*PCP*, 268, 544–45)

Philip eagerly embraces such evidence that life resolves itself into a series of *non sequiturs*. It overwhelms his half-hearted quest for a holistic fiction of the self and justifies his detached intellectual skepticism. The "point" of the novel's title for Philip resides in its pointlessness.

Anthony Beavis is the direct descendant of Philip Quarles. In 1933, he too seems prepared to accept the idiot's text as the final word: "Somewhere in the mind a lunatic shuffled a pack of snapshots and dealt them out at random, shuffled once more and dealt them out in different order, again and again, indefinitely. There was no chronology. The idiot remembered no distinction between before and after. . . . The thirty-five years of his conscious life made themselves immediately known to him as a chaos—a pack of snapshots in the hands of a lunatic" (*EG*, 22–23). Anthony has a great deal invested in this premise. The passage quoted here is occasioned by the involuntary association he makes between the smell of his girlfriend Helen's body and another smell twenty years earlier in the presence of his friend Brian Foxe. The connection that triggers this memory, we learn later, is the irresponsible sexuality that has characterized his relationships both with Helen and with Brian's fiancée, Joan Thursley. In the first case the result is Helen's deep unhappiness; in the second it was Brian's suicide, for which Anthony has been trying to deny his own responsibility since the event. His characteristic rationalization is that one is literally not the same person from day to day: "What right had the man of 1914 to commit the man of 1926?" (151). In order to avoid accepting the consequences of his acts, he must continue to reassure himself of the rule of discontinuity and arbitrariness: a discrete present, disjoined from past or future; a Lucretian world of "particles of thought, desire and feeling moving at random among particles of time, coming into casual contact and as casually parting" (25).

Faulkner's contemporary tale of sound and fury was literally told in part by an idiot. Huxley's omniscient narrator distributes the chapters of *Eyeless in Gaza* like a pack of snapshots dealt out at random by a lunatic. Each of the fifty-four "snapshots" comprising Anthony's life is precisely dated, like the letters of an epistolary novel, allowing the reader some temporal orientation. There are relatively distinct periods of narration (1902–4, 1912–14, etc.), within which events follow chronologically. And since the novel's final chapter is also its latest, there is an overall movement forward in time. Still, the immediate impression is of randomness. No two consecutive dates or events are given in consecutive chapters. And except where chapters are obviously linked by a verbal motif or a common subject, the principle by which they follow one another appears at first sight to be casual rather than causal. Discontinuity is built into the novel's structure as an objective correlative of Anthony's own self-justifying fiction.

But the apparent chaos of the form is a mimetic reflection of more than just Anthony's personal incoherence. It mirrors a radical disjunction in the world of the novel. This is a fallen world steeped in original sin, its characters severed from the sources of grace and meaning. Yet there is pattern here too. Each of the three climaxes in Anthony's life is marked by a literal fall: the dog's fall from an airplane, splattering its blood over him and Helen as they lay sunbathing after making love; Brian's fall from the top of a cliff to his death; and Mark Staithes's fall from his mule in Mexico. In the first instance, as Helen recounts the event: "And then, bang, like a sign from heaven, down comes the dog! . . . And we had no clothes on. Like the Garden of Eden" (305–6). In *Eyeless in Gaza* the body *is* the fall, especially the body as instrument of love or procreation. The fallen dog becomes the central symbol of the body's utter contingency; its smashed and bleeding carcass the novel's emblem of fleshliness.

This incident resonates through time and the narrative structure in a dense network of reflexive associations. If the flesh is sordid and disgusting, so will be its fruits. That night Anthony has one of his recurrent nightmares: he is unable to swallow a mouthful of food which becomes increasingly, horribly viscous. Upon awakening he realizes that the dream this night has been connected with the dog. Furthermore, the dog's body swarming with flies recalls Brian's corpse at the foot of the cliff. Guilt has made life indigestible for Anthony. He can no longer, as it were, swallow his own lies.

One line of association leads to Helen. At a butcher's shop in 1926, she has resolved to steal a kidney. But as she grabs it, "the idea came to her that for some reason she might have to take the horrible thing in her mouth, raw as it was and oozy with some unspeakable slime . . ." (52). The overtones of this scene are amplified in 1927. As three of the men who are later to become her lovers look on, a now rampantly pubescent Helen sensuously teases a pet kitten. But the kitten suddenly sickens and dies, reminding Helen of "those filthy kidneys" (343). By the next year she has become pregnant by her mother's lover, Gerry Watchett, and has had a nearly fatal abortion. In her delirium she identifies her dead fetus with the dying kitten and the kidneys (ch. 39). That a dog should drop from an airplane like an obscene birth and douse her in its blood is all of a piece with her experiences of the flesh. Even her one successful affair, with the German communist Ekki, is ended by the vulnerability of his body—tortured to death by the Nazis.

The day after the dog has fallen, Helen visits her mother in the filthy flat that Helen compares to "a dog-kennel" (288). Bankrupt, addicted to morphine and alcohol, and hanging precariously onto memories of the past, Mary Amberley has fallen a long way from the bewitching sexual vampire who in 1914 could goad Anthony into seducing his best friend's fiancée. But the seeds of her dissolution are inherent in the attitudes with which she has always used that potent instrument, her body. Sex for Mary is a masochistic degradation of the self: "she really *wanted* to be treated as he was treating her—like a prostitute, like an animal" (280). To be reduced to living in a "dog-kennel" is no less a logical extension of this than is the phallic hypodermic syringe she uses to punish and caress her body with morphine (ch. 34). If one lives by the body, one dies by it: Mary becomes, along with the dog, the novel's *memento mori*. How fitting that when Anthony first meets her in 1902 the setting is a cemetery and Mary is pregnant (ch. 4).

When Mary and Anthony meet for the second time, in 1912, she lectures him on the destructiveness of marital relations and the dangers of excessive parental affection. Brian's mother, she remarks, "had a dog's life" with her late husband (227). But she predicts that Brian will suffer even more from the outpouring of her love. Mrs. Foxe, who specializes in sympathy for crippled children as if to prove that real love is of the spirit, not of the flesh, succeeds only in crippling her own son physically and emotionally. Brian's stutter is the outward form of a discontinuity that manifests itself more seriously in the gap between his sexual feelings for Joan and his inability to act on them. He feels betrayed by his body and paralyzed by guilt. Because Joan is unable to suppress her own normal sexual desires, she has her affair with Anthony which in turn leads to Brian's suicide. Indulge it or deny it, the body betrays.

Despair of the flesh had appeared before in Huxley's fiction. For Mr. Cardan, "the body, the doomed, decaying body, is the one, appalling fact" (*Those Barren Leaves*, 337). The theme is represented most dramatically by the Savage in *Brave New World*. But *Eyeless in Gaza* contains its most articulate and insistent spokesman. Mark Staithes is another masochist, punishing himself for his family's fortune. ("One of the dogs!" he complains of his playboy brother. "A dog among bitches," 314.) He writes advertisements about bad breath and body odors, and revels in describing the origins of perfume: how civet is extracted from the genital secretions of cats. Animal excrement, what women use to make their bodies sexually tempting, is at the heart of Mark's misanthropic vision: "We're like dogs on an acropolis. Trotting round with inexhaustible bladders and only too anxious to lift a leg against every statue" (409). As an alternative to nihilism, he convinces Anthony to accompany him to Mexico where they might risk their lives in a revolution. Once again, however, the flesh that Mark despises imposes its disorder. He falls from his mule, contracts gangrene, and is saved only by the fortuitous arrival of Dr. Miller who amputates his leg.

"And perhaps, after all," Anthony writes, "this is the real reason for our belief in personality:—the existence and persistence of bodies. And perhaps whatever reality there is in the notion of coherent individual continuity is just such a function of this physical persistence" (148). But mere physical continuity is just as tenuous and fragile as the dog's flesh. Homosexuality fares no better than heterosexuality; the lives of Anthony's friend Beppo and his uncle James are hellish. Sex and pain and death all have the same root. In Mexico Anthony and Mark see a peasant child suffering under the pain of meningitis. Anthony suddenly remembers Helen in the throes of orgasm: "Tortured by pleasure, tortured by pain. At the mercy of one's skin and mucus, at the mercy of those thin threads of nerve" (494). The body, far from providing a source of order, is its own chaos—another element of the fundamental disjunction reflected in Anthony's life and the narrative structure.

And yet the novel is not unremittingly grim. One recalls the scene in 1902 on the occasion of Mrs. Beavis's death, where Brian touches Anthony to express the feeling that his stammer prevents him from speaking (ch. 6). This moment is genuine in ways that much of the social satire is not. And though Brian dies early in the novel's chronology, the scrambled structure keeps him alive until Chapter 48.[6] His fundamental goodness and humanity remain to counterpoint the squalor almost until the end.

Similarly, fully one-fourth of the chapters are devoted to Anthony's post-1933 diary. This is the voice of a regenerate man trying sincerely to change himself so as to be able to change the world. Even before Anthony's conversion, however, he reveals himself to be less crass than simply weak. He does not so much actively conspire with evil and disorder as passively acquiesce in them. This is especially true of his moral cowardice with Brian and Joan. "The decision had made itself," he rationalizes. "Looking back, he felt that he had had nothing to do with the matter" (511). There is a hint of desperation in Anthony's attempt to turn alienation into a virtue. Much of it is a mask to hide the real self he is afraid to acknowledge. In the very first chapter he strikes this false note as he rephrases Wordsworth: "I would wish my days to be separated each from each by unnatural impiety" (9). But this assertion of discontinuity is countered by a more oblique allusion to Tennyson. "What are you looking at?" Helen asks, as he pores over his old snapshots. "At my old corpses," Anthony replies (5). That men may rise on stepping-stones of their dead selves to higher things is only an intuition for Anthony at this point—a slight crack in the mask. But it is symptomatic, as arrogance and self-doubt alternate in the difficult process of his attaining to self-realization.

In the days following the dog's fall Anthony begins to see through his own fictions for the first time. Like Milton's Samson Agonistes in the soliloquy from which Huxley took his title, Anthony becomes willing to admit that his blindness and bondage may be his own fault. And by the time he meets Miller in 1934 he is ripe for conversion. Here Huxley uses Milton again, providing Anthony with a series of "fortunate falls" as necessary preconditions for his redemption. Mark's fall leads Anthony directly to Miller, his redeemer; but the earlier falls also serve as stepping-stones. The dog jolts Anthony into an awareness of the pain he has been inflicting on Helen, "this hurt and suffering woman, this *person* . . ." (154). Afterwards he even begins sorting his photographs, putting his past into some kind of order. These feelings don't last long but the movement is in the right direction, and once started he can never go back. Finally, Brian's fall completes the pattern. At first Anthony had been content to let it be thought an accident, another gratuitous event in the discontinuous universe that justified his failures. But once he accepts responsibility for it, he becomes able to take his own leap—the leap of faith to "go and make myself ridiculous with Miller" (582).

The introduction of Miller causes Anthony to reassess all his previous assumptions. One of his earliest diary entries compares his pessimistic first reading of Pavlov ("We were all dogs and bitches together") with his new sense that "it merely restated the doctrine of free-will. For if reflexes can be conditioned, then, obviously, they can be re-conditioned" (84). Miller is as much a behaviorist as Pavlov, and he proposes nothing less than a revisionist history of the novel's events. What had seemed arbitrary and discontinuous, implying the inevitability of victimization and degradation, can be seen to have resulted from misuse of the self. Cause and effect is the law governing human fate. Anthony had staked everything on the laws of chance. For him the game was run by a lunatic dealing the cards out at random. Miller revises the terms of the metaphor: "Not that anything ever happens by chance, of course. One takes the card the conjurer forces on one—the card which one has oneself made it inevitable that he should force on one" (550).

So Anthony accepts Miller's arguments, admitting responsibility for what he has been and resolving to learn how to love others without hurting them. He becomes a pacifist, predicating large-scale changes on love and unity rather than violence and separation. He takes up meditation as a means of seeing the oneness underlying all diversity. And his point of view in the last chapter clearly reveals the logic of the novel's structure. Discontinuity has a continuity, disorder an order. Every event in the novel is an effect, the cause of which is implicit in its other events, no matter how scrambled their chronology: the fragments cohere into a whole. The self exists in disparate forms at different moments; but ultimately it is the same self. We work at sorting out the book just as Anthony struggles to resolve the chaos of his life.

But there remain critical problems—the weakness of Miller as *deus ex machina*; Huxley's apparent failure to retain his authorial distance from Anthony; the novel's unconvincing final chapter.[7] If Miller lacks credibility, Anthony's conclusions as his protegé must also be suspect. And since so much of the novel, including its structural logic, seems to depend on our accepting Anthony's final point of view, it would appear that Huxley could hardly allow critical detachment at the end. In truth, Miller cannot be taken entirely seriously nor can the concluding chapter. Yet Huxley manages to achieve a narrative perspective sufficient to indicate his own misgivings about the way Anthony has chosen, and at the same time he preserves the mimetic relationship between structure and theme. The novel exists in the sort of delicate balance suggested to Huxley by the form, substance, and even the title of Søren Kierkegaard's earliest masterwork.

2

If any man needs to keep a diary, I do. . . .

—Either/Or[8]

"Kierkegaard is very queer, I think. I read some selections in German last year and a French translation of that episode in the huge novel *Enten Eller* called *Le Journal du séducteur*, a very odd and good book." [9] So Huxley wrote in February 1932; eight months later he was "accumulating notes and writing experimental pages" for what was to become *Eyeless in Gaza*. [10] In between he had put together an anthology, *Texts and Pretexts*, in which he cites Kierkegaard under the chapter headed "Memory": "Life can only be understood backwards; but it must be lived forwards" (*T&P*, 154). Memory would become an important theme in *Eyeless in Gaza*, as would the difficulty of bringing one's understanding of the past to bear upon one's living in the present.

But as Huxley indicated by calling it a "novel," more than just the themes of Kierkegaard's book appealed to his imagination. Published in 1843, *Enten Eller* (*Either/Or* in English) is presented through the elaborate fiction of a pseudonymous editor, Victor Eremita, who explains how he found a series of manuscripts in an old secretary. There are two sets of papers: one written by a young man, consisting of various fragments ("Diapsalmata"), aesthetic essays, and a journal ("Diary of the Seducer"); the other a packet of three lengthy letters written to the young man by an older man, a judge. Kierkegaard labels the authors "A" and "B" respectively. A's papers present an aesthetic view of life; B opposes that with his ethical view. Hence the title.

A is the more interesting character. Melancholy, romantic, and ironical, he propounds with literary flair the virtues of a life of freedom based on a refusal to commit oneself. "True eternity," he argues, "does not lie behind either/or, but before it" (*E/O* I, 38). Boredom and finitude are the twin evils of his world. One avoids them by militating against consistency, memory, friendship, marriage, anything that binds one to oneself or others. The aesthetic sensibility remains free by remaining detached.

In contrast B is a moralist who preaches to A on the error of his ways. He redefines the question of either/or: not an immediate choice between the aesthetic and the ethical ("for he who lives aesthetically does not choose"), but an absolute choice "whereby one chooses good *and* evil/or excludes them" (*E/O* II, 172–73). The man who would live beyond good and evil or before either/or refuses to posit the very terms which make choice possible. Choosing the ethical, on the other hand, means choosing oneself as freedom. Since he who lives aesthetically is *ipso facto* in despair, the answer is to *choose* despair and in so doing reconstitute the self in its eternal validity.

If A is more attractive, B is more persuasive; yet Kierkegaard draws no conclusions and *Either/Or* offers no real resolution. In his "editor's" preface Victor Eremita criticizes the traditional novel in which characters represent opposing views of life: "Instead of these views being allowed to speak for themselves, the reader is enriched by being told the historical result, that one has convinced the other. I regard it as fortunate that these papers contain no such information." In fact he speculates that all the papers may be "the work of one man . . . who had lived through both of these phases, or who had thought upon both" (*E/O* I, 13–14).

Anthony Beavis is certainly such a man. "I know what I ought to do," his first diary entry begins, "but continue to do what I know I oughtn't to do" (12). This entry is dated April 4, 1934. A's first entry in his "Diary of the Seducer" is also dated April 4 (*E/O* I, 309). Furthermore, Victor Eremita explains in his preface how he calculated the year to be 1834 (*E/O* I, 10). Why this remarkable similarity? Huxley introduces this chapter and Anthony's next diary entry (ch. 7) with the heading, "From A. B.'s diary." The Anthony Beavis who writes in his diary is the same man he has been in the past but he is also the new man he has become. He has lived, in Kierkegaard's terms, both the aesthetic life and the ethical: the "A" and the "B." He is, precisely, "A. B." Although Dr. Miller assumes the role of B for part of *Eyeless*, the older man who provides the ethical arguments, he actually appears directly in only two chapters, in Mexico. Otherwise he exists solely through Anthony. Recalling Kierkegaard's suggestion that his A and B are two phases of a single man, we realize that Huxley's A. B. embodies both terms of the either/or.

Kierkegaard's A shares with the early Anthony a dualism of character: philosophical self-assurance combined with personal self-doubt. "There is nothing more dangerous to me than remembering," begins one of his "Diapsalmata" (*E/O* I, 31), reminding us of the opening chapter of *Eyeless*. A pursues this theme in "The Rotation Method," where he urges the would-be aesthetic man to practice diligently the art of forgetting. Mastering one's memory, he promises, will "insure against sticking fast in some relationship in life, and make possible the realization of a complete freedom." The other requirements of such freedom? One must guard against friendship ("the essential thing is never to stick fast") and avoid marriage. Beware of relationships with the possibility of many members ("when you are one of several, then you have lost your freedom") and never accept an official position of any kind. Above all, one must constantly vary oneself—"this is the essential secret" (*E/O* I, 291–95).

Anthony might easily have studied A's cynical text. In 1912 at Oxford he jealously guards his "freedom," avoiding involvement in the Fabians and rotating his momentary allegiances from Brian to Mark to Gerry. Why, he asks himself, "should one be bullied into making choices when one didn't want to choose; into binding oneself to a set of principles when it was so essential to be free; into committing oneself to associate with other people . . . ?" (117). The need to be free will later dominate his book, *Elements of Sociology*, as well as his sexual relationships. The dangers of uninvited memory will underline the importance of a theory of varying, discontinuous selves.

But discontinuity has its darker side for A as it does for Anthony. The "Diapsalmata," while self-indulgently melancholy in the best romantic tradition, can also provide powerful existential revelations: "My life is absolutely meaningless. When I consider the different periods into which it falls, it seems like the word *Schnur* in the dictionary, which means in the first place a string, in the second, a daughter-in-law. The only thing lacking is that the word *Schnur* should mean in the third place a camel, in the fourth, a dust-brush" (*E/O* I, 35). B is sensitive to these notes of anxiety in A's writing and warns him that the games he plays "might end with your nature being resolved into a multiplicity," with a loss of "the unifying power of personality." One who neglects to choose may in time find himself without the possibility of choice because others have chosen for him: "because he has lost his self" (*E/O* II, 164, 168).

Anthony, too, begins to understand how easily the freedom of unattachment can devolve into the vacuum of discontinuity. "I've had a queer feeling," he tells Mark, "that I'm not really there, that I haven't been there for years past." Always before he had celebrated the absence of a coherent sense of self on the grounds that "if one gets rid of the 'you', one gets rid of responsibility and the need for consistency. One's free as a succession of unconditioned, uncommitted states . . ." (364–65). But Anthony's fall into consciousness makes all his previous self-justifications seem hollow; and as his blindness turns to insight, the pun in the novel's title becomes manifest. He has not simply been "eyeless" to the truth of his life but "I-less" as well, a condition which ultimately proves far more difficult to repair.

Anthony's discontinuity fiction provides one rationale for the scrambled chronology of *Eyeless*; another is its correlative in *Either/Or*. Kierkegaard's "editor" describes how he "let chance determine the order" of A's papers. "I have left them in the order in which I found them, without being able to decide whether this order has any chronological value or ideal significance." But he also notes that there are certain correspondences in their chance arrangement (*E/O* I, 7–8). The structure may be as intentionally random as the personality of A is self-consciously diverse. Still, an underlying unity reveals itself.

"Really and by nature every man's a unity," Miller says (14). The problem for Anthony is to recompose the fragmented elements of his self into that natural state. And if Kierkegaard's A is the model for Anthony's drama of I-lessness, B provides the script by which Anthony activates his new idea of selfhood. The crux of B's argument is in his second letter, "Equilibrium Between the Aesthetic and the Ethical in the Composition of Personality," a title that recalls Huxley's 1927 essay and the key chapter in Anthony's book. "What then must you do?" B asks. "I have only one answer: despair" (*E/O* II, 212). The man who chooses despair chooses himself absolutely. "He does not become another man than he was before, but he becomes himself, consciousness is unified, and he is himself" (*E/O* II, 181). He is a new man and at the same time the man he has always been. Hence, "the self he chooses contains an endless multiplicity, inasmuch as it has a history, a history in which he acknowledges identity with himself" (*E/O* II, 219–20). The Anthony Beavis who goes with Mark to Mexico, perhaps to die, and ends instead by following Miller out of the jungle, brings into being a new self, a unity, in which he acknowledges identity with the multiplicity of selves he has been. "Only when I choose myself as guilty do I choose myself absolutely," B asserts (*E/O* II, 221). Anthony accepts his part in Brian's death and Helen's pain, the personal past he has tried to deny. The formal coherence of *Eyeless in Gaza* follows directly from B's formula. The one and the many coexist within the structure of the novel as within the composition of the self.

B's ensuing description of the man who has chosen himself closely resembles Anthony in the final chapter. "When the individual has grasped himself in his eternal validity . . . the temporal vanishes from before his eyes." He is filled with "an indescribable bliss. . . . He relapses into contemplation . . ." (*E/O* II, 235–36). Anthony finds this timeless bliss in his meditations, particularly in his long mantra of "peace." And when the striking of the clock calls him back to the temporal world, he is able "dispassionately, and with a serene lucidity," to consider what lay ahead of him. "Whatever it might be, he knew now that all would be well" (620). As B says, the ethical man "possesses calmness and assurance," and is "infinitely secure in himself" (*E/O* II, 259).

Moreover, B takes pains to warn against the lethargy that may result from excessive indulgence in the pleasures of mystic contemplation. "The self which is the aim is not merely a personal self but a social, a civic self . . . he takes a hand in the affairs of life" (*E/O* II, 267). Anthony, of course, devotes himself to a civic life, proselytizing in the cause of pacifism and attempting to recast his passive, detached sociology in the mould of Miller's active, committed anthropology. He realizes, too, the danger of meditation's becoming for him just another "bolt-hole from unpleasant reality" (503). He is still in part the man he has always been, and must take special care to avoid slipping back into his old patterns.

So Anthony becomes "A. B.": the embodiment of both the aesthetic and the ethical lives he has led. Like Kierkegaard before him, Huxley contains the two points of view in a single book and to some extent in a single character, showing both personal fragmentation and a means for resolving it into a unity via a literary structure that is itself both random and coherent. But the fact that Kierkegaard's book exists in a *critical* as well as a paradigmatic relationship with Huxley's novel forces us to take another more searching look at the born-again Anthony Beavis.

B, for instance, violently condemns the man who chooses the way of mysticism. "The falseness of such a life" he finds "appalling," "a deceit against the world" (*E/O* II, 246–48). In fact he argues that the mystical is just another form of the aesthetic life, self-absorbed and lacking in continuity. Now Anthony knows his social responsibilities and the need for meditation to be merely a means toward an end. Yet Huxley concludes the novel with Anthony's long meditation on "peace as a dark void beyond all personal life . . . richer and of finer quality than ordinary life" (619). This is the same man who is about to go to a meeting to speak on the concrete realities of loving one's neighbor.[11] And although Anthony does recall himself to the mundane matters awaiting him, his imagery is significant: "Slowly and cautiously he allowed himself to lapse out of the light, back through the darkness into the broken gleams and shadows of everyday existence" (620). This is Plato's cave, a second-rate reality separated by a long darkness from the light of truth. To "disdain the reality of existence," as the mystic does, is to violate one of B's central premises (*E/O* II, 248).

Or consider Huxley's use of A's "Diary of the Seducer." A's seducer befriends "poor Edward" and encourages his courtship of Cordelia just to facilitate his own plans, whereas Anthony does not intentionally use his friendship with Brian this way. The immediate result is the same, however. Joan, like Cordelia, believes the seduction to be an indication of true love. Since this episode obviously belongs to the "aesthetic" period of Anthony's life, its relation to A's diary seems straightforward. Yet as we have noted earlier, the date of the first entry in "Diary of the Seducer" is almost exactly the date of the first entry in "A. B.'s diary." In other words, while A's seducer is linked thematically to the old Anthony, he is linked structurally to the "new." The theme of Anthony's April 4 entry is a question: "how to love?" (15). The theme is the same in A's April 4 entry except in the form of a cynical answer: "No impatience, no greediness, everything should be enjoyed in leisurely draughts; she is marked out, she shall be run down" (*E/O* I, 312–13). Date, diary and theme, the common denominators, all appear to undercut Anthony's new moral stance. His conversion, this allusion suggests, is less than a total success. There is still a lot of "A" in "A. B."

The point is that neither Huxley nor Kierkegaard concludes his work with a simple absorption of A into B, a defeat of the aesthetic by the ethical. In his editor's preface Kierkegaard's Victor Eremita advises the reader to reflect upon the book's title.

> This will free him from all finite questions as to whether A was really convinced
> of his error and repented, whether B conquered, or if it perhaps ended by B's
> going over to A's opinion. . . . Whether A's soul continued to be tossed
> about in wild abandon, or whether it found rest, I cannot say, since the papers
> indicate nothing. Nor is there any clue as to how things went with B, whether
> he had strength to hold to his convictions or not. When the book is read,
> then A and B are forgotten, only their views confront one another. . . .
> (*E/O* I, 14)

B seems to have the better of the argument, but Kierkegaard's commentators
are almost unanimous in agreeing that B's proposals are inadequate to solve
A's problems, to produce an absolute and instant new man.[12] And the
situation of *Eyeless in Gaza* is similar. Two points of view, both flawed
(though one less so than the other), are left standing in dialectical tension
within a fictive structure that allows for a balance of views. At times in
Huxley's novel the juxtaposition of alternatives suggests a standoff—"only
their views confront one another"; but then again there are occasions when
the result is ironically telling at Anthony's expense.

At the end of Chapter 3, for example, Anthony forces from his mind
the image of Brian's dead body by stroking Helen: "One, two, three, four—
counting each movement of his hand, he began to caress her. The gesture
was magical, would transport him, if repeated sufficiently often, beyond
right and wrong . . ." (25). In the next chapter he counts billboards on the
train to his mother's funeral in 1902 as a way of transporting himself beyond
the pain of the immediate moment. It should not be surprising, then, that
in the final chapter he uses the same technique in his meditation: "One, one,
one, he repeated" (614). The former Anthony counts for sensual pleasure, the
latter for universal unity. But the primary effect is to indicate that he has
not really come a long way from 1933—or even from 1902. His characteristic
gesture is still a mechanism of incantation and escape.

Similarly, as early as 1912 Anthony is reading St. Teresa and boasting
of his belief in the value of "completeness" (121). Diary entries in 1934
again show him reading St. Teresa and advocating "complete knowledge"
(522). In 1926 one of the cynical premises of his sociology book is that
human progress is a myth: "Looking closely, one could detect the uniformities
under the diversity, the fixed rules of the endlessly shifting game" (312).
The rhetoric of his early cynicism is no different from that of his later
optimism. Only the contexts and interpretations have changed. Anthony in
fact cites Miller's argument that the measure of change lies precisely in
one's interpretations. "So that one can see, for example, either irremediable
senselessness and turpitude, or else actualizable potentialities for good—
whichever one likes; it is a question of choice" (513). Where the old Anthony
chose to see senselessness, the new chooses to see good. But we are also faced

with an either/or: to choose to see either negative or positive potential in Anthony's various manifestations.

In his final meditation he sees into the heart of things and acknowledges a harmony of unity and diversity within the divine order. The world is a sea of strife but below it lies "a submarine night of living calm" (620). Back in 1912, however, Huxley presents another version of Anthony's metaphysics which makes it difficult to take the final one seriously. Having lied to Brian so that he can dine with his upper class friends, Anthony gets drunk and imagines himself "a divine and remotely happy fish," viewing the world serenely from within "its timeless aquarium." The scene ends with a nasty self-parody of the final scene, his pretensions to mysticism undercut by his strained levity and drunken cries: "We see into the life of things. The life of things I tell you" (135–36).

Anthony's "transcendence" in this scene is partly a function of alcohol. Later he finds it in drugs. Miller has anaesthetized Mark in order to amputate his leg, and Anthony thinks how peaceful and serene he looks, how "free." He marvels at the irrelevance to Mark of the "revolting rasp and squeak of the steel teeth biting into the bone," and sees only the positive fact—Mark has transcended his pain (563). Anthony seems willing to accept the serenity of escape at any price. Significantly, the next chapter finds him making notes in his diary on the varieties of meditational techniques. Again the juxtaposition is revealing: amputation and meditation, chloroform and prayer. The terms are different but the dynamics are the same.

The relationships between chapters like these cast doubt not only on the extent of Anthony's change but on the validity of his new system of belief—and by implication Miller's as well. Huxley, like Kierkegaard, explores dialectically the possibility that Miller, like B, does not have all the answers. In almost any sequence of chapters alternating between narrative and diary, Huxley allows us to see the immediate relationship between before and after, either/or.

In Chapter 40 Anthony writes about a film on reproduction that Miller has shown him to "proclaim the glory of God" (490). Since the previous chapter concerned Helen's abortion in 1928, the point of this juxtaposition seems to be a Millerian lesson about the misuse of the self. But it is in the next chapter, in 1933, that Anthony and Mark see the little Mexican girl suffering from meningitis. This is a powerful, terrible scene: the child screaming and thrashing about, the mother trying helplessly to make her stop, the pain unceasing. What is its comment on Miller's "glory of God"? One is reminded of another of Huxley's favorite writers, Dostoevsky, and Ivan Karamazov's rejection of God because of the sufferings of innocent children. But *Eyeless* lacks Dostoevsky's eloquent rebuttals—Anthony plays a poor Alyosha to Miller's travesty of Father Zossima.

The disjunction is made even more vivid by the chapter that follows. There Anthony meditates on the subject of force and pain versus love, and concludes that love always wins out (ch. 42). However, we have just been shown in striking terms the impotence of a mother's love in the face of her child's pain, and the juxtaposition makes Anthony's optimism seem incredibly facile. In the end Anthony accepts that evil is the condition of life; but evil defined only as "separation." Nothing in Miller's theology or anthropology can reconcile the tortured child with the glory of God.

The trouble with many of Miller's theories is that they run up against the hard facts of what even Hugh Ledwidge realizes is a "reality . . . profoundly different" (518). He is often annoyingly naive and dogmatic. When he discusses politics with Mark, Miller smugly asserts "that if you treat other people well . . . in the long run they'll *always* treat you well" (580—my italics). When he diagnoses Anthony's problems as chronic constipation, bad posture, and negative thinking, and prescribes a meatless diet and meditation, he is probably not entirely wrong. But the body in *Eyeless* has an entropy of its own that is not easily reversed. One can choose oneself as ethical or healthy—still the body decays. Miller seems not to notice this fact. His doctrines of free will and cause and effect fail to account for children who gratuitously contract meningitis and dogs that fall on people from airplanes. These are matters beyond the scope of ethical philosophy, but they are facts central to the novel. Kierkegaard's aesthetic man celebrates the arbitrary in defense of his refusal to choose; his ethical man dismisses it in favor of the need to choose. Kierkegaard himself gives it due credence in his preface: the accidental discovery of the papers, their chance arrangement. Anthony in his aesthetic phase stakes his lot with chance, the idiot who deals out the cards at random, while Miller insists that one always chooses the card one receives. Huxley, like Kierkegaard, embodies both in the structure of his book. *Eyeless in Gaza* has fifty-four chapters—equivalent to a full deck plus two jokers. [13]

Though the novel does not accept Miller uncritically, Anthony seems to. But his decision to become Miller's disciple is not so much a new direction as a continuation of old patterns. In this he resembles his predecessor, Philip Quarles: "At different times in his life . . . he had filled the most various moulds. He had been a cynic and also a mystic, a humanitarian and also a contemptuous misanthrope; he had tried to live the life of detached and stoical reason. . . . The choice of moulds depended at any given moment on the books he was reading, the people he was associating with. Burlap, for example, had redirected the flow of his mind into those mystical channels. . . . Then he had seen through Burlap and flowed out again . . ." (*PCP*, 268–69). Anthony, too, is easily influenced by others. At one phase in his life he models himself after Mary Amberley, at another he aspires to be Gerry Watchett. Now the mould is Miller; and one day he may just flow out again.

In any case the novel leaves considerable doubt about the strength of his commitment to Miller's doctrines. "Use conditions function," Miller preaches (85): if you repeat anything often enough, it will come to be true for you. This is Anthony's hope as he constantly, loyally mouths the party line. But the essential weakness of his conviction is shown over and over again in the diary. He really doesn't like people very much, though he would like to be able to, and his is a continual battle against backsliding. That he chooses to fight the battle is all to his credit. He is clearly a better person for having chosen to confront himself, accept his past, and change his ways. Nonetheless, the last line has a hollow ring: "Whatever it might be, he knew now that all would be well." Nothing in the novel offers much support to this sentiment. For the moment it is a useful fiction for Anthony that allows him to do what he had formerly been incapable of doing. But it resolves nothing at all. In the end we don't know whether he actually goes to speak at the pacifist meeting; or if he does, what might happen if he were physically attacked as had been threatened. Nor can we even guess for how long he might maintain his newly found faith.

As in *Either/Or*, all we have are two views confronting one another: ours of the character and his of himself; the aesthetic and the ethical; the work's structural coherence and its fragmentation; the author's sympathy and his distance. "In this respect," says Victor Eremita, "these papers have no ending" (*E/O* I, 14). As well as philosophical substance, what Kierkegaard seems to have provided for Huxley via the model of *Either/Or* was the possibility of avoiding the kind of static and unself-critical ideological positions that so marred Huxley's subsequent work. The result in *Eyeless in Gaza* is a compelling record of one man's ongoing struggle with himself.

Notes

1. Garnett, rpt. in *Aldous Huxley: The Critical Heritage*, ed. Donald Watt (London: Routledge & Kegan Paul, 1975), 250–51; Woodcock, *Dawn and the Darkest Hour: A Study of Aldous Huxley* (London: Faber, 1972), 15–16.

2. See, e.g., Peter Bowering, *Aldous Huxley: A Study of the Major Novels* (London: Athlone, 1968), 20–21.

3. Peter Firchow, *Aldous Huxley: Satirist and Novelist* (Minneapolis: University of Minnesota Press, 1972), 149–56; Pierre Vitoux, "Structure and Meaning in Aldous Huxley's *Eyeless in Gaza*," YES, II (1972), 212–24; and Woodcock, 198–204.

4. *Eyeless in Gaza* (London: Chatto & Windus, 1936), 614. Citations from the novel will be noted by page numbers in my text.

5. "Spinoza's Worm," in *Do What You Will* (London: Chatto & Windus, 1929). All subsequent references to Huxley's texts are to the Chatto & Windus editions and include the following: *Proper Studies* (1927; rpt. 1949), *Point Counter Point* (1928), *Those Barren Leaves* (1925; rpt. 1969), *Texts and Pretexts* (1932).

6. Brian's death in 1914 and the hiatus in the chronology between 1914 and 1926 remind us of the novel's historical dimension. Though the Great War is hardly mentioned, Brian's fall denotes an end of prelapsarian innocence and a trauma from which sufficient time is needed to recover. Not coincidentally, when Anthony accepts his role in Brian's death, he goes out to preach pacifism in the face of another impending war.

7. See Jerome Meckier, *Aldous Huxley: Satire and Structure* (London: Chatto & Windus, 1969), 157; George Stevens, in *The Critical Heritage*, 262–63; and Woodcock, 205.

8. Søren Kierkegaard, *Either/Or*, trans. David F. and Lillian M. Swenson, rev. Howard A. Johnson, 2 vols. (Garden City, N.Y.: Doubleday Anchor, 1959), I, 32.

9. *Letters of Aldous Huxley*, ed. Grover Smith (London: Chatto & Windus, 1969), 356.

10. Sybille Bedford, *Aldous Huxley: A Biography*, 2 vols. (London: Chatto & Windus, 1973), I, 264.

11. Compare Anthony's language and situation here to Huxley's satirical portrait of Marjorie Carling's mysticism, and particularly her meditation on "peace," in *Point Counter Point*, 496–97.

12. See, e.g., Louis Mackey, *Kierkegaard: A Kind of Poet* (Philadelphia: University of Pennsylvania Press, 1971), 87–95; Gregor Malantschuk, *Kierkegaard's Thought*, ed. and trans. Howard V. and Edna H. Hong (Princeton: Princeton University Press, 1971), 226–29; and Ronald Grimsley, *Søren Kierkegaard: A Biographical Introduction* (London: Studio Vista, 1973), 37–38.

13. I am indebted to Donald Buschlen for this clever observation.

Huxley and Hearst

Frank Baldanza

1

ALTHOUGH ALDOUS HUXLEY and his wife Maria were tacitly refused American citizenship for their pacifist views, they were unofficial California citizens soon after their arrival in 1937. The climate was ideal for Huxley's always precarious health, and if their initial motive was to flee the European war, they remained out of choice. Old friends like Frieda Lawrence, Gerald Heard, and Anita Loos and newer ones like Christopher Isherwood were initial magnets. The great universities and research, scientific, and intellectual establishments like Robert Maynard Hutchins's Center for the Study of Democratic Institutions; the availability of large sums for movie work (Huxley even wrote for Disney); the rich supply of "quacks" (Huxley's term) with peculiar spiritual-dietary-medical theories; the expatriate community, particularly the Stravinskys; and the Huxleys' passion for automobiles—all these attractions and many others combined to ground them firmly in the Los Angeles and desert areas; they urged Maria's family to join them. Perhaps the best informal gauge of Huxley's California citizenship was his choice of a drive-in wedding chapel for his second marriage.

Why, then, does his first American novel, *After Many a Summer Dies the Swan* (1939), stand in certain of its details as a major satiric attack on L.A. as a state of mind? The most immediate explanation in terms of its composition is that the notes for the novel, begun shortly after his arrival in California, were based on the shock of initial responses, and the composition was faster than any work since the early *Crome Yellow*.[1] His wife Maria wrote to Edward Sackville-West that "this one is about longevity, and is going to be comic too. . . . He is going to put in a lot about California life. . . . He is in a good mood."[2] Several months later Huxley wrote his English publisher that he was "hard at work on a short phantasy . . . but built up of solidly realistic psychological elements; a wild extravaganza, but with the quality of a most serious parable . . . at once comic and cautionary, farcical, blood-curdling and reflective."[3]

Reprinted from the *Journal of Modern Literature* 7 (1978): 441–55, with the permission of the journal and the author's estate.

It is this combination of "wild extravaganza" with "a most serious parable" that constitutes the primary intrinsic reason for the satiric views of California life—aside from the general fact that satire is most frequently Huxley's basic *métier*, and Los Angeles happened to be the material at hand. The novel consists of three basic elements braided together, two of which are decidedly non-novelistic. One may assume Huxley knew that the material most seriously significant to him—the didactic sermon-essays of the pan-mystical Jeffersonian democrat, William Propter—were least amenable to novelistic presentation and would need to be carried along by some extravagantly piquant appeal in other elements of the narrative. Consequently, Huxley situates Propter on the fringes of a huge ranch owned by millionaire Jo Stoyte and dominated by his hilltop castle, a vulgar wedding cake of masonry containing a mad jumble of art treasures. Stoyte's obsessive fear of death and general emotional immaturity (primarily revealed in his relations with his baby-faced and -minded mistress Virginia Maunciple) are related to his imperious power drive, his childish sentimentality, and his mad need to plunder the world for antiques—all these characteristics being the opposite of Propter's mystical quietism, asceticism, and humble social service to the needy. Thus by a neat thematic dovetailing, the sensational narrative of the goings-on at Stoyte's castle—widely recognized as a fictional treatment of supposed events at William Randolph Hearst's estate, San Simeon—represents the obverse of Propter's values, a kind of negative illustration. The third element—the narrative of the Fifth Earl of Gonister, who has prolonged his life for 201 years by eating minced carp guts—is managed largely by journal entries; again, the thematic dovetailing is obvious, because the Fifth Earl is as obsessed with longevity as Jo Stoyte—he is also, like Stoyte, a compulsive land grabber and a collector of art. An English visiting scholar, Jeremy Pordage, some of whose features suggest he is partly a self-satire by Huxley, serves as a link between all three strands, since he reads the Earl's manuscript journal among the Hauberk papers at Stoyte's castle and informs Dr. Obispo, the longevity researcher, of the Earl's experiments on himself. It is Jeremy who provides the satiric response to L.A. on his arrival at the beginning of the novel.

I shall concern myself largely with that third of the novel devoted to Jo Stoyte, in an attempt to specify the parallels with Hearst and San Simeon and those between Virginia Maunciple and Hearst's mistress of over thirty years, Marion Davies. We shall never know whether Huxley first decided to treat Hearst and then the longevity idea grew out of that choice, or vice versa. But Hearst himself was widely known to fear aging and death—he rarely attended funerals, and he kept himself closely informed on longevity and rejuvenation experiments. It is actually doubtful whether Hearst was quite so rigid in these matters as his employees thought him, but when one of a group of transplanted palm trees died during their installation at San

Simeon, in order to avoid any suggestion of death, the landscaper hurriedly sprayed the leaves with green paint until he could replace the tree.

2

The first question in Huxley's treatment of Hearst is how he came upon his material. The most obvious answer is that Huxley and Maria spent at least one weekend at San Simeon themselves, he probably preoccupied with the manners and the antique treasures, and Maria noting housekeeping details ("cotton sheets in a house with an old master in the lift" [Bedford, 379]). The considerable publicity about the estate and widespread gossip about the Hearst-Davies arrangement were, of course, what must have attracted Huxley's attention; these interests were soon to be concentrated on Orson Welles and Herman J. Manciewicz's film *Citizen Kane*, which premiered in New York on May 1, 1941. Fortuitously, in July 1939, Maria gave a large party as a joint celebration of Aldous's birthday and the completion of revisions on *After Many a Summer*, with Orson Welles, newly arrived in Hollywood, as one of the guests (along with Charlie Chaplin, Paulette Goddard, Lillian Gish, Helen Hayes, Charles MacArthur, and many others). However, despite Welles's presence at this party, it appears that the idea of basing a movie on Hearst was originally the inspiration of Manciewicz, a journalist, movie scriptwriter, and playwright for Welles's Mercury Theatre, who had been an ardent Hearst-watcher for many years and a frequent guest at San Simeon. He had written a movie script on Hearst in New York as early as 1925, and he appears to have broached the idea of a Hearst movie to Welles in December 1939, two months after Huxley's novel appeared. His work on this new script in the Spring of 1940 thus appears actually unrelated— though it is disquieting to learn that Manciewicz prided himself on being the first person to read all important books by publication date.[4]

At any rate, Huxley's novel was published before Manciewicz and Welles discussed the idea for the film, so we can rule out *Citizen Kane* as an immediate influence. It is, of course, impossible to discover where and when and from whom Huxley first heard of Hearst, though the most likely link was Anita Loos, an old friend of Huxley's who was also a neighbor of Marion Davies in Santa Monica and a frequent guest at San Simeon. Huxley considered Anita the "doyenne of Hollywood," and it was she who Americanized the language in this very novel. It is certain that gossip about Hearst was very nearly universal. For example, Robert Maynard Hutchins, a friend of Huxley's, was asked by Cissy Patterson to leave San Simeon at one point because he had "insulted" his hostess Marion Davies by calling her "stupid" twice in one evening (she had defined "theosophist" as "not to eat any meat").[5] Huxley on another occasion wrote to Hutchins (himself a target of

Hearst's anti-Communist–academic smear) about his distress over the Hearst participation in the red-baiting controversy on the proposed appointment of Bertrand Russell to a position at CCNY. Hearst was at this time a *bête noire* of liberals. These events did not necessarily precede Huxley's choice of a subject, but are related simply as illustrations of the staple of Hearst talk among intellectuals.

Before looking at the details of Huxley's representation of the man, we might note that, in previous novels, he frequently drew material from characters and incidents known to his family and friends (including the death of his mother), and usually in a seemingly naive manner, so that he seems to have been genuinely surprised when the supposed source persons were offended: notable examples were Lady Ottoline Morrell's long animosity over Huxley's supposed treatment of her entertainments at Garsington in *Crome Yellow*, and his wife's offense at allusions to his crush on Nancy Cunard (and Maria's collusion in some of his marital peccadilloes) in *Point Counter Point*. In such cases, he was concentrating on the structural and thematic function of such materials within the imaginative fiction; incidents drawn from one real person or situation were blended into an amalgam of materials drawn equally from quite different sources, which he felt exonerated him from charges of "using" friends. They, however, often assumed malice on his part and took the blended-in details drawn from other sources as distortion. The same problem occurred in *After Many a Summer*: President Herbert Mulge of Tarzana College, a classic satiric vignette of the piranha-opportunist educational administrator, all unctious, phony idealism on the surface, is said to be drawn from "two of the Southland's leading educators," and Huxley's portrait "did not endear the author to his models."[6] Hearst himself seems to have left no record of his feelings about the novel.

We may assume that Huxley was employing the Hearst stories in his usual way, though in this case he may have been somewhat more conscious of "using" his material. For example, he asked his publisher to change the name of Stoyte's mistress in the novel to "Maunciple" throughout the proofs because the original name he had used, "Dowlas," had "a fortuitous resemblance to that of a notorious lady in this neighbourhood" (*Letters*, 446). He may have had in mind both Marion Davies's stage name and her actual family name, Douras. Again, describing to his son Matthew in 1949 a most repellent picture of Hearst and Marion Davies in their old age, he added, "the reality sounds infinitely more gruesome, and also more improbable, than the fictions of *After Many a Summer*" (*Letters*, 593). In her memoirs, Miss Davies mentions having heard of the novel but says she never read it.

3

The arrival of Jeremy Pordage in Los Angeles to catalogue Jo Stoyte's Hauberk papers provides Huxley with his opening satiric salvo, with the recluse-scholar's shock and bewilderment at the hamburger-joint landscape and the movie mansions. The culminating set-piece of this passage is the chauffeur's gratuitous tour of the Beverly Pantheon, a fictional savaging of Forest Lawn Cemetery, later made the subject of Evelyn Waugh's *The Loved One*. When Jeremy Hutchinson (is the Christian name a fortuitous coincidence?) visited Huxley during the composition of this novel in March 1939, he says, "Within an hour of arriving [precisely on Jeremy Pordage's schedule!] I was being conducted round Forest Lawn with Aldous caressing the marble pink bottoms of the statuary and pointing out the 'staggering sensuality' as the eternal Wurlitzer sounds came out from behind the trees . . ." (Bedford, 369). It is rather a pity that Huxley only discovered in 1952, too late for use in this novel, another feature of the establishment: in showing the place to Edith Sitwell, he and his guest hooted on learning that the wedding chapel is warmed by heat generated in the crematorium. Stoyte's ownership of the Beverly Pantheon is a brilliant Huxleyan irony, given Stoyte-Hearst's necrophobia, though Hearst had no interest in Forest Lawn.

Pordage's speed in arriving at Stoyte's castle is due to Huxley's having moved it nearly two hundred miles south from the location of Hearst's San Simeon to the San Fernando Valley just outside Los Angeles (Powell, 7). Guests who visited Hearst had a much more difficult, complicated itinerary (San Simeon was two hundred miles from a city and forty-three miles from any town), though given his lavish, baronial hospitality, those who arrived in the middle of the night in his private Pullman cars slept undisturbed until the morning journey up La Cuesta Encantada (The Enchanted Hill).

On Pordage's immediate approach to the Object (his name for the castle), Huxley conveniently produces William Propter as an in-house hitch-hiker to initiate Jeremy to his host's foibles. The burden of his message is that Jo Stoyte bullies people as overcompensation for having been teased as a school-child for his fatness. While this sounds like cheap parlor Freudian-ism, even Hearst's most reliable and objective biographer, W. A. Swanberg, indulges in "childhood trauma" theories, as does Manciewicz with his famous "Rosebud" gimmicks in *Citizen Kane*. But those familiar with Huxley's other works will recognize this passage as patent publicity for Sheldon's system of psycho-physical classification, for which Huxley was a rabid partisan. Stoyte is a perfect endomorph to balance Obispo's mesomorphy and Pordage's ectomorphy. Incidentally, Pauline Kael's description of Hearst's physical presence, when she bumped into him on a dance floor, tallies with Propter's description of Stoyte.

In dealing with the real San Simeon as a model for Stoyte's castle in the novel, one can only echo what Huxley wrote to Matthew about Hearst's old age—it is simply too gruesome and improbable to be done any kind of justice in the most extravagant fiction. The lusts behind its building began early: at ten, Hearst said to his mother, on their first European tour, that he would like to live in Windsor Castle—this was not a chance remark, for one biographer assures us "that he spent more for housing and decoration [on all his properties, including a castle in Wales with 135 rooms] than any man in history, king or commoner."[7] By conservative estimate, San Simeon alone cost thirty million dollars. On the same boyhood European tour, he also, not half-jokingly, asked his mother to buy the Louvre. Hearst's lifelong, madly compulsive purchase of antiques is almost impossible to encompass mentally. His fifty-year average expenditure of one million dollars or more per year on antiques of all sorts sometimes constituted "a quarter of the entire sales of objects of art in the world."[8] The most spectacular coups were a tenth-century Spanish cloister from Segovia purchased sight unseen, for which Hearst built twenty-one miles of railroad to ship out the stones in 10,700 crates and later the Cistercian monastery of Santa Maria de Oliva, near Siguenza, in 14,000 crates. Many items were held in two five-story warehouses in the Bronx, others in five California warehouses; Hearst never saw thousands of his antiques. At one point, his twelve thousand objects were catalogued in 150 "fat black looseleaf notebooks" which contained photographs and descriptions under 504 categories; it took ten or eleven clerks just to maintain the notebooks.[9] He is said to have possessed either the largest and/or the finest collection in the world in each of these categories: Gothic mantles, tapestries, old silver, Majolica and Hispano-Moresque plates, Mexican silver saddles, antique furniture, paneled rooms, and stained glass.[10] Even his armor collection was impressive, if not superlative. San Simeon was in a continuous state of building from its inception in 1919 on the site of Hearst's father George's ranch; wing by wing, room by room, it was designed around the accommodation of treasured antiques. The ranch contained 45,000 acres when he inherited it, and he expanded these holdings to 240,000 acres, with fifty miles of seacoast—half the size of Rhode Island; at one point, he is said to have purchased twenty-three ranches in one day.[11]

Jeremy's initial tour of the castle bristles with familiar details taken from its prototype.[12] The Stoyte Home for Sick Children on the grounds is based on the two million dollar Marion Davies Clinic for Children in Los Angeles (now part of the UCLA Medical Center at Westwood [Davies, 57–58]). The host's pause at the clinic to buy thirty thousand acres of ranch land is a typical Hearstian gesture, and the construction of a tomb for embalmed Spanish nuns is a Huxleyan arabesque on Hearst's purchase of the Spanish cloister and monastery. If Huxley's imaginary treatment could ever conceivably outdo the reality of San Simeon, it is in the quality of the paintings: Huxley places major Rubens and El Greco canvases in the Great Hall, probably based on the Assembly Room at San Simeon, which features large tapestries on the life of Scipio Africanus. Paintings did not especially interest Hearst, but Huxley could not resist indulging his obsession with painting. While Hearst had an old master in the elevator to the Celestial Suite (said to be a former confessional), it was not of the quality of the Vermeer Huxley places there.

But at no point does Huxley aim at direct literalness—Stoyte is short and Hearst was very tall; the former is an oil baron, the latter was a journalistic one; the castle boasts an Early English entrance porch, whereas San Simeon was imitation Spanish baroque and Asian. Huxley was in part trying to avoid a legal suit, though he perhaps did not know that Hearst held a settled conviction that it was futile to sue in all such cases. For example, Hearst tried hard to buy out *Citizen Kane* before it was exhibited, and when he failed at that ploy, he froze it out of ordinary theatre exhibition channels. But aside from legal questions, Huxley certainly knew that psychological and moral truths do not depend on literalness.

Chapter Four opens with a desperate migrant family going to work in an orange grove within view of the castle, an egregious fictional liberty in terms of fact, but one dictated by thematic necessity (and obviously justified by the initial change of location for San Simeon). By contrasting Stoyte's opulent extravagance with the hunger of the displaced Kansas farm family, Huxley is able to underline the theories of his spokesman in the novel, William Propter (modeled on his friend Gerald Heard). Later, in Chapter Ten, when Stoyte angrily objects to Propter's attempts to help the migrants, Propter delivers a set lecture on Jeffersonian-democratic, decentralized, rural self-reliance as the only viable means to social and economic justice and spiritual health—with a demonstration of his model solar energy machine (which shows Huxley to be as prescient in ecological matters as *Brave New World* proved him in technology). Huxley attributes Stoyte's desire to see the Okies continue to suffer as a complex response to the poverty of his own childhood; only by their staying poor can he gauge his own achievements in having risen so far. This is another departure from Hearst's life, since as a boy his father would flip him a twenty-dollar gold piece to treat playmates to ice cream. The real-life basis for Stoyte's violent hatred of Okies was Hearst's 1934 campaign, alongside the movie moguls, to defeat Upton Sinclair's "End Poverty in California" campaign for the governorship. Hearst printed fake movie stills of hoboes getting off a train in the Los Angeles *Herald-Express*, saying they had come "to help launch the Sinclair revolution" (Swanberg, 448). It is significant that Stoyte in this novel accuses Propter of impractical idealism and communism, precisely the terms in which Hearst attacked Sinclair.

To return to Chapter Four of the novel, while the Okie father beats his children in a rage of frustration, Stoyte at his luxurious swimming pool is squeezing the smooth, voluptuous legs of his mistress (this technique of swift and violent, but significant, contrasts between simultaneous actions was a fundamental feature of *Point Counter Point*). Huxley's description of

Stoyte's desire to preserve a dream of Virginia's baby-like innocence, while at the same time jealously and exclusively enjoying her favors, is devastatingly accurate in terms of Hearst's relations with Marion Davies, his chorus-girl discovery who has been called "the most accepted and certainly the wealthiest mistress of all time."[13] Especially in his minute supervision of every detail of her movie career, Hearst's personal image of Marion is clear: he never permitted her mature, maternal roles, and reacted strongly when she wished to play the prostitute Sadie Thompson in *Rain*; he summarily refused to allow her to play a pie-in-the-face scene. Miss Davies tells us Hearst forbade kissing on the mouth in her films, supposedly for health reasons, though the rule was relaxed in her later career, in a scene with Clark Gable. His favorite vehicles for Marion were candy-box-pretty costume pieces in which she appeared as a peach-bloom virgin, often surrounded by authentic antique settings—almost as part of his collection. Miss Davies's own devastating declarations in her memoirs of a total lack of talent are perhaps a bit too modest; good critics feel that she had a real knack for light-hearted comedy, but that Hearst suppressed any public, cinematic display of an ebullience which bubbled through the endless partying of her private life. Huxley very accurately catches the obscenely incestuous father-daughter overtones of the relationship, only exaggerating the age difference a trifle—Hearst was thirty-four years older than Miss Davies, Stoyte thirty-eight years older than Virginia. The portrait of Virginia is remarkably close to the real Miss Davies in her love of present pleasures and her mischievousness, though Huxley exaggerates her confused piety and entirely neglects Miss Davies's truly magnanimous charities as well as her dependence on alcohol. He may not have known some of these details, though he mentions her heavy drinking in a letter to his son ten years later; one can only speculate on whether he ignored her charities in order to concentrate most of the benevolence in the novel on the good works of William Propter; of course, Miss Davies's philanthropy tended either to be personal and impulsive or else to operate through present institutional channels like the Boy Scouts, whereas Huxley, in Propter, is calling for a radical change in the structure of society.

The satanic Dr. Obispo (whose name comes from the county and town of San Luis Obispo near San Simeon) is said to be modeled after a Hollywood physician (Powell, 7); his administration of shots of testosterone to Jo Stoyte beside the pool echoes Hearst's own consuming interest in medical efforts at longevity, especially in the monkey-gland operations of Dr. Serge Voronoff, which Obispo himself mentions in conversation (Swanberg, 432). Obispo's laboratories on the castle grounds are an invention; Hearst, notoriously tender-minded about the suffering of animals, would delay large dinner parties to nurse an ailing pet. He forbade the killing of the large numbers of mice at San Simeon (the butler put out harmless cage traps and released the mice each morning), and he would certainly not have permitted their use on the grounds for medical experiments. On one occasion, Louella Parsons had to sit for an hour in her auto until a stubborn moose who was sunning himself in the middle of the drive moved on.

Although all the other principal characters at the castle are apparently based at least in part on real prototypes, I can find no source-figure for Obispo's assistant Peter Boone, though his function is clear in terms of aesthetic structure—in the drama of ideas, his naive, malleable leftist good will makes him an easy mark for some of Propter's ideas. Years after the completion of the novel, a question arose about restoring Peter to a dramatic version of *After Many a Summer* from which he had been excluded; Huxley wrote the playwright that Pete's hopelessly idealizing Platonic worship was a necessary counter balance to the types of love represented by Obispo and Stoyte.

The incident of feeding the baboons is a brilliant example of how Huxley adapted San Simeon material to his fictional needs. Hearst had the largest private collection of wild animals in the country; at one time, San Simeon featured spotted deer, buffalo, yaks, elks, antelope, kangaroos, camels, giraffes, zebras, polar bears, lions, tigers, cheetahs, emu, moose, elands, goats, monkeys, orangutans, spotted leopards, black panthers, a she-elephant, wildcats, chimpanzee, gorillas, eagles, cockatoos, and ostriches. Miss Davies describes in her memoirs her pleasure in teasing an elderly "ape" (actually, a chimpanzee) right under a large sign reading "DO NOT TEASE THE ANIMALS." One can only assume this teasing occurred when Hearst was not present, just as Marion and Carole Lombard would run off to the ladies' room to take a swig of Scotch or gin cooling in the water tank, since W. R. only permitted one cocktail before dinner. One of her favorite sports, after tug-of-war with Jerry the chimpanzee, was throwing stones at him. In the novel the visitors throw potatoes to an old baboon, and as he deserts his youthful mate, a young male takes the chance for quick copulation while the elder's back is turned. The parallel to Stoyte, Virginia, and Obispo is masterful. The real Jerry was a misanthrope who would go into paroxysms when Hearst approached; he was later shipped out because on several occasions he threw his excrement at lady guests, including Marie Dressler—one wonders how a satirist like Huxley could have neglected that detail. And how nicely it would have fit in with the climactic horror scene in which the Fifth Earl of Gonister is slowly developing into an ape! Jerry's mate at San Simeon bore him one young chimp which died in infancy; this may have been Huxley's source for the dead young chimp in the novel.

Following the scene at the baboon cage, Stoyte's bursting into Virginia's bedroom while Obispo is translating from the de Sade volume, split between Chapters Ten and Twelve, is, in terms of the novel, an ominous forecast of what will happen later at the swimming pool when Stoyte interrupts their making love.[14] But the incident also seems to have parallels in the daily behavior of Hearst and Miss Davies. Hearst kept very close tabs on her; he often would phone to discover if Marion were at the place she told him she was going; he is said to have had detectives and employees shadow her, and he showed frequent signs of watchfulness when they were in a large party. It was on one such occasion that she is said to have remarked, "Hearst come, Hearst served." Miss Davies herself tells us she was open to flirtatious glances and suggestive badinage from male guests over jig-saw puzzles, but the moment W. R. entered the room, everyone became instantly correct and sober. Her biographer suggests that Marion Davies's occasional, brief liaisons with handsome young hangers-on and leading men were tacitly tolerated by Hearst on the implicit understanding that no depth of feeling was involved and that the arrangements were short-term diversions (Guiles, 94–95, 163–64).

Thus Obispo's seduction of Virginia in her bedroom is probably to be taken generically rather than literally. We can, however, verify certain details from the bedroom. Miss Davies's room at San Simeon contained a very impressive painting of the Madonna, said to be the finest of a very large number of Madonnas in terra-cotta, stone, wood, and other media at San Simeon. The soda fountain in her room is Huxley's addition, though it has some justification because Miss Davies frequently remarks in her memoirs on her insatiable passion for ice cream and her capacity to eat more at one sitting than anyone who ever challenged her to a contest. When Aimee Semple McPherson attacked Marion in a radio broadcast about a basement bar in her 110-room beach home at Santa Monica, Miss Davies converted it to a soda fountain. One detail from the seduction scene certainly has an authentic ring: when Obispo calls Stoyte an old buzzard, Virginia reacts very angrily. In the same way, Marion Davies was fiercely loyal to Hearst, and she genuinely respected him. Her social position was a painful and precarious one, despite her twenty million fortune; at the moment of Hearst's death, she was summarily cut off from any say in the management of the empire, despite clearly contrary indications in his will. Had Marion Davies decided to leave or expose Hearst at any point, he would have had no recourse. It is widely known that she gave him one million dollars or more during a time of extreme financial pressure.

In turning to the climactic scene of the novel—an incident which almost certainly had no basis in real events at San Simeon—we must remember that analyses such as this one draw on materials like Miss Davies's memoirs and authoritative and reliable biographies like those of Swanberg and Guiles which were unavailable to Huxley. That one should find his imaginative treatment as incisively true to the general tone and psychological reality of the situations is in itself remarkable. We must assume, however, that the author drew his material largely from oral sources; consequently, it is in rumor that we shall find the probable source of the climax of the novel.

Stoyte surprises Virginia and Obispo in a compromising position beside the swimming pool, but his line of vision masks the exact identity of the man. Long suspicious of Peter's bumbling attentions to Virginia, he seems to assume it is Peter beside her. In a furious rage, Stoyte runs to find his pistol and encounters a series of frustrations in locating it. When he does return, Obispo has gone to seek Virginia's comb, and Peter has come on the scene. Thus, given his earlier suspicions, Stoyte naturally shoots *him*. The irony of Obispo's going free is a devastating confirmation of his satanically successful cynicism—augmented by the fact that he, as a physician, is able to cover up what happened and exonerate Stoyte, but at a very high price.

The most probable rumor that might have suggested this incident to Huxley was one surrounding the death of Thomas H. Ince, an independent film producer whom Hearst was consulting on Miss Davies's career. During a cruise on Hearst's yacht, *Oneida*, Ince was taken ill of acute indigestion, supposedly accompanied by heavy drinking—though *all* the facts in the incident seem disputed—and was removed at San Diego. He died of a heart attack. Hearst reportedly allowed no drinking on his yacht, so if Ince had drunk, it must have been surreptitiously. The early newspaper reports said he had taken ill on a visit to the ranch; it is to be surmised that perhaps Hearst interests wanted to prevent any suggestion of alcohol (during Prohibition) and any publicity that might link Hearst and Miss Davies, because there had been no public admission of their long-standing liaison, though testimony at a recent court trial threatened exposure. Rumors sprang up about a wild drinking party and grew to more and more sensational proportions. Newspapers began speculating. Swanberg wrote in 1961 that "one can still hear solemn stories in Hollywood today that Ince was murdered, one of the most ridiculous of them being that Hearst found him pressing unwelcome attentions on Miss Davies and shot him fatally" (376). We must remember that Obispo's attentions to Virginia were largely unwelcome until after he aroused her. But this particular rumor does not account for the mistaken shooting of the wrong man. Indeed, Miss Davies's biographer Guiles adds, "The murder rumor is substantially the same in all of the accounts given to the author by those surviving members of the Davies-Hearst circle who will discuss it, excepting one detail: whether it was a case of mistaken identity or not" (160). The rumors assume that Hearst was jealous of Miss Davies's supposed liaison with Charles Chaplin, who bore some resemblance to Ince: "The story places Marion and Ince in the lower galley sitting at a table, talking. The galley light was relatively dim and Ince's back was to the galley steps or 'ladder.' Hearst, it was said, suddenly missed Marion and his suspicions got the better of him. He began searching the vessel for her, saw her engrossed with someone whom he immediately took to be Chaplin, pulled out a pistol, and shot him" (Guiles, 160).

Though this rumor is close to the novel version, it does not include the substitution of one man for the other during Stoyte's absence when he went to find his gun. The closest version of the rumor is this one: "Hearst was . . . uncommonly jealous of other men's attentions to Marion; detectives had kept him informed of her dalliance with Chaplin during his absence. . . .

It is believed that during the birthday party Hearst noticed that Marion and Charlie had slipped off together and were later discovered by Hearst *in flagrante* on the lower deck. In her famous stutter, Marion let out a prophetic scream—'M-m-m-murder!'—which brought the other guests running as Hearst ran for his revolver. In the ensuing confusion, Ince, not Chaplin, dropped, a bullet in his brain."[15] In addition to shooting the wrong man, this rumor maintains that Louella Parsons, who saw the incident, received a life contract as a Hearst columnist as the price of her silence—a parallel to Obispo's capitalizing on the cover-up. Reliable sources today express extreme skepticism about these rumors, but we must remember they were probably the staple of Huxley's approach at the time.

Huxley was an indefatigable practitioner of the novel of ideas, and even in his fairly close representation of a very real and very famous set of people, he did not choose Hearst and Davies only for sensational scandal appeal, though he clearly meant to use that appeal. The portion that treats the castle, seen in the context of the other two-thirds of the novel, represents values diametrically opposite to those of William Propter, the axis where Huxley's values cohere. Stoyte, Virginia, and Obispo are plunged into the futile realm of human striving, neurotic pursuit of power and material possessions, sensual pleasures, and overriding fear of time and death; Obispo as an evil intelligence uses human reason to attempt to prolong these very evils, and in his use of medicine in the service of what Huxley sees as abominable aims, he is in the process of creating monstrous abortions, like the Fifth Earl, becoming a fetal ape at 201. Propter, in his mystic, ascetic renunciation of worldly goods, honors, and appetites, uses his intelligence on beneficent projects. The passages given to Propter bulk much larger in the whole book, since Huxley had by this point in his career moved away from the uncommitted skepticism of his early works. The Hearst-Davies portions are solidly given in the tone of the early manner, but seen now from the perspective of intensely held values.

Notes

1. The notes were begun in April 1938; the writing, with interruptions for film work, took from June 1938 until May 1939, when Huxley was correcting the typescript, finishing the revisions by July. The novel was published in October.

2. Quoted in Sybille Bedford, *Aldous Huxley* (Knopf, 1974), p. 365.

3. *Letters of Aldous Huxley*, ed. Grover Smith (London: Chatto and Windus, 1969), pp. 440, 441.

4. Pauline Kael, "Raising Kane," in *The Citizen Kane Book* (Little, Brown, 1971), pp. 29, 33, 37.

5. Marion Davies, *The Times We Had*, eds. Pamela Pfau and Kenneth S. Marx (Bobbs-Merrill, 1975), pp. 205–6. Miss Davies tells us in her disarming manner that George Bernard Shaw made similar remarks on her intelligence.

6. Lawrence Clark Powell, "Aldous Huxley's *After Many a Summer Dies the Swan*," *Westways* (December 1970), p. 7.

7. W. A. Swanberg, *Citizen Hearst* (Charles Scribner's Sons, 1961), p. 508.

8. John Tebbell, *The Life and Good Times of William Randolph Hearst* (E. P. Dutton, 1952), p. 267.

9. Geoffrey T. Hellman, "Onward and Upward with the Arts: Monastery for Sale," *New Yorker* (1 February 1941), p. 29.

10. Mrs. Fremont Older, *William Randolph Hearst, American* (D. Appleton-Century, 1936), p. 544.

11. The official guidebook gives the figure of 275,000 acres, but I have always taken Swanberg's facts where I encountered discrepancies.

12. Huxley may use the term "castle" with mischievous intent, though the word appears on the official guidebook; Hearst always forbade the term, insisting with typical sentimentality about childhood experiences that San Simeon was a ranch.

13. Fred Lawrence Guiles, *Marion Davies* (McGraw-Hill, 1972), p. 4.

14. Marion could speak nonsense French as a joke with Fifi d'Orsay (*"C'est aujourd'hui, n'est-ce pas? Mais certainement sur la table. C'est aujourd'hui parce que c'est l'hiver"*), and Hearst believed it to be genuine (Guiles, 189). The famous secret French naval treaty, the publication of whose contents led to Hearst's expulsion from France, is claimed by Marion as her own theft: she says she slipped it into her "sissy britches" on a visit to the Foreign Ministry partly because she wanted to learn to read French.

15. Kenneth Anger, *Hollywood Babylon* (Dell, 1976), p. 99. Another commentator, in trying to sort out the rumors, says, "if everyone rumored to have been in the stateroom had been there, it would have been more crowded than the one in *A Night at the Opera*, and the conspiracies that supposedly surrounded John Wilkes Booth and Lee Harvey Oswald pale in comparison." George Eels, *Hedda and Louella* (Putnam's, 1972), p. 87n.

Brahmins from Abroad: English Expatriates and Spiritual Consciousness in Modern America

DAVID ROBB

One of the major intellectual and cultural dilemmas of the interwar period of the 1920s and 1930s involved the quest for an adequate source of value in a world that had come to be understood as intrinsically valueless. Symptomatically, many Western intellectuals, academics, writers and artists evidenced a longing to believe in some transcendent idea or principle that would give structure and meaning to their experience. This longing, according to Franklin Baumer, was brought on by the failure to reconcile the "man-society" connection with the "man-universe" connection.[1] For some, this longing for belief was satisfied by either a kind of religious adherence to political and economic ideologies or by a return to traditional religious creeds. Others were led to an exploration of a broad combination of religious, scientific and psychological elements which together represented a new, modern syncretic spiritualism.

Arthur Koestler explored this dilemma in his 1946 collection of essays, *The Yogi and the Commissar*. Koestler likened the entire range of attitudes towards life to a physicist's light spectrum. On the infra-red end, he locates the commissar. This end of the spectrum encompasses the lowest vibrations which are also the hottest. The commissar, argues Koestler, believes in change from without; that all the ills of mankind from the unequal distribution of wealth to the elimination of Oedipus complex can be accomplished by the application of logical reasoning, social engineering and, if need be, violent revolution.

At the other end of the spectrum are the ultra-violet frequencies, a range where the beam of light becomes invisible to the naked eye. At this end is the Yogi, who believes that the ills of mankind can only be addressed by securing the proper internal disposition, a disposition which is oriented only towards the truth which is understood to be the "godhead."[2]

The underlying problem, Koestler suggests, is the fundamental opposi-

Reprinted from *American Studies* 26 (1985): 45–60, with the permission of the author and publisher.

tion between the conception of change from without and change from within. These opposing notions of change help to explain periodic historical swings between the two extremes of the spectrum and offer a vehicle for understanding such mid-range combinations as political liberalism, Fabianism and the social gospel. Koestler believed that twentieth-century man was inexorably moving towards the Yogi end of the spectrum, sometimes consciously and at other times unconsciously. According to Koestler's diagnosis, the West was suffering from a bad case of anti-materialistic nostalgia which was repelled by logic, optimism and rationalism, and attracted to various forms of romantic mysticism.[3]

My concern is with a small group of English expatriates who, from the late 1930s through the 1960s, contributed to the spread of mystical religious ideas in America. This group included Aldous Huxley, who by the time of his emigration was a world-renowned novelist and essayist; Gerald Heard, a well-known BBC science commentator and man of letters; and Christopher Isherwood, the leading novelist in a group of young, leftist, interwar writers referred to as the Auden group. Collectively they created a minor literary movement that brought to the attention of American readers a wide variety of religious subjects including spiritualism and psychic phenomena, mysticism, pacifism, oriental philosophy, self-help therapies and consciousness-altering drugs. In addition to their importance as noteworthy twentieth-century authors, they represent facets of a more generalized religious awakening in the West. As a group, they helped to stimulate this religious awakening in America and shape its distinctive eclectic form. As case studies, they provide instructive examples of modern spiritual longing and help to elucidate the form and substance of contemporary divergent religious belief in America.

The reason for treating these three as a group has little to do with their age—a total of fifteen years separates Heard, the eldest, from Isherwood, the youngest. Even from a literary perspective, they represent different "generations." What these three did have in common was their experience of the interwar period—the disquieting knowledge that they had survived the Great War and a sense of foreboding about the inevitability of a second war. Each found himself ultimately frustrated with the England of the interwar years; each developed a commitment to pacifism which served as a catalyst for his interest in religion; each settled in America (more specifically, Los Angeles) where all three remained in constant contact for approximately twenty-five years; each explored in his personal life and writing the spiritual aspects of human existence; and each contributed to the nascent American interest in mysticism, spiritualism and Asian religions. Thus, as individuals and as a group, they are important in the history of the twentieth century "religious renaissance" among Western intellectuals in the 1930s, 1940s and 1950s.

The very idea of a modern religious renaissance necessarily involves a variety of complex and arguable comparisons. Noting that "One of the most significant tendencies of our time, especially in this decade, has been the new turn toward religion among intellectuals and the growing disfavor with which secular attitudes and perspectives are now regarded in not a few circles that lay claim to the leadership of culture," the editors of the *Partisan Review* asked a group of prominent intellectuals in 1950 to comment on the notion of a religious renaissance.[4] The responses were anything but unanimous. Nevertheless, the fact remained that a variety of individuals, generally regarded as intellectual and cultural leaders, had demonstrated an apparent reawakening of interest in spiritual matters. These included Carl Jung, Arnold Toynbee, Arthur Koestler, Pitirim Sorokin and Albert Einstein, just to name a few. Certainly Huxley's unexpected spiritual turn generated much notoriety. As Ben Ray Redman wrote in 1944, "We shall do better to study the case of Huxley as an important case-history of our time. . . . Such a study may shed light upon what is happening not only to Huxley but to many others of our generation, for his abdication is only one among many."[5]

Whether it constitutes a religious renaissance or not, the twentieth century has witnessed a growing interest in the scientific study of religious phenomena coupled with a syncretic approach to human spirituality. This type of spiritual interest which is broad in focus, minimally religious in the traditional sense of the word and extensively known due to its diffusion in popular culture, consists of attempts empirically to validate spiritual experience by reconciling religious insights with scientific and psychological theories. Relying heavily on anthropological data, philosophical speculation and psychological observations, this empirical analysis of religion has occupied some of the more imaginative minds of our century. Applying analytical skills to traditional western religions and to the rediscovered Asian traditions, these scientific spiritualists have taken as their task the analysis of religious experience within a scientific-empirical framework. Abandoning religious vocabulary, the resulting scientific spiritualism has become one of the more appealing forms of religiosity for Western intellectuals who seek forms of spiritual belief compatible with their secular and scientific frames of mind. Many of these secularized spiritual orientations have stressed their separation from normative religious traditions by insisting that they are not religions at all but "alternative ways of knowing," new metaphysical systems for a nuclear age or simply forms of psychological self-help. Regardless of the form, the last four decades have seen a notable growth in the West of divergent or *ad hoc* "religions" that have appealed to a highly educated and secular audience.

Franklin Baumer terms this modern spiritual interest a "layman's religion."[6] According to Baumer, this layman's religion is an individualized combination of beliefs and practices chosen from such diverse sources as Christianity, oriental religions, political ideology, psychological theories and anthropological observations. As such, the layman's religion expresses a personal belief system rather than adherence to formal dogma or theology.

Moreover, it exhibits at least two significant characteristics: it is polymorphic and anti-dogmatic.[7]

The polymorphic quality of modern spiritual belief is hardly surprising given the popularity of comparative religious studies, the vast treasure of ethnological literature about the role and function of religion in other societies and the interest in exploring the psychology of religious experience. Because intellectuals share at least a passing acquaintance with these subjects, their spiritual beliefs tend to incorporate, or at least acknowledge, the insights of all religions while avoiding the notion of privileged revelation. Individual modern believers are more likely to ponder these collected insights and reduce them to a set of common denominators so as to form what has been termed a "minimum working hypothesis."[8]

As an obvious corollary to these polymorphic qualities, Baumer suggests that a layman's religion would resist the tendency to dogmatize. Each individual believer understands himself or herself to be responsible for fixing in his or her own mind the limits of one's own belief system. Therefore, no attempt is made to seek common agreement on other than the most general articles of belief. At best, modern intellectuals may agree on a common ethical system or simple rules of behavior as opposed to more complex patterns of belief. For example, such behavioral rules may incorporate elements of vegetarianism, pacifism or communitarianism.

As a mode of life, the layman's religion, in whatever form, is composed of a number of beliefs, practices and disciplines—some disparate, some related—all of which together are used by the individual believer to mediate his own felt spiritual vacuums or psychological dead-ends. Because the individual believer feels that he has the latitude to piece together a belief system to meet his or her own unique set of individual needs, it is highly unlikely that his choice of elements would consist of those which are not compatible with his own personality and needs. As such, the process of constructing a layman's religion, inasmuch as it is a heterodox and individualistic process, is in the mainstream of modern intellectual life.[9]

Gerald Heard, now a largely obscure and forgotten figure, in the 1930s was a well-known science commentator for the BBC as well as a prolific writer. E. M. Forster's assessment of Heard as one of the "most penetrating minds in England"[10] was shared by many including W. H. Auden, who in 1933 was at work on a poem that portrayed Heard as Virgil guiding Auden through the complexities of modern life.[11] But while Heard's admirers hailed him as a profound synthesizer of science and religion, his detractors excoriated him as an intellectual gadfly and philosophical raconteur. In reviewing Heard's thirty-five books and numerous articles and essays, one is immediately struck by the variety of genres he pursued. Heard the raconteur (writing under his real name, Henry Fitzgerald Heard) wrote a total of nine books including mysteries, science fiction and eerie short stories. However, it was as Gerald Heard the mandarin that he wrote most of his twenty-six other books devoted to scientific, philosophical, historical and religious topics.

In spite of his copious literary canon, Heard essentially devoted his life to the rewriting of a single "book." That "book" was a series of accounts of the modern dilemma, which Heard characterized as the dichotomy between humanity's growing control over the material world and its corresponding lack of control over the spiritual or psychological world. Heard believed that the application of a scientifically validated form of contemplative or mystical spirituality, underscored by a teleological belief in the continuing evolution of human consciousness, would lead to the development of a more advanced form of intelligence capable of transcending the political, economic and social consequences of one's individualized consciousness. Heard pursued this theme in each of his major works and, over time, as he was able to digest greater and greater amounts of historical, anthropological and psychological data, his expositions became more detailed and complex. The fundamental outline of Heard's thesis, however, is contained in a trilogy of his early works: *The Ascent of Humanity* (1929), *The Social Substance of Religion* (1931) and *The Source of Civilization* (1935).

An ardent proponent of evolutionary theory, Heard believed that while physical evolution had come to a halt, the evolutionary process itself continued on in the realm of consciousness. As the result of his evolutionary investigations, Heard became convinced that it was always the less specialized forms of life that prevailed. Overspecialized species, by completely adapting to a single change in their environment, became incapable of subsequent adaptions to other inevitable changes. Therefore, these species remained locked in a static state of development and ruefully awaited the day of their extinction. Unspecialized species, on the other hand, were far better able to adapt to change and consequently survive for further evolutionary development. Just as behavioral overspecialization produced effects harmful to physical evolution, so conceptual overspecialization produced effects harmful to psychological evolution.

History, for Heard, provided the record of man's capacity for adaptation and change. Thus, in the tradition of Comte, Spengler and Toynbee, his major works consisted of impressionistic, metaphorical world histories in which he repeatedly honed his teleological theories. "The real advance," wrote Heard, ". . . is in man's spirit and can be disclosed through the evolution of his standards."[12] Heard believed that man's consciousness had evolved from a primitive, pre-individual group consciousness to a fully individualized form of consciousness. Unfortunately, the development of man's intensified self-consciousness, which resulted in his obsession with material progress, overshadowed the need for social merger with his fellow beings— the essence of self-negating spiritual development. Heard feared that humanity was in danger of capsizing mentally because of the gross imbalance between man's enormous material growth and his corresponding lack of spiritual growth. Moreover, Heard was convinced that modern ideologies such as capitalism, Marxism, nationalism and scientism were all conceptual overspecializations of this individualized human consciousness that had arrested man's psychological evolution. By comparison, conceptual unspecialization consisted of man's capacity for adaptation, wonder, curiosity and all-embracing love.

Because modern science provided evidence of man's developing capacity for curiosity and wonder, Heard enthusiastically reported on science in the broadest possible sense, describing the latest discoveries in physics, biology, psychology and anthropology, and speculating on their implications for the future.[13] These implications, asserted Heard, pointed to the underlying development of a new consciousness which, he believed, would be a transcendent super-consciousness. Further, this emerging consciousness, in combination with new discoveries in physics and psychology, could lead to the integration of scientific cosmology with the free and benevolent political and economic orders necessary for constructive social action.[14]

Convinced that religion was the expression of man's capacity for love and proof of the historical quest for psychological wholeness, Heard penned nine books and countless articles on spiritual themes. Consistent with his negative view on the effects of individualized consciousness, he argued in *The Social Substance of Religion* (1931) that the growth of individual consciousness occurs in inverse proportion to the intensity of the psychic field which a social group is able to create. Traditional religion was no longer able to create the necessary psychic field because, equally affected by individualized consciousness, it had become "increasingly intellectual, the approach of a creature who thinks of itself as being nothing but a self-conscious individual to an equally defined self-conscious individual creator, a relationship of bargaining or conversation, almost never of union."[15]

Because traditional religion and the social forces created out of man's individualized consciousness were inappropriate for achieving further progress in the evolution of human consciousness, a new source of creative power had to be tapped. Heard believed that this new source of power, which lay in the subconscious mind and could be awakened by deliberate techniques, was a kind of mysticism or yoga found in religion but also accessible through psychological understanding and conditioning.[16]

Heard's concern for improvement in the human condition was more than academic. As a leading figure in the British interwar peace movement he was increasingly disheartened by the seemingly inevitable drift towards war and the failure of the pacifist movement to capture the mass imagination. From Heard's point of view, war was simply the crudest expression of individual consciousness—the pitting of one's individuality against another's with the provision that only one survive. Thus, if war was essentially a "symptom of a diseased individualized civilization,"[17] the most efficacious preventative required the transformation of individual consciousness. This transformation,

or "new pacifism," as Heard called it,[18] began with proper individual conditioning as prescribed in his book *The Third Morality*; a blend of asceticism,
meditation and good works which Heard termed a "new athleticism."[19]
Unfortunately, while many found Heard's approach novel, few seemed willing to follow the required regimen. Ultimately frustrated with the general
European situation and his inability to influence its outcome, Heard emi-
grated to America in 1937 and took up residence in Southern California.

Heard was entranced with the cosmopolitan diversity of the Los Angeles
area partly because he was convinced that mankind's greatest advances were
nourished by the social and psychological alchemy of such melting pots.
Writing of Los Angeles, his thoughts drifted back two millenia to another
similar place. "There was once a coast curiously like this, when the world
went through its last world crisis. On the Levant, the palestinian coast in
the senescence of the Classical Age, crank religions and fraud cults prolifer-
ated. But there also had risen Stoicism and Christianity and there amid all
the charlantry, emerged the new chemistry. . . . Indeed, it may be that
only out of such a welter of conflicting credulity that profound creation can
arise."[20]

Scoff as we might, there is ample evidence to suggest that Heard
envisioned Southern California as a potential modern Holy Land and, as he
began to attract his own personal following, he increasingly saw himself as
a kind of guru or "neo-brahmin," as he called his version of the modern
spiritual leader.[21] In 1943, with donated funds, Heard purchased a small
ranch at Trabuco Canyon some miles inland from Laguna Beach. Renovated
to look much like a small monastery complete with courtyard, cloisters,
cells, library, refectory and meditation hall, Heard ensconced himself with
a small group of followers for the purpose of training a cohort of neo-
brahmins who would be equipped to reenter the world as modern spiritual
mediators or guides for the perplexed.[22] Heard maintained Trabuco College
(as it was called) until 1949, at which time he reentered the world as a
writer, essayist, lecturer and radio personality. Heard found his audiences
on college campuses, in the congregations of liberal Protestant churches and
among the urbane and cosmopolitan as well as among the troubled and the
disaffected. For the rest of his life, Heard criss-crossed the country winning
friends and outraging others. His audiences were consistently curious, if not
always enthusiastic. Admittedly, his influence was diffuse. Over time, as
biographical detail is fleshed out by additional research, we may learn more
about this intriguing figure. What we do know is sketchy but suggestive.
As Eckard Toy reported some years ago, Heard captured the spiritual imagination of a number of prominent conservatives such as William C. Mullen-
dore, Chairman of the Board of Southern California Edison Company, Henry
and Clare Booth Luce and Robert Greenleaf of AT&T.[23] There is evidence
that Heard not only provided spiritual guidance to such individuals but also
introduced some of them (under his guidance) to the effects of hallucinogenic

drugs. With the personal and financial support of these followers, Heard devoted the remainder of his life to what he called "growing edge" research into such areas as psychotherapy, hallucinogenic drugs and parapsychology. Perhaps not surprisingly, Heard's work brought him to the attention of Michael Murphy and Richard Price, co-founders of the Esalen Institute. Not only was Heard apparently involved in the early formulation of Esalen's unique brand of psychosomatic hygiene, but he occasionally served as an early Esalen seminar leader. Heard's involvement with Esalen was indicative of his interest in a theology of human transformation and in propounding a kind of religious knowledge that was grounded in psychotherapeutic techniques. Although his bombastic style often obscured his message, the core of Heard's belief centered on the notion that a universal religion embracing both the traditions of the East and the West offered the best hope for revitalizing man's evolutionary progress.

In all probability, Heard will be remembered less for his own work than for his influence on other more talented writers, especially Aldous Huxley, whose deserved literary reputation as the preeminent satirist of the 1920s is based on a series of stingingly funny and irreverent early works: *Crome Yellow* (1921), *Those Barren Leaves* (1925), *Point Counter Point* (1928) and *Antic Hay* (1923). The publication of *Brave New World* in 1932 underscored his growing international stature. For the next four years, however, Huxley published little, travelled much, underwent treatments for a variety of physical and psychological ailments and struggled fitfully with his next novel. When *Eyeless in Gaza* finally appeared in 1936, Huxley's readers were puzzled to find a clumsily constructed but nevertheless serious novel about personal morality, spiritual cause and effect, pacifism and mysticism. This was followed by several pacifist works including a widely publicized pamphlet entitled *What Are You Going to Do About It?* (1936), *The Encyclopedia of Pacifism* (1936), a full-length pacifist manifesto, *Ends and Means* (1937) and a host of later works on religious and spiritual topics. Huxley critics have since decried this transformation and, in one degree or another, have denounced it as a betrayal, an example of the wages of cynicism turned cowardly, or worse, a modern intellectual loss of nerve.[24] In general, the portrait of Huxley as a cowardly crank conveniently ignores the mystical elements that are apparent in his early works, especially *Those Barren Leaves*, and appears to be partly based on some degree of nonapproval or displeasure with his later philosophical positions.

Huxley had been introduced to pacifism, as he was to so many other things, by Heard. Initially, his pacifism was a kind of personal humanitarian response to the worsening worldwide political situation. As such, Huxley's early pacifism was largely concerned with customary and pragmatic approaches to peace, including the use of diplomacy and power politics, embargoes and even military intervention on a limited scale. However, as the possibility of war loomed larger each year, the pacifist movement was unable to sustain its support by the use of arguments appealing to practical common sense alone. Soon pacifism became for Huxley, as it did for many others, a kind of creedal position which required an almost religious adherence.[25] In November of 1935 Huxley wrote that pacifism "finally resolves itself into a religious problem—an uncomfortable fact that one must be prepared to face. . . ."[26] A major contributing factor to the change in Huxley's pacifism may have been his exposure to Mahatma Gandhi's principles of nonviolent living. Although Englishmen were well aware of Gandhi and his movement, the acceptance of his principles was effectively impeded by an ingrained British contempt for subject native races.[27] For this reason, the application of Gandhi's nonviolent philosophy to British pacifism had to await reintroduction by two American pacifists, Devere Allen and Richard Gregg. Ironically, Gregg's work on Gandhi became so influential that the integration of spiritual nonviolent principles with British pacifism came to be known as "Greggism" rather than "Gandhi-ism."[28] Although the transcendental principles of "Greggism" were oriental, the optimistic belief that such principles could be used to transform Western culture may have owed some small debt to this American distillation.

Evidence suggests that the exposure to Gandhi's principles of nonviolent living was a contributing factor in Huxley's spiritual transformation. Two of Huxley's pacifist works, the *Encyclopedia of Pacifism* and *Ends and Means*, are filled with descriptions of nonviolent living and examples of nonviolent resistance to evil—what Gregg termed "moral jiu-jitsu" and what Huxley referred to as the "moral equivalent of war." The end results of a life lived in accordance with these principles and practices, Huxley asserted, were the development of the "non-attached" man (as described in *Ends and Means*) and the achievement of a kind of social rejuvenation based on Gandhi's theories of village-scale economic and political activity (Khadar) as advocated by the character of William Propter in *After Many a Summer Dies the Swan* (1939).

Like Heard, Huxley undoubtedly found the deteriorating European situation less than conducive to the development of his ideal "non-attached" man. Thus, in company with Heard, he embarked on an extended lecture tour of America in 1937. Finding the intellectual and cultural eclecticism of southern California much to his liking, he stayed and focused his energies on the further exploration of spiritual and social transformations.

The key to Huxley's brand of social rejuvenation was the ability to live a "non-attached" spiritual life, first described in *Ends and Means* and given further novelistic treatment through characters such as William Propter in *After Many a Summer Dies the Swan* (1939) and Bruno Rontini in *Time Must Have a Stop* (1944). In essence, Huxley insisted that truly good works could only be performed by truly good people. Thus, although he never completely abandoned his interest in spiritually based social transformations, Huxley became increasingly concerned with personal sanctification. This new insistence on a proper internal disposition seemed naive to many. Coupled with his perceived aloofness, his ironic sense of humor and his residence in Los Angeles, some critics came to the conclusion that he had become just another Hollywood spiritual huckster.

The seriousness of Huxley's quest and the quality of his spiritual acuity were vindicated by two insightful religious biographies, *Grey Eminence* (1941) and *The Devils of Loudun* (1952). *Grey Eminence* was the spiritual biography of Francois Leclerc du Tremblay, a seventeenth-century French mystic who served as Richelieu's secretary of state and whose machinations, Huxley asserted, were responsible for unnecessarily prolonging the Thirty Years' War. While the book serves as a general warning against all political action, it expressly cautions against combining religious devotion with exterior political ends. *The Devils of Loudun*, which recounts a documented case of seventeenth-century demonic possession resulting in the *auto-da-fey* of a town priest who was probably guilty of nothing more than being roundly disliked, served to warn of the dangers inherent in practicing intense spiritual disciplines without possessing an adequate psychology. Just as worldly action was likely to be harmful without the proper prerequisite spiritual disposition, so a self-absorbed spiritualism limited by an overly dogmatic world view was equally dangerous.

Perhaps Huxley's most lasting contributions to modern American religious belief revolve around his attempts to explicate the experience of direct awareness of the Godhead. Huxley wrote *The Perennial Philosophy* (1945) not as a coherent statement of his mystical beliefs but as an anthology of mystical thought. Mysticism, or direct intuitive experience of the Godhead, was the only religious approach for those, like himself, whom Huxley described in his novel, *Time Must Have a Stop*, as "not congenitally the members of any organized church, who have found that humanism and blue-domeism are not enough, who are not content to remain in the darkness of spiritual ignorance, the squalor of vice or that other squalor of mere respectability. . . ."[29]

The Perennial Philosophy reportedly sold 23,000 copies within weeks of its American publication.[30] Gai Eaton, who gave the book a negative review, nevertheless noted that the publication of *The Perennial Philosophy* "must have doubled, in the course of a few weeks, the number of people in England and the United States who have some slight interest in Oriental doctrines. . . ."[31] In the Collected Works Edition of Huxley's books, published in England in 1968, sales of *The Perennial Philosophy* were second only to *Brave New World*.[32]

The Perennial Philosophy was distasteful to many critics because of the apparent self-confidence with which Huxley picked and chose among those bits and pieces of historically disparate religious traditions which fit his criteria of significance. Huxley, himself, appeared to have been conscious of the pick-and-choose nature of his approach. "The construction of an all-embracing system of metaphysics, ethics and psychology is a task that can never be accomplished by any single individual, for the sufficient reason that he is an individual with one particular kind of constitution and temperament and therefore capable of knowing only according to the mode of his own being. Hence the advantages inherent in what may be called the anthological approach to truth."[33]

By asserting that the anthological approach to truth was advantageous in understanding mystical experiences, Huxley also implied that different mystical experiences might be equally valid. In fact, he came to recognize any number of trans-personal experiences as potential spiritual aids. Moreover, his long held belief that individual temperament and thought were related to physical traits was reinforced by new physiological discoveries suggesting that thought processes and emotional states were, in part, chemically based. Dietary controls or drugs could be used to correct emotional imbalances as well as to stimulate desirable psychological states. Thus, Huxley concluded, there might be little physiological or psychological difference between drug-induced visions or those of the religious ascetic. It is not my intention to chronicle Huxley's involvement with mind-altering drugs which spanned the last ten years of his life. Taken as a whole, evidence suggests that his involvement was more theoretical than actual.[34] However, Huxley was careful to point out that drug-induced visionary experiences alone constituted an insufficient insight into true mystical wisdom because spiritual knowledge was incomplete unless it was translated into a will to act for good in the world. Perhaps as his final statement on the relationship between spiritual insight and social transformation, he wrote in his last novel, *Island* (1962), that spiritually transformed action could be made to serve as a kind of looking glass through which the unenlightened might begin to perceive a higher level of being.

Huxley was particularly fond of a phrase attributed to the artist Goya, *Aun Apprendo*, "I am still learning." The phrase was characteristic of Huxley's basic intellectual restlessness. Huxley tended to treat religion as a profound curiosity, the value of which lay in its latent ability to transform human existence. The ultimate transformation was the experience of an intuitive mystical union with the Godhead. However, because this transformation itself transcended religion, knowledge and understanding of it could be obtained through any number of ways. Perhaps not surprisingly, several hours before his death, in what was undoubtedly the final experiment in a life of research into the human condition, Huxley, at his own request, was administered a small dosage of LSD.

Heard's and Huxley's role in the pacifist conversion of Christopher Isherwood provided a postscript to their own spiritual transformation. Isherwood had become one of the brightest novelists in a group of young, leftist writers and poets that had come to prominence in the 1930s. In his novels and in several plays (written in collaboration with W. H. Auden) Isherwood captured the literary imagination of the political left by framing his works from the viewpoint of the weak and victimized—those living on the fringes of normal existence. An early advocate of an armed popular front against fascism, Isherwood's pacifist conversion was precipitated by his 1938 trip to China, with Auden, to gather material for a book on the Sino-Japanese War which was later published as *Journey to a War* (1939).

Although the journey to China had been Isherwood's first experience of people actually involved in war, it was the Munich Crisis (occurring exactly at the time of his return) that demonstrated the real possibility that war might actually involve him. By the end of 1938, Isherwood felt a growing disillusionment with politics and acknowledged that he was groping towards some sort of self-realization he could not define but which was, nevertheless, a rejection of power, force and the tyranny of majorities.[35] This realization led to the abandonment of organized political movements and the search for a new set of personal values. Isherwood began his search by leaving England in January 1939, again with Auden. After spending a few months in New York, he headed for Hollywood. As he explained to John Lehmann in London: "I myself am in the most Goddamawful mess. I have discovered what I didn't realize before, or what I wasn't till now, that I am a pacifist. That's one reason why I am going out to Hollywood, to talk with Gerald Heard and Huxley. Maybe I'll flatly disagree with them, but I have to hear their case, stated as expertly as possible. . . ."[36]

Isherwood was initially attracted to Heard's brand of "new pacifism" because of its notion that all pacifists should become psychologically sound, study medicine and practice actual forms of healing in opposition to all the destructive forces loose in the world. Such notions appealed to Isherwood who desperately felt the need for self-discipline and an active style of pacifism.[37] From May through June of 1939, Isherwood met rather intensively with Heard who expounded on the practice of yoga, on the need for spiritual discipline, on mysticism and on God. Heard's spiritual instruction proved to be exciting and provoked Isherwood's curiosity with its non-dualistic view of morality, its non-dogmatic approach to knowledge and its "try it for yourself" attitude towards spiritual discipline. "[W]hat Gerald recommended was a practical mysticism, a do-it-yourself religion which was experimental and empirical. You were on your own, setting forth to find things out for yourself in your individual way."[38]

Finally, Isherwood asked to be introduced to Swami Prabhavananda, of whom both Heard and Huxley had spoken highly. As a result, Isherwood came into contact with the Vedanta Society and the individual who was to have the greatest lasting influence on his subsequent spiritual development. Isherwood's thirty-seven year association with Prabhavananda has been chronicled in his autobiographical memoir, *My Guru and His Disciple* (1980), a remarkable portrayal of a deep, mutually enriching relationship and a testament to Isherwood's fundamental belief in the saving power of human relationships.

Although Isherwood applied for and received conscientious objector status, by the time America entered the war his age disqualified him from any alternative service and left him at loose ends. At Prabhavananda's suggestion, he moved into the Vedanta Center and from 1943 through the end of the war assumed the role of what Isherwood called a "demi-monk." During this time, Isherwood devoted his energy to editing the Vedanta Center's small magazine and assisting Prabhavananda with several English translations of Hindu scriptures including the *Bhagavad-Gita*.

It was during this same period that Somerset Maugham published *The Razor's Edge* (1944), which portrayed a young American's search for enlightenment through Vedanta. After his enlightenment, the hero of the story, Larry, becomes a cab-driving neo-brahmin dispensing transcendental wisdom to all who will listen. It was rumored that Maugham, who had consulted with Isherwood on several aspects of Vedantic philosophy, had also used him as a model for Larry. The fact that Isherwood denied this did nothing to lessen speculation.[39] Public interest was further stimulated by the film version of the book which appeared in 1946, starring Tyrone Power as Larry.[40]

A no less worldly publication than *Time* magazine featured an extended article on Heard, Huxley and Isherwood in its review of Isherwood's translation of the *Bhagavad-Gita*. Featuring a photo of Isherwood with Prabhavananda on the steps of the Vedanta temple in Hollywood, the review observed that Heard, Huxley and Isherwood in company with Maugham and American playwright John van Druten, had created a spiritually-oriented "minor but noteworthy literary movement."[41]

As a novelist, Isherwood tended to view the world in terms of individual perceptions and human interactions. Admittedly less intellectual than Heard or Huxley, Isherwood's beliefs were generally formulated in response to particular persons. Thus his conversion to Vedanta was largely a matter of intuition and feelings, which resulted from his contact and experiences with Huxley, Heard and of course Prabhavananda. Because of these human attachments, Isherwood's conversion was more emotional and tended to focus almost exclusively on the specific belief system that Prabhavananda represented.

In a short article entitled "Hypothesis and Belief," Isherwood attempted to answer the skeptical remonstrances of his more intellectual friends.[42] In this essay, he observes that when any member of the intellectual class becomes affiliated with a set of religious beliefs, he is immediately forced to deal with his skeptical friends who either mock him, express curiosity or open hostility or sympathetically mourn the new believer's loss of all critical faculties. The convert, rather self-consciously, either becomes quietly retiring, openly evangelical or remains as he always has been and thereby shocks his friends who expect a demonstration of virtue equal to that of the greatest saint. In any case, the convert must always expect his friends to ask, "Do you really believe all that?" and the answer will always be, "No, not yet." He will answer this way, Isherwood wrote, because the very meaning of "belief" involves its validation through experience. Until any convert reaches this point, all of his new-found religious teachings are merely hypotheses. In this way, the intellectual convert retains the same degree of skepticism and discrimination as his more "scientific" friends. While the scientist validates his hypotheses via the testimony of his instruments and laboratory findings, the convert verifies his hypotheses via the testimony of all the great religious figures in history. Just as you would assent to your doctor's remedy, argued Isherwood, so you should at least attempt to follow the hypotheses of the world's great religious teachers. If at the end of three or four years no improvement has been realized, then you are entitled to discard it all as a worthless placebo.

Despite his discomfort with the more Indian aspects of the Vedanta Society, Isherwood never found reason to cast off his new beliefs. Vedanta appealed to Isherwood because it was morally non-dualistic and theologically nonexclusive. Isherwood characterized Vedanta as a kind of "algebra," a way of grouping religions in general, of isolating their variables and relating them to each other.[43] That algebra was the key to its nonexclusiveness. Vedanta offered its adherents a choice of paths to choose from in order to realize one's true self. Echoing Huxley, Isherwood wrote that it was all "a matter of psycho-physical type . . . more than anything else, which religion you choose."[44]

Having chosen Vedanta, Isherwood found himself engaged in the attempt to merge his religious beliefs with his fiction. His results with the religious novel were mixed. On several occasions, he portrayed his own spiritual dilemmas. These appear in his more autobiographical works such as *Prater Violet* (1945), *Down There on a Visit* (1962) and most recently, *My Guru and His Disciple* (1980). In addition to these, he also completed three "constructed" novels, *The World in the Evening* (1954), *A Single Man* (1964) and *A Meeting by the River* (1967), which made its way to the stage. Of these, *A Single Man* may be Isherwood's best.

A Single Man is about a day in the life of George, an aged, homosexual Anglo-American literature professor. George is fighting desperately to retain his physical, intellectual and emotional vitality in the face of his own aging and inevitable mortality. In spite of his fear of death, George is determined to cling to life and to transcend the loneliness that is the consequence of individualized consciousness. George does this by attempting to establish a deep personal link with one of his students. At the end of the day, in a dream sequence, George experiences a kind of mystical consciousness which he taps in sleep. "[O]ver George and the others in sleep come the waters of that other ocean—that consciousness which is no one in particular but which contains everyone and everything, past, present and future, and extends unbroken beyond the uttermost stars."[45] The success of the book lies in that George's dilemmas are not only real but also modern; and in a modern age which allows little time for contemplation, the suggestion that spiritual insights are purely intuitive, perhaps even dreamlike, lends a sense of credibility to the work.

Much of the interest in the religious thought of Heard, Huxley and Isherwood was undoubtedly due to its unique blending of mystical and modern empirical elements. Like modern researchers, the three men approached their religious investigations with a good deal of skepticism. Religious experiences and spiritual claims were continuously subjected to rational or scientific validation. Thus metaphysics and cosmology were measured against the discoveries of modern physics and astronomy; religious institutions and symbol systems were analyzed in the light of modern anthropological findings; and personal religious experiences were understood in psychological terms. This blend of the religious and the empirical was as attractive to many as it was repellent to others.

It will always be difficult to assess adequately the influence exerted on modern American spiritual belief by Heard, Huxley and Isherwood. The very meaning of the word "influence" denotes the power to effect change through indirect or imperceptible means. Thus the evidence of influence is more often than not merely suggestive and seldom conclusive. Perhaps the volume of skeptical and sometimes virulent attacks on the work of the three has been indicative (albeit in a negative way) of the influence they were perceived to have exerted on American thought and culture. Because Isherwood was primarily concerned with the novel, he was spared much of the ideological criticism that was directed at Heard and Huxley. Nevertheless, the non-Western religious themes woven into Isherwood's novels have tempted some to dismiss his work as merely curious. Huxley, in particular, has been criticized both for his oversimplification of mystical and oriental doctrines and for his alleged popular advocacy of psychedelic drugs. Ironically, both Huxley and Heard ultimately advocated a kind of spiritual aristocracy that reserved the most intense spiritual experiences for those who were intelligent and well-bred enough to truly benefit from them.

It is becoming increasingly clear that significant numbers of Americans now exhibit religious preferences and beliefs that incorporate many elements of the "layman's religion." The impetus for this modern spiritual eclecticism can be traced to several sources, including increased exposure to Asian culture and philosophy. But in the early part of the latter half of the twentieth century, the work of Gerald Heard, Aldous Huxley and Christopher Isherwood played a noteworthy role in introducing American reading audiences to the problems of modern spiritual belief and the possibility of constructing a highly individualized and syncretic religious response.

Notes

1. Baumer, *Religion and the Rise of Skepticism* (New York, 1960), 225. Baumer credits Arthur Koestler with coining these two terms.

2. Arthur Koestler, *The Yogi and the Commissar and Other Essays* (New York, 1946), 4.

3. Ibid., 13.

4. See the editorial statement, "Religion and the Intellectuals," *Partisan Review* 27 (February 1950), 103. The resulting written symposium appeared in the February, March, April and May-June issues of 1950.

5. "From Time into Eternity," *The Saturday Review* (2 September 1944), 8.

6. See Baumer's *Religion and the Rise of Skepticism*, especially Chapter 5, "A Layman's Religion."

7. Ibid., 273.

8. The phrase was used by Aldous Huxley as the title of an article in 1944 and formed the basis of his 1945 study of mysticism, *The Perennial Philosophy* (1945; rpt. New York, 1970).

9. Use of the terms "heterodox" and "individualistic" in characterizing the main thrust of modern intellectual thought is found in Samuel Hynes, *The Auden Generation* (New York, 1977).

10. Nigel Nicolson, ed., *Diaries and Letters of Harold Nicolson* (New York, 1967), II, 87.

11. Ibid., 153.

12. Gerald Heard, *The Ascent of Humanity* (New York, 1929), 9.

13. In addition to his role as a scientific commentator with the BBC, Heard wrote several books of popular science including: *This Surprising World, A Journalist Looks at Science* (1932), *Science in the Making* (1935), *Science Front, 1936* (1936), *Exploring the Stratosphere* (1936) and *Is Another World Watching? The Riddle of the Flying Saucers* (1951).

14. Gerald Heard, *The Emergence of Man* (London, 1931), 298.

15. Gerald Heard, *The Source of Civilization* (London, 1935), 17.

16. Ibid., 18–20.

17. Gerald Heard, "The Significance of the New Pacifism," in Gerald K. Hibbert, ed., *The New Pacifism* (1935; rpt. New York, 1972), 17.

18. Ibid., 22.

19. *The Third Morality* (New York, 1937), 295.

20. Gerald Heard, "California," *Enquiry* (April, 1950), 29.

21. For a full discussion of the "neo-brahmin" see Gerald Heard, *Pain, Sex and Time* (New York, 1939).

22. Much more remains to be learned about Heard's associations during this period. Significantly, Alan Watts, a popularizer of oriental philosophy in his own right, received an early introduction to the subject in the 1940s from Heard, Huxley, Isherwood and Prabhavananda. Watts also spent some time with Heard at Trabuco College. See Alan Watts, *In My Own Way* (New York, 1973), 208.

23. Eckhard Toy, "The Conservative Connection: The Chairman of the Board Took LSD Before Timothy Leary," *American Studies*, 21 (Fall, 1980), 65–77.

24. See Donald Watt, ed., *Aldous Huxley, The Critical Heritage* (London, 1976), and Jerome Meckier, "Mysticism or Misty Schism? Huxley Studies Since World War II," *The British Studies Monitor*, 5 (1974), 165–177. Meckier notes that most Huxley critics have relied on some form of the "two Huxley theory" which is based on the notion that the Huxley of the early novels and the Huxley of the later spiritual works are irreconcilable. Huxley's harshest critics have charged that his fall was attributable to a failure of nerve, to his aloofness and to his gullibility.

25. There are two excellent studies of the religious overtones in the pacifist movement: Joyce Berkman, "Transformations in Pacifist Consciousness in England, 1914–1939," in W. Warren Wagar, ed., *The Secular Mind: Transformations of Faith in Modern Europe* (New York, 1982); and Martin Ceadel, *Pacifism in Britain 1914–1945: The Defining of a Faith* (Oxford, 1980).

26. "To Victoria Ocampo," 19 November 1935, Letter 389, Grover Smith, ed., *Letters of Aldous Huxley* (London, 1969), 398.

27. Isherwood recognized this same feeling in himself when he first became attracted to Vedantic religion. See Christopher Isherwood, *An Approach to Vedanta* (Hollywood, California, 1963), 35.

28. Martin Ceadel provides an excellent history of the British pacifist movement in *Pacifism in Britain 1914–1945*.

29. Aldous Huxley, *Time Must Have a Stop* (New York, 1944), 294.

30. This figure is reported by Sybille Bedford in *Aldous Huxley, A Biography* (New York, 1974), 446.

31. *The Richest Vein* (London, 1949), 167.

32. Watt, 478–79.

33. Huxley, *The Perennial Philosophy*, 153.

34. According to Huxley's second wife Laura Archera Huxley, he had only about ten or twelve drug-induced psychedelic experiences over the ten-year period of his experimentation. Huxley critics have charged that Huxley's published works *The Doors of Perception* (New York, 1954), and "Drugs That Shape Men's Minds," *Saturday Evening Post*, 18 October 1958, were irresponsible and had a pernicious effect on impressionable young readers.

35. Isherwood, *An Approach to Vedanta*, 11–12.

36. Quoted by John Lehmann, *The Whispering Gallery* (New York, 1955), 330.

37. Isherwood, *An Approach to Vedanta*, 16.

38. Ibid., 23.

39. Isherwood's denial was contained in a letter to the editor, *Time*, 17 December, 1945, 4.

40. Several years later, Power met with Gerald Heard to discuss his own interest in Vedanta which had been stimulated by his research for the role of Larry in the film. "Mrs. Fritz to Gerald Heard," 13 August 1951. Box 29, Folder 1. Gerald Heard Papers. University of California at Los Angeles.

41. "Universal Cult," *Time*, 12 February 1945, 96.

42. Christopher Isherwood, "Hypothesis and Belief," *Vedanta and the West*, 7 (1944), 87–91.

43. Christopher Isherwood, "Discovering Vedanta," *Twentieth Century* (Fall, 1961), 70.

44. Ibid.

45. Christopher Isherwood, *A Single Man* (New York, 1964), 155–56.

Life as Time's Fool: Time in Aldous Huxley's Novels

Barry Leal

In the first of two survey articles written in the early nineteen-seventies, Jerome Meckier remarks that Huxley criticism lacks studies on a number of important themes. He lists three in particular, among them 'the functions of time in [Huxley's] novels and philosophy'.[1] By 1972, when Meckier's article was published, the question of time in Huxley had indeed received scant attention. In the nineteen-fifties Margaret Church had contributed two short articles[2] on the subject, both limiting themselves to dealing with time as a philosophic concept. Most of Church's attention is directed to contrasting the concept of 'clock time' espoused by Huxley with the relativistic psychological approaches to time adopted by Marcel Proust and Virginia Woolf. Research by the present writer suggests that, since Church's articles, no other analyses have been attempted. The subject has received some mention in several monographs,[3] but there has been no systematic study, however brief.

Meckier's suggestion about the need to study the theme of time in Huxley is made in the context of an article that stresses the unity of the various stages in Huxley's career. 'Despite constant change', asserts Meckier, 'the later developments are visible from the start, while the scepticism and satire of the early novels never vanish' (166). As we shall see in the present article, the truth of Meckier's assertion receives clear confirmation from an analysis of the theme of time in Huxley, especially when the unifying element is seen as the concept of 'life as time's fool'. Huxley's preoccupation with the concept,[4] drawn from Shakespeare's *Henry IV, Part 1*, is obvious in the last twenty or so years of his life as he actively pursues the means of loosening time's hold on life. It is, however, also inherent in the satire and experimentation with time of the earlier novels.

Time is the dominant emphasis in the first short chapter of *Crome Yellow*. Denis Stone, though rather a misfit in the group he is to join at the

Reprinted with permission from the *Journal of the Australian Universities Modern Language Association* 70 (1988): 276–95.

country house, is distressed at the unfilled time he is spending in the train that 'creep[s] indolently forward'.[5] 'It was two hours cut clean out of his life, two hours in which he might have done so much, so much—written the perfect poem, for example, or read the one illuminating book' (1). Time is construed as having an existence independent of man, whose life must be subjugated to it if the possibilities it contains are to be fully grasped. Indeed, the extent to which Denis Stone has made life subservient to time is seen in the fact that his last reflexion before the train stops is that he has no reason for claiming a right to be alive. His life has come to have no inherent value.

Misfit though Denis Stone is in the society of Crome Yellow, his initial attitudes nevertheless announce the ways of thinking of his friends, in particular Ivor Lombard. A creature of time, exploiting every passing moment, fearful lest one instant should escape his grasp, and bereft of firm beliefs or values, Ivor Lombard is 'forever moving, restlessly and rapidly' (107). He spends his summers rushing from one invitation to another, making quick but unenduring amorous conquests and dazzling his hosts with his brilliant but superficial wit. It is significant that he should attribute his need to leave Crome Yellow to the demands of 'Hard fate!' (149), a synonym for Time, to which he has manifestly subjected himself.

Similar emphases are found in *Antic Hay*, the very title announcing the pointless, often ludicrous, activity engaged in by the characters to be presented. In the text, Shearwater pedalling his exercise bicycle and Gumbril with Myra Viveash driving about London without any clear destination in mind provide perhaps the best examples of this activity. Of these characters Myra Viveash is most subject to the demands of time and activity, starkly revealing the emptiness that such an attitude brings. Early in the novel she is pictured as laughing 'expiringly from her inward death bed'[6] with her eyes having 'a formidable capacity for looking and expressing nothing' (59). Moreover, her penultimate remark in the novel indicates her own consciousness of the bankruptcy she has discovered in a life lived within the narrow confines of time, which, like the river she is watching, 'flow[s] darkly past' (354). The dominance of time over life and the deleterious effects it produces are further suggested by the image: 'Like time the river flowed, staunchlessly, as though from a wound in the world's side' (253). Frantic activity has emptied life of its vitality.

As its title suggests, absence of vitality is also a feature of Huxley's third novel of the nineteen-twenties, *Those Barren Leaves*. For Calamy, the would-be mystic in this novel, the general social activity of the group he frequents lacks any definite direction, being characterized as 'futile noise and bustle'.[7] The clearest example of this is to be found in his hostess, Mrs. Aldwinkle. 'Perpetually haunted by the fear that she was missing something' (16) and anxious lest the moment will elude her when 'the secret of the Universe' (63) is unexpectedly revealed, Mrs. Aldwinkle resists surrendering time to such barren activities as sleep and meditation. Rather does she pursue with an increasingly desperate sense of urgency the thoughts and words of her guests as she searches for ill-defined illumination. Calamy comes to consider her, along with most members of her group, as a water beetle 'scampering [. . .] across the invisible skin of depths' (341). For him, on the other hand, it is 'necessary to think, necessary to break through and sink into the depths' (341). Such a search for profundity leads Calamy at the close of the novel to reject his society's subservience to time. In doing so he becomes the first character in Huxley's fiction clearly to reject contemporary social norms. His remark to Mary Thriplow that 'within the atom there is neither space nor time' (344–5) may in fact be seen as indicating the reality independent of time to which he aspires.

Written at a period when Huxley's thought was being strongly influenced by Lawrence, *Point Counter Point* contains only a limited number of references specifically to time. However, the theme of the hidden depths of life, introduced by Calamy in *Those Barren Leaves*, receives extensive and developed treatment. What was for Calamy incomprehensible, mysterious and obscure in life is for Philip Quarles astonishingly complex and rich. Although time and habit have made him morally insensitive, taking the 'wrongness out of almost all the acts he had once thought sinful',[8] he has retained a consciousness that 'every object and event contains within itself an infinity of depths within depths' (301). With Philip Quarles, Calamy's protest against a life that is directed by time-determined fashions and prejudices becomes much more clearly focused and expressed. What he seeks above all is to avoid superficial and partial views of reality and to attain to one that is comprehensive:

'Each sees [. . .] a different aspect of the event, a different layer of reality. What I want to do is to look with all those eyes at once. With religious eyes, scientific eyes, economic eyes, *homme moyen sensuel* eyes . . .' (266)

The Lawrence-inspired figure of Rampion has a similar but differently expressed ideal of the comprehensive, together with a violent antipathy towards the path of technological progress along which modern society is rushing. Railing against modern notions of progress in time, he pleads for his ideal of 'a real complete man or woman' (418), a timeless ideal which he insists must be kept completely separate from the inordinate sense of haste that governs modern life.

Viewed from the perspective of the writer's preoccupation with time, *Point Counter Point* marks the end of a particular period in Huxley's thought. The novels of the nineteen-twenties are principally novels of satirical social portrayal, in which attitudes to time play an important part. We have seen that the protests raised against these attitudes, expressed at first tentatively through Calamy, then with greater conviction in Philip Quarles and Rampion, grow in intensity. They do, however, prove largely ineffective and remain voices crying in the wilderness of contemporary society. The novels of the thirties and beyond, on the other hand, carry preoccupation with time beyond protest against inadequate attitudes and show a desire to experiment with time. In them one finds not just satire of society and isolated protest but also an effort to transcend in some striking and imaginative fashion the early vision of life as time's fool. The first examples of this experimentation are to be found in *Brave New World* and *Eyeless in Gaza*.

One of the outstanding successes achieved by the conditioning processes described in *Brave New World* is to make people believe that they are benefiting from 'progress' in their society while at the same time depriving them almost totally of any valid standard of comparison. '[. . .] progress *is* lovely, isn't it',[9] Lenina Crowne unthinkingly asserts, producing a response conditioned by 'five hundred repetitions once a week from thirteen to seventeen' (82). Although she visits the Reservation in Mexico to learn what society was like in pre-Fordian days, comparison becomes impossible through the effects of prior conditioning, soma, and the inordinately squalid conditions of the Reservation's inhabitants. Despite its conditioned belief in progress, the society of which Lenina is a product is one in which time is frozen, any independent thought of past or future and any criticism of present society being strongly discouraged. 'Was and will make me ill [. . .] I take a gramme and only am' (86), says Lenina as she swallows her soma. In a society in which comfort and happiness have replaced truth and beauty (187) there is no reason or room for any perspective on time to be sought. Time as a concept has been deprived of any relevance and the population is locked into an unchanging social situation believed to be incomparably good.

The extent of the irrelevance of any concept of time outside the present is seen in the success achieved in arresting the aging process. Not only do the inhabitants of *Brave New World* live in an unchanging society; each one also lives in an unchanging body, which continues in its youthful state until death suddenly strikes at the age of sixty. 'We keep their internal secretions artificially balanced at a youthful equilibrium', explains Bernard, '[. . .] and then crack! the end.' (90–91). In such a situation the future is inconceivable, while the past is at best irrelevant and at worst dangerous.

What Huxley has done in this cautionary tale of science fiction is to extrapolate the already unacceptably limiting attitudes towards time held by his own society. The earlier novels had illustrated clearly enough life's subservience to limited views of the present in Britain of the nineteen-twenties. Now, in the frozen stability of the twenty-sixth century, the dominance of the untranscended present is absolute, and many of the logical consequences of twentieth century attitudes are revealed. The works of Shakespeare, the Bible and other literary monuments of the past are considered subversive and mere reference to the past is viewed with intense disapproval. It is significant that one of the discoveries which is made by John the Savage but which remains inaccessible to those that are 'civilized' is that of 'Time' (113).

Eyeless in Gaza, published some four years after *Brave New World*, presents experimentation with time in a somewhat different fashion. The lack of respect for the chronological order of events is the most obvious experimental technique employed, but there are numerous other investigations of problems associated with time that receive rather more subtle emphasis. They contribute to the gradual elaboration of a philosophy that for Huxley will ultimately lead to at least a partial liberation of life from the constrictions of time.

The preoccupation of Anthony Beavis with time is stressed in the very first pages of the novel. His contemplation of snapshots from early in the century induces him initially to reflect upon changing fashions, and he notes in particular the disparity between the rather absurd reality now presented by the snapshot and the delicate emotional reaction that he has retained towards those depicted. His concern with the relationship between historical and psychological visions of reality leads on the one hand to a note that progress can never be actually experienced by one human being and on the other to an attack on Proust, pictured as 'for ever squatting in the tepid bath of his remembered past'.[10] Proust's retrieval of the past is not regarded by Anthony Beavis as in any sense a liberation from the present, but rather as continued subservience to time. 'I would wish my days to be separated each from each by unnatural impiety' (9), he remarks to Helen Ledwidge. Whereas *Brave New World* may be considered as a vigorous protest against an uncritically accepted present, *Eyeless in Gaza*, through the character of Anthony Beavis and through its structure, aspires, albeit tentatively, to a liberation from time itself.[11]

Later chapters of the novel treat this theme of liberation from time, but frequently from a more generalized social perspective and in a manner which tends to lead to an outlook of black pessimism. In a chapter which bears the same date as the first chapter, August 30th, 1933, Anthony Beavis, reading his diary, finds himself still obliged to agree that the history of society is in fact a history of successive slaveries, imposed in the name of a quest for freedom. His reluctant conclusion is that man's situation in time is such that he is bound to one servitude or another, and this not just on a social level, but also in his personal life. For Beavis 'five words sum up every biography: *Video meliora proboque; deteriora sequor*' (12). This moral emphasis is, moreover, reinforced at the end of the novel when Anthony Beavis reflects that 'Evil [. . .] is the condition of life, the condition of being aware, of knowing what is good and beautiful' (615).

The approach taken to time in *Eyeless in Gaza* is consequently much broader in scope than in the earlier novels. Treatment of specific historical situations gives way to reflexions on time of the most general nature, and, in common with certain other writers of that turbulent period in European politics, Huxley reflects upon the nature of 'the human condition', most specifically in connection with the question of time. Despite the general gloom of Beavis's reflexions on the subject, there are some glimmers of hope, perceived principally through the first of Huxley's 'ideal' figures, James Miller M.D., who appears to have succeeded in ordering his life in accordance with principles properly regarded as independent of external circumstances. Miller stresses 'progress, not only as a citizen, a machine-minder and machine-user, but also as a human being' (220). True progress, as Huxley is to assert later in *Ends and Means* (1937), is moral progress,[12] which cannot be imposed from without. In one of the last chapters of the novel Beavis in fact goes further and suggests that moral progress needs a religious basis, his remarks foreshadowing at one point (chapter 50) Huxley's work of a decade later, *The Perennial Philosophy*. Liberation from the domination of time-conditioned values has come to be found in some form of religious belief.

The assertion by Anthony Beavis at the end of *Eyeless in Gaza* that 'Evil [. . .] is the condition of life' is central to Huxley's next novel *After Many a Summer*. The second of Huxley's 'ideal' figures, Mr. Propter, identifies time as 'the medium in which evil lives and outside of which it dies'[13] and even goes on to claim that 'time is evil' (106). Believing, in consequence, that good is located outside of time, he pursues his quest for 'psychological eternity' (105), a timeless inner experience of good that remains independent of, but not without effect upon, the processes of the world of time. The only 'good act' that Propter is prepared to admit is one which contributes towards liberation from the evil of the temporal.

These views of Propter, which in many ways are indicated to be close to those of the author, are recognizably gnostic in tone and substance, and do in fact suggest to the scholarly Jeremy Pordage 'the worst kind of theology' (106). However, Propter's scholarship and moral rectitude command considerable respect among those whom he frequents and prevent his views from being dismissed out of hand. Even more impressive than these moral and scholarly achievements is the fact that Propter is described as 'disinterestedly friendly, at once serene and powerful, gentle and strong, self-effacing and yet intensely *there*, more present, so to speak, radiating more life than anyone else' (122). Ironically perhaps, Propter's location of good as being *outside* time has served to relate him more effectively to life in time than is the case with those who never seek to transcend the temporal in their search for meaning. In that respect he is clearly in the lineage of James Miller, the active pacifist of *Eyeless in Gaza*. This theme of the beneficent effects of the mystic on day-to-day living is to become, moreover, a constant emphasis in Huxley's later writing.[14]

Despite his professed religious belief, Jo Stoyte, whose ostentatiously displayed wealth is responsible for bringing the characters of the novel together, is pathologically obsessed by his own mortality. His desperate search for longevity, through the experimentation of the scientist Obispo and the researches of Pordage, contrasts neatly with Propter's concept of 'psychological eternity' and allows Huxley not only to poke fun at the notion of automatic progress in time but also to present an extreme case of a man who has allowed his life to become completely subject to time. The discovery in England of the foetal apes that the Fifth Earl of Gonister and his house-keeper have become after living for some two hundred years not only shows the vanity and stupidity of clinging to lives uninformed by values outside time but also suggests that the physical life of the individual is essentially a process of degradation rather than improvement. The discovery tends to confirm many of the contentions of Propter and illuminates his earlier state-ment that 'the longer you live, the more evil you automatically come into contact with' (108). The echoing of Obispo's laughter in the underground chamber is a fitting commentary not just on Jo Stoyte's quest for longevity but also on the futility of the scientist's research. Both have been the fools of time.

Time Must Have a Stop is the first of Huxley's novels to refer specifically to time in its title. It is also the first to quote the passage from Shakespeare's *Henry IV, Part 1* which contains both the novel's title and the concept of life as time's fool:

> But thought's the slave of life, and life time's fool,
> And time, which takes survey of all the world,
> Must have a stop.[15]

Towards the end of the novel Sebastian Barnack gives an illuminating com-mentary on this passage, and through his words Huxley's developing views on time receive their clearest expression.

Huxley claims that the initial contention of the passage that thought is the slave of life has received considerable recognition and attention in the twentieth century from 'Bergson and the Pragmatists, Adler and Freud, the Dialectical Materialism boys and the Behaviourists' (291). The other two statements, however, which he sees as containing ethical and metaphysical dimensions, have been neglected, and at enormous cost to society and the individual. It is in this context that Huxley launches a savage attack on the deliberate subjugation of the present to the future by the major ideologies of his time. Faith in the Future, 'the only faith of a majority of twentieth-century Europeans and Americans' (291), is held responsible for untold misery as it sacrifices the possibility of present happiness to an ideal distant in time.[16] Equally as unacceptable as worship of the past, idolatries of future time perpetuate and reinforce the subjugation of life to time. 'Before or behind, time can never be worshipped with impunity' (292).

The title of the novel, however, refers to the third statement in the Shakespeare quotation and it is this metaphysical emphasis that attracts most attention. The ramifications of 'time [. . .] must have a stop' are seen both in certain of the novel's theoretical statements in the notebooks of Sebastian Barnack, and in the experience of his uncle, Eustace Barnack. Through them Huxley contends that for those who choose to consider time as an absolute, whether in the present, past or future, life will necessarily be relegated to the role of fool. Liberation from foolishness in time comes only when one seeks a timeless, metaphysical dimension. As Sebastian expresses it: 'the life of the spirit is life out of time, life in its essence and eternal principle' (276), and somewhat later 'the divine Ground is a timeless reality' (292). His uncle's attitudes in life and death show that for him these realities remained quite inaccessible.

Eustace Barnack's life is an illustration of his nephew's reflexion that 'the habit of sensuality and pure aestheticism is a process of God-proofing. To indulge in it is to become a spiritual mackintosh, shielding the little corner of time, of which one is the centre, from the least drop of eternal reality' (284). Prematurely aged, his face betrays the life of self-indulgence he has led: 'the face was like a loose rubber mask sagging from the bones, flabby and soft and unwholesomely blotched' (38). In a life given over to sensuality and art he is incapable of serious conversation. Typically, he dies of a heart attack following a bout of eating and drinking.

The aspect of *Time Must Have a Stop* that has most disconcerted critics because of its unexpected and experimental nature is the description of Eustace's *post mortem* experience.[17] Eustace is aware that the sense of time and individuality to which he has always clung and which he has taken with him into death is alien to the penetrating brilliance of the light that appears and promises 'an eternity of joy' (138). However, he is unable to renounce it, even though he is now aware that it brings with it an increasingly intolerable sense of absence. He glimpses 'eternities of the insatiable, despairing knowledge of absence within absence, everywhere, always, in an existence of only one dimension' (137). Through several chapters, interposed among those that treat the world of the living, the dead Eustace ponders this one-dimensional existence in time, and eventually, despite the continuing consciousness of absence, chooses to keep 'his little property of memories and images. To treasure and enjoy them interminably—to enjoy them to the point of identification, to the point of being transubstantiated into them' (156). For him existence within the limitations of time is preferable to the 'crystal of luminous silence [. . .] shining in all the interstices of the jagged laughter' (227) of the universe. His ultimate fate is consistent with his acceptance of life as time's fool.[18]

The importance to Huxley of *Time Must Have a Stop* is well known[19] and its association of morality, mysticism and time indicates the direction his thought is to take in succeeding years. The first clear example of this direction is his erudite philosophical and theological work *The Perennial Philosophy* (1946), which introduces two important concepts on which the author is to base his thought for the rest of his life. The first is 'the Order of Things', which is given specific fictional expression in *Ape and Essence*; the second is 'the Eternal Present', which, allied with the concept of grace, constitutes the major emphasis of Huxley's second last novel, *The Genius and the Goddess*. The two concepts combine to provide philosophical underpinning to the social system of Pala in *Island*. Taken together they have clear theological implications which, in the postwar years, give a particular emphasis to Huxley's continuing reflexions on the subject of time.

Ape and Essence is Huxley's second novelistic excursion into the future. Written some sixteen years after *Brave New World*, it presents a vision of the future that takes into account the events of this intervening period, notably the rise of national-socialism, the Second World War, and especially the dropping of the atomic bomb.[20] It is consequently scarcely surprising that the picture of society painted in *Ape and Essence* should be so uniformly depressing.

In a sense *Ape and Essence* pursues and generalizes the fate of the fifth Earl of Gonister and his housekeeper in *After Many a Summer*.[21] It does this in two ways: the 'ape-mind' has become dominant in what remains of Californian society; and apes have themselves taken over many of the activities of this society, being found particularly in positions of power. The contrast with *Brave New World* could scarcely be greater: though both situations document and attempt to eliminate through the course of time what is specifically human, this occurs in one novel through advances in psycho-chemical conditioning and in the other through a reversion to bestiality before and after a nuclear war. *Brave New World* and *Ape and Essence* present two different but possible scenarios for a future produced by what passes for technological progress. Together they form Huxley's most vigorous fictional attack not only on the directions being taken by technology, but also on the very concept of automatic progress in time.

In *Ape and Essence* Huxley's attack on the inevitability of progress in time is consistently mediated by a stress on 'the Order of Things'. Reference to this concept dear to *The Perennial Philosophy* is found as early as the introductory chapter entitled 'Tallis', where the narrator states his belief that Gandhi had been killed 'because he tried to bring us back to the concrete and cosmic facts of real people and the inner Light'.[22] Shortly afterwards, at the beginning of 'The Script', the Narrator warns the audience 'Somehow you must be reminded / Be induced to remember, / Be implored to be willing to / Understand what's What' (25). The Ape social system in California, continuing the tendencies of its pre-nuclear-war counterpart when all sense of reality came to be lost (93), refuses such understanding. As in *Brave New World*, it undertakes a largely successful campaign of repression of what is human, represented most dramatically and most provocatively by the 'NO' patches worn by women most of the year.

There is, however, an underlying confidence in this novel expressed through both the protagonist Poole and the Narrator that, though access to 'the Order of Things' may be hindered by this 'progress' of society in time, it is always available to the individual and hence remains independent of the passage of time. In the last pages of the novel Poole assures Loola: 'Whatever Belial may have done with the rest of the world, you and I can always work with the Order of Things, not against' (148). It is a measure of Huxley's despondency with the state of postwar society that the most productive protest he imagines against society's madness is expressed solely in individualistic terms.

The largely atemporal nature of humanity's moral tendencies is further emphasized in the novel by the introduction into the narrative of Belial and 'the Other One' (138) as personal forces encouraging man in one direction or the other. Poole's statements expressing confidence in the eternity of the Order of Things as well as his faith in its Maintainer are counterbalanced by the Arch-Vicar's exclamation: 'Progress! I tell you, that was too rare an invention to have been the product of any merely human mind—too fiendishly ironical! There had to be Outside Help for that. There had to be the Grace of Belial, which, of course, is always forthcoming [. . .]' (93). Experience of Californian society early in the 22nd century does in fact induce Poole to modify his enlightened 'Liberal-Protestant' (146) views on the existence of the Devil and see in much more traditionally religious and a-historical terms the powers competing for man's allegiance. It is interesting to reflect that the first view of California by the passengers on the *Canterbury*, the exploratory ship from New Zealand, is that of three oil derricks 'silhouetted against the sky, like the equipment of a modernized and more efficient Calvary' (35).

As in his previous writing, Huxley suggests—though with much less emphasis and conviction—that life in time, unilluminated by a vision of the extra-temporal Order of Things, tends towards degradation.[23] The Arch-Vicar reminds Poole that 'from the second century onwards no orthodox Christian believed that a man could be possessed by God [. . . .] He could only be possessed by the Devil' (95). There is nothing in modern history that enables Poole to refute the validity of this belief.

Huxley's short novel *The Genius and the Goddess*, published in 1955, may be described as a meditation on the idea of grace, which is conceived as a divine gift enabling the recipient to live a fuller, more satisfying life. However, the events of the story, as well as the words of the protagonist, John Rivers, broaden the concept of grace from something narrowly 'religious' to a quality that includes every aspect of life. 'Spiritual grace, animal grace, human grace—three aspects of the same underlying mystery; ideally all of us should be open to all of them',[24] says John Rivers, commenting on the extraordinarily beneficent effects of his sleeping with Katy Maartens. In discovering that 'love may be chosen as the instrument of divine intervention'

(98), Rivers also discovers the importance of the Present, since it is only in present time that the Eternal can manifest itself.

The theme of the Eternal Present—the sense of eternity in the present moment—is drawn to the reader's attention at the very outset of the novel. As in the first pages of *Eyeless in Gaza*, pre-occupation with the past is vigorously attacked. Reminiscence is classified by John Rivers as 'a dangerous drug' (9). This lesson is mediated to Rivers by the two women in his life: by his wife Helen who 'knew how to live—to live now and here for the greater glory of God' (10), and by Katy Maartens, who had, in a sense, used him sexually as a channel for grace to flow. Indeed, the relationship with Katy Maartens, at least in its initial stages, is construed by Rivers as a form of protest against the inexorable passage of time, which destroys life rather than bringing to it a creative impulse. As Katy Maartens enters John Rivers's room in desperate need of solace, time is described as 'bleeding away' (88), and the chimes of a distant clock become 'a man-made insult added gratu-itously to a cosmic injury—a symbol of time's incessant passage, a reminder of the inevitable end' (88). Eternity, however, expresses itself creatively in the present through direct experience, on this occasion through intense sensuality. A little earlier in the novel John Rivers, almost certainly having in mind his later experience with Katy Maartens, had made a rather impas-sioned plea that the eternal quality of the 'isness' (45) of persons and things be recognized. 'At every instant every transience is eternally that transience' (46), he proclaims, utterly opposing Goethe's Platonic contention that '*Alles vergängliche ist ein Gleichnis*' (46).[25]

The diverse elements in this short fictional apology for the transitory— for the here and now—make it rather more than a mere variation on the traditional theme of *carpe diem*. Behind the attitude proposed are both the long reflexion on mystics set down in *The Perennial Philosophy* and a psychology of religion that invades the vocabulary of almost every page. John Rivers himself states that 'the uprush from within of something strong and wonderful, something that's manifestly greater than yourself' (98) can be expressed only in the vocabulary of the theological (98), and he does not hesitate to use terms like 'soul', 'devils', 'predestination', as well as stressing, as we have noted, concepts of 'grace' and 'God'. Moreover, to underline the spiritual importance of the here and now Rivers has recourse to the Old Testament to quote 'God's own definition of Himself: I am that I am' (46). For Huxley, recognition of the divine in the transitory enables man, whose apparent fate on earth is to 'degenerate into one or other of the varieties of the human gorilla' (49),[26] to avoid becoming a fool of time.

In his last novel, which bears the concrete but appropriately generic title of *Island*, Huxley attempts to give social reality to what might be called a philosophy of spiritual materialism. The society of Pala is frozen in time in the sense that its members devote their attention solely to the materiality of the present, but this present is perceived as participating in the eternity of God and thus manifesting Huxley's ideal of the Eternal Present.[27] As Will Farnaby rather crudely expresses it at the end of the novel: 'Eternity [is . . .] as real as shit';[28] God is, moreover, seen to be 'self-evidently the fact confronting him' (318). In Pala man is acknowledged to be a creature of time, but time is not permitted to govern his experience of reality. This is perhaps the most basic way in which in this novel Huxley has combined what he sees as the best elements of Eastern and Western cultures.

The cries of the mynah bird that greet Will Farnaby when he reaches Pala encapsulate the philosophy of life adopted by the island's inhabitants. 'Attention!' and then 'here and now, boys', the bird repeats to the bewildered Farnaby, wrapped in a shroud of guilt and remorse as he recalls his past. The life of the islanders is directed totally to awareness of present realities, in which they discover a sense of the divine. This discovery is exemplified in rather bizarre but striking fashion in the Palanese manner of giving thanks for food. '[. . .] we don't say grace *before* meals. We say it *with* meals', explains Shanta, and she continues: 'Or rather we don't *say* grace; we chew it' (197). Close attention to the qualities of the food as it is being consumed has the effect not only of heightening awareness of matter but also of permitting access to what is termed the 'not-you' (198)[29] in the environment and in one's own organism. 'Chewing grace' is experienced by the Palanese as a liberation from the tendency of the Western individual to dematerialize reality into concepts that cloak the living, divine qualities of matter. It is significant that the Palanese educator, Mr. Menon, sees as his principal problem: 'how can we educate children on the conceptual level without killing their capacity for intense non-verbal experience?' (203)[30]

The refusal of the Palanese to allow themselves to be dominated by concepts—and especially by concepts of time—is seen also in their staunch refusal to subjugate, in the name of progress, present reality to an uncertain and probably miserable future. 'The wave of the future' (59), which ultimately overwhelms them due to pressure from petroleum interests, holds little attraction, since it promises the extinction of the freedom and happiness that they have achieved in their present way of life. By encouraging the Palanese to come back into 'touch with the rest of the world' (58) where 'mass production, mass slaughter, mass communication and, above all, plain mass' (58) prevail, the Ambassador of neighbouring Rendang Island is in reality inviting them to return to a state of subjection to time.

The extent to which the Palanese are conscious of the importance of not allowing themselves to be controlled by time is seen in their interest in the ability of certain individuals to distort clock time quite radically. Mrs. Narayan explains to Farnaby that she, only an average student in the art, is able to 'distort time to the point where one minute is subjectively the equivalent of thirty minutes' (205) and hence to complete certain intellectual tasks much faster than normally might have been expected. In this way time is being brought into the service of man rather than dominating him by the demands ascribed to it.

A further indication of the attitude to time adopted by the inhabitants of Pala is seen in their approach to dying. For Dr. MacPhail thanatology is 'the ultimate science' (141), since death is an experience that each person must have. The Western fear of death and of the future is illustrated by Will Farnaby's recollections of his Aunt Mary as, stricken with cancer, she prepared to face what Will terms 'the Essential Horror' (252). In the West death is conceptualized into an object of terror that waits in the uncertainty of the future, and hence evokes anguish, dread and fear. In Pala, as Susila tells Will Farnaby, 'going on being aware—it's the whole art of dying' (239). At no stage, least of all at the approach of death, is present existence ransomed to fear to the future. The death of MacPhail's wife Lakshmi late in the novel is a good example of the process. As she imperceptibly drifts from life, she provides a telling contrast to the 'bitterly querulous self-pity' (254) displayed by Farnaby's aunt.

Shortly before his own death in 1963, Huxley managed, with great difficulty, to finish a short essay entitled 'Shakespeare and Religion'. The last paragraphs of this essay form a meditation on the memorably succinct passage that gave *Time Must Have a Stop* its title. In particular Huxley writes:

> Thought is determined by life, and life is determined by passing time. But the dominion of time is not absolute, for 'time must have a stop' in two senses, from the Christian point of view in which Shakespeare was writing. It must have a stop in the last judgment, and in the winding up of the universe. But on the way to this general consummation, it must have a stop in the individual mind, which must learn the regular cultivation of a mood of timelessness, of the sense of eternity.[31]

The last words of this passage form Huxley's final considered response to the question of the individual's attitude to time. While necessarily remaining a creature of time, man must remain open to the eternal. *Island* is, after all, simply an elaboration of this precept.

Both the continuing preoccupation of Huxley with time and the length of the intellectual and spiritual road that he travelled in his consideration of it may be gauged by comparing the above words with those written in 1917 as a post-script to a letter to Lewis Gielgud:

> The notion of Time as a God. Time the creator and destroyer in one, the father of truth. A good religion, it seems to me, and the only sensible and rational one.[32]

One may perhaps detect a touch of irony in these words, but there is none of the mysticism of the later years nor even of the protest of *The Olive Tree*

(1936), where he writes: 'Time is our tyrant'. Through it man has become 'the inhabitant of an artificial universe that is, to a great extent, walled off from the world of nature.'[33] In his meditation on time Huxley passes from tentative acceptance to firm protest, thence to the various stages of mysticism that have been outlined in this article.

In this progression, which reveals an aspect of the unity of the writer's work, Huxley emerges as an anti-Platonic and an anti-Hegelian thinker. In *The Doors of Perception* he speaks somewhat pejoratively of Plato (12) and in an earlier essay of *Themes and Variations* (1950) he states his philosophic justification for doing so:

> In the philosophy and practice of any genuine spiritual religion the significant and decisive dualism is not the Platonic dualism of body and mind, but the mystics' dualism of time and eternity [. . .] the Platonic dualism with its practical corollary of escape from the body, through ecstasy or death, into pure spirituality is admissible; but salvation is complete only when time, body and manifoldness are accepted and transfigured through being apprehended in their relation to eternity.[34]

In this chosen realm of time and eternity Huxley rejects with increasing conviction the time-bound non-transcendent approaches of Hegel's disciples who espouse what is referred to in *Ape and Essence* on two occasions as 'Hegel's patent History' (11, 32). In *Ends and Means* (1937) Huxley specifically attacks Hegelian-inspired views of history which identify the real and the rational. He writes:

> Spying, delation, torture, arbitrary imprisonment and execution—in every dictatorial country these are the ordinary instruments of domestic policy. They occur; they are therefore 'historical'. Being historical they are, in some *tief*, Hegelian way, reasonable and right. (67)

Such social and political considerations helped Huxley formulate the idea of 'non-attachment' in *Ends and Means*, Propter's goal of 'psychological eternity' and the later concept of 'Eternal Present'.

There are consequently in Huxley's mature approach to time elements that are political and social as well as others that are psychological, philosophical and spiritual. In what we have termed his 'spiritual materialism' Huxley seeks to hold together without contradiction the many demanding realities of the world and the timeless reality that underlies them. Without such an approach to life we cannot, asserts Huxley through the words of Sebastian Barnack, 'prevent time from turning our lives into a pointless or diabolic foolery' (*Time Must Have a Stop*, 292).

Notes

1.   Jerome Meckier, 'Housebreaking Huxley: Saint versus Satirist', *Mosaic*, vol. 5, 1972, p. 176.

2.   Margaret Church, 'Aldous Huxley's Attitude Towards Duration', *College English*, vol. 17, April 1956. Margaret Church, 'Concepts of Time in Novels of Virginia Woolf and Aldous Huxley', *Modern Fiction Studies*, vol. 1, 1955, pp. 19–24.

3.   e.g. Jerome Meckier, *Aldous Huxley: Satire and Structure* (London, Chatto and Windus, 1969), *passim*; Peter Bowering, *Aldous Huxley: a Study of the Major Novels* (London, Athlone Press, 1968), especially pp. 152–3.

4.   Peter Bowering remarks: 'That man is a victim of circumstance, that life is "time's fool" is something Huxley always insisted on. At first this insistence is wholly negative but it becomes, in the end, an urgent plea to act on those levels where free will does not operate.' op. cit., p. 161.

5.   *Crome Yellow*. London, Chatto and Windus, 1958, p. 1.

6.   *Antic Hay*. London, Chatto and Windus, 1949, p. 59.

7.   *Those Barren Leaves*. London, Chatto and Windus, 1960, p. 267.

8.   *Point Counter Point*. London, Chatto and Windus, 1954, p. 215.

9.   *Brave New World*. London, Chatto and Windus, 1960, p. 215.

10.   *Eyeless in Gaza*. London, Chatto and Windus, 1955, p. 8.

11.   Jerome Meckier considers Huxley's experiments with time in both *Brave New World* and *Eyeless in Gaza* as 'aimed at time's capacity to divide and separate' (op. cit., 1969, p. 164).

12.   *Ends and Means*. London, Chatto and Windus, 1965, p. 6.

13.   *After Many a Summer*. London, Chatto and Windus, 1968, p. 106.

14.   In *Grey Eminence* (1941), for example, Huxley asserts: 'The mystics are channels through which a little knowledge of reality filters down into our human universe of ignorance and illusion. A totally unmystical world would be a world totally blind and insane' (London, Chatto and Windus, 1956, p. 98).

15.   *Time Must Have a Stop*. London, Chatto and Windus, 1966, p. 290.

16.   In such writing one recognizes some of the principal emphases of Albert Camus in the postwar period, especially in such works as *L'Homme révolté*. There is an interesting study to be done on comparing the moral teachings of Huxley and Camus. The similarities may well help to explain the great popularity of Camus in Anglo-Saxon countries.

17.   For a brief account of the mystification of many critics see: Peter Bowering, op. cit., pp. 160–1. The novel has also earned considerable praise. Jerome Meckier considers it 'a considerable accomplishment' (op. cit., 1969, p. 6), while for Harold Watts it is 'the best novel Huxley wrote in his career, subsequent to *Brave New World*' (*Aldous Huxley*, Boston, Twayne, 1969, p. 108).

18.   Huxley had in fact thought of calling the novel *Time's Fool* (in letter to Cass Canfield, 7th December, 1943. Grover Smith (ed.), *Letters of Aldous Huxley*. London, Chatto and Windus, 1969, p. 499).

19.   'I personally think the most successful [novel] was *Time Must Have a Stop*. I don't know, but it seemed to me that I integrated what may be called the essay element with the fictional element better there than in other novels.' (*Writers at Work*. The *Paris Review* Interviews, 2nd series. Introduced by Van Wyck Brooks. London, Secker and Warburg, 1963, p. 172).

20.   In his 1946 foreword to *Brave New World* Huxley specifically comments on the lack of reference in the work to nuclear fission (op. cit., p. x).

21.   Jerome Meckier makes this point when he writes: 'the world of *Ape and Essence* is

an extension of the simian existence of Jo Stoyte and the Fifth Earl in *After Many a Summer'* (op. cit., 1969, p. 202).

22. *Ape and Essence.* London, Chatto and Windus, 1966, p. 7.

23. As early as 1935 Huxley suggests in a letter to E.M. Forster dated 17th February that 'progress' may be 'aiming directly for some fantastic denial of humanity.' Grover Smith (ed.). op. cit., p. 391.

24. *The Genius and the Goddess.* London, Chatto and Windus, 1955, p. 99.

25. Such ideas are also found in *The Doors of Perception* (1954) where Huxley applauds the *Istigkeit* ('Is-ness') concept of Meister Eckhart. He relates this to his present situation, where he perceives 'a transience that was yet eternal life, a perpetual perishing that was at the same time pure Being, a bundle of minute, unique particulars in which, by some unspeakable and yet self-evident paradox, was to be seen the divine source of all existence.' (*The Doors of Perception; Heaven and Hell.* London, Chatto and Windus, 1960, p. 12).

26. At the end of the novel the resuscitated Henry Maartens is described as 'that stupendous clockwork monkey' (p. 127).

27. The concept of 'Eternal Present' is treated specifically in chapter 12 ('Time and Eternity'), of *The Perennial Philosophy*.

28. *Island.* London, Chatto and Windus, 1962, p. 267.

29. Huxley deals with the importance of co-operation with 'not-I' forces in various sections of his writing but specifically in *Adonis and the Alphabet* (London, Chatto and Windus, 1956), pp. 39–73.

30. This statement echoes to some extent Huxley's affirmation in *The Devils of Loudun* (1952): 'For Lallemant, the life of perfection is a life simultaneously active and contemplative, a life lived at the same time in the infinite and the finite, in time and eternity. This ideal is the highest which a rational being can conceive—the highest and at the same time the most realistic, the most conformable to the given facts of human divine nature.' (p. 93)

31. 'Shakespeare and Religion', in Julian Huxley (ed.) *Aldous Huxley 1894–1963* (London, Chatto and Windus, 1965), p. 175.

32. Grover Smith (ed.), op. cit., p. 119.

33. *The Olive Tree.* London, Chatto and Windus, 1936, p. 124.

34. *Themes and Variations.* London, Chatto and Windus, 1954, p. 139.

Aldous Huxley and the Nuclear Age: *Ape and Essence* in Context

SANFORD E. MAROVITZ

On 10 August 1945, four days before Japan surrendered unconditionally and ended World War Two, Aldous Huxley wrote to Victoria Ocampo, editor of a literary journal in Buenos Aires: "Thank God we are to have peace very soon. But I confess that I find a peace with atomic bombs hanging overhead a rather disquieting prospect. National states armed by science with superhuman military power always remind me of Swift's description of Gulliver being carried up to the roof of the King of Brobdingnag's palace by a gigantic monkey."[1]

In 1948, this early Swiftian allusion would indirectly but significantly reappear in *Ape and Essence*, although Huxley had already begun to develop the idea behind it in *Science, Liberty and Peace*, arguing vigorously against the view of Einstein among others that the destructive power of atomic weapons is so great that men will no longer want to wage war. All men are like delinquent fourteen-year-old boys in their quest for gain and power, he says, and they have always found new measures of defense against new weapons, although "there may be no defence against atomic missiles."[2] However intensely "the nationalistic boy-gangster is frightened of what atomic power may do to him and his world . . . he continues to think in terms of gang rivalry and his own supremacy. 'If,' he argues, 'our gang can get its scientists to perfect the rocket and the atom bomb, . . . then all that need be done is to press a few buttons and bang! the war to end war will be over, and I shall be the boss of the whole planet' "(*SLP*, 37–8). All war departments in technologically advanced nations will operate on this basis, Huxley predicts, designing and building more formidable weapons, experimenting and testing secretly until the buttons are inevitably pushed.

Clearly the awesome power of nuclear arms was at the front of Huxley's mind when he wrote these words, and therefore it was probably to be expected that his concern would find its way into his next work of fiction, which appeared the following year. In *Ape and Essence*, he provides an alternate

Reprinted with permission of author and publisher from the *Journal of Modern Literature* 18 (Winter, 1992): 115–25. © 1994 Temple University.

195

version of the future, a not-so-brave and ravaged old world, the consequence of a nuclear holocaust. To some extent, this work echoes *Brave New World*, published sixteen years earlier. It includes a preoccupation with sex, a look into the future, witty snatches of dialogue, a perverted form of traditional religious practices, considerable didacticism in expository form, and the presence of an alien figure from outside the dystopian setting. But by virtue of its theme—derived from the then-recent nuclear explosions over Japan— the circumstances of *Ape and Essence* are considerably darker and more caustic than those of *Brave New World*, and its message should have been far more compelling. Ironically, however, whereas the stylistically cheerier *Brave New World* ends grimly with the suicide of John the Savage, the effect of the sardonic grotesquerie in *Ape and Essence* is ameliorated by a conclusion that seems to hold promise for a fleeing couple in love and possibly, by extension, for later generations of post-atomic humanity.

Nevertheless, this slight opening for individual hope, following the scenes of carnal barbarism and social perversion that Huxley vividly paints in quick succession, is much less convincing as a prediction of our future than as a relatively happy ending for the book. Reading *Ape and Essence* in the context of Huxley's other contemporary comments on war, nationalism, totalitarianism, and particularly nuclear armament—no one of which can be discussed meaningfully in his thought without reference to the others— leaves one uncertain over the strength of the author's commitment to ad- dressing seriously the moral questions that the work provokes. His real intention in writing this dramatic piece of fiction is clouded, and it is difficult indeed to determine whether his personal investment in it was chiefly that of the moral philosopher or of the imaginative author. In a broader sense, these ambiguities open to question the extent that Huxley's concern over the possibility of nuclear war affected his thought and writing during the post-war years. That his commitment to peace and disarmament was absolute, one may be sure, but that his principal aim in writing *Ape and Essence* was to convert that commitment into a dire warning to the public—as it seems to be—is not as clear. Instead, in that novel and especially after it, Huxley showed little inclination to surrender other more intense personal interests to the overriding issue of the Bomb. Unlikely as this may appear, the evidence speaks for itself.

Ape and Essence was received poorly by many readers, even devotees of Huxley's earlier work. Donald Watt generalizes accurately on the critical response when he points out that reviewers "frequently . . . recoiled from the horrid forecast of the book, the 'ape,' in many cases without acknowledg- ing its generating idealism, the 'essence,' "[3] that is, as represented by the escaping Loola and Poole, the saving remnant, nourished by the divine light of sustaining love (echoing Shelley's "Epipsychidion" and "Adonais"). Anthony Bower acknowledges the importance of Huxley's implicit message in *Ape and Essence* but regrets the lack of a more serious resolution to the problem than "a blend of Eastern mysticism and Western technology." "Splitting the atom could as well be a cause for optimism as for pessimism: the greater the knowledge of science, the greater the chance of [its] . . . leading to the establishment of a sane world order."[4]

But Huxley had already rejected this eventuality as plausible when he wrote a year earlier in *Science, Liberty and Peace* that he believes man in a position of power is more tempted to use it for self-aggrandizement than to conform with political agreements meant to restrain him. Consequently, he asserts that atomic energy is and will be for the foreseeable future "politically and humanly speaking, in the highest degree undesirable" (*SLP*, 62). More-over, in *Ape and Essence* itself, the narrator specifically states that the birth of badly deformed babies "could as well be the product of atomic industry as of atomic war."[5] Emphasizing the importance of environmental conserva-tion to overcome world hunger, Huxley wrote to Fairfield Osborn (author of *Our Plundered Planet* [1948]) earlier in the year, "while mankind could do very well without atomic energy, it cannot dispense with bread" (*Letters*, 578; 16 January 1948). Clearly, Huxley was aware of nuclear power as a potential source of peacetime energy soon after the Bombs were dropped, but he did not trust it—and that was long before Three-Mile Island and Chernobyl. The novel opens in Hollywood on the day of Mahatma Gandhi's assassination, and Gandhi's humanitarianism thus implicitly contrasts with the egotism and materialism of life in the film capital. Gandhi was killed, the narrator states, because he was caught up in "the sub-human mass-madness of nationalism" (8), a form of regimented insanity that can be cured only from the periphery, not the center. If one works with the system, he becomes caught up in it, used by it, and later dropped; or he begins to apply its policies in attempting to fulfill his own aims. Gandhi's assassination was a prophetic symbol, a warning to anyone who might advocate a policy other than war to achieve peace (9).

The narrator and a filmscript writer discuss a new film being made of the life of Saint Catherine of Siena; in it, the effect of her church politics are minimized in favor of a love theme because otherwise it would be [t]oo depressing . . . [for t]he public" (12). Because these lines anticipate ironically Huxley's own concession to a similar argument a year later, when *Ape and Essence* was being adapted for stage production, they are more significant than their immediate context in the novel might suggest in helping to determine his original aim. When the producer requested in 1949 that Huxley add "human interest" to the staged version being prepared in France and tone down "the atomic-bomb impression that the play gives" (*Letters*, 599), Huxley concurred with minimal reluctance, suggesting that perhaps nuclear holocaust had not originally been his principal concern after all.

The form of *Ape and Essence* is that of a filmscript with narrator. Shortly after the script opens, the idea of the play is stated—in a passage from Shakespeare's *Measure for Measure* (II.ii, 117–22):

> But man, proud man,
> Drest in a little brief authority—
> Most ignorant of what he is most assur'd,
> His glassy essence—like an angry ape,
> Plays such fantastic tricks before high heaven
> As make the angels weep. (34–5)

The play is set in California in February 2108, a little over a century after World War III nearly destroyed the earth. Baboons in human roles, with scientists chained, immolate themselves with atomic missiles that finish off what gas clouds from biological warfare missed, and a Belial-worshipping culture emerges from the ruins. Like the failed civilization that it replaces, this culture is ruled by fear, which, ultimately, the narrator says, "casts out even a man's humanity" (51).

Central in the action of the script is Dr. Alfred Poole, an exploring scientist from New Zealand stranded in California when hordes of barbarians attack; his companions leave him behind in fleeing to their boat. He is captured, and as the barbarians commence to bury him alive for their amusement, the Narrator observes, specifying the role of the media in the moral schizophrenia of contemporary Western society:

> Cruelty and compassion come with the chromosomes;
> All men are merciful and all are murderers.
> Doting on dogs, they build their Dachaus;
> Fire whole cities and fondle the orphans;
> . . .
> Whom shall we persecute, for whom feel pity?
> It is all a matter of the moment's mores,
> Of words on wood pulp, of radios roaring . . . (75)

Huxley later called this attitude a "schizophrenic breach in our moral sensibility"[6]; we sympathize and suffer over harm to individuals—even animals—but have minimal or no feelings for large-scale destruction of life when it is "distant, . . . abstract and generalized" (*Human*, 84). After being rescued, Poole eventually persuades Loola, a dim-witted but voluptuous young woman, to escape with him to the north, where they can live as human beings rather than as slaves and beasts, but first he observes the policies and practices of the post-nuclear culture in California.

"[E]ven without the atomic bomb," he learns from one of the rulers, "men would have destroyed themselves by destroying the world they lived in" through over-industrialization, overpopulation, disregard for conservation and the environment, and through "Progress and Nationalism" (123–25). In attempting to conquer nature, their Belial nature conquered them. Huxley had anticipated this idea in *Point Counter Point* twenty years earlier; in that novel, Mark Rampion says, "Christianity made us barbarians of the soul, and now science is making us barbarians of the intellect."[7] Philip Quarles (to some extent Huxley's persona) notes of Rampion that his children "have a passion for machinery. . . . It's as though the young were absolutely determined to bring the world to an end—mechanize it first into madness, then into sheer murder" (*Point*, 437).

These perverted practices are implemented by the Belial culture of *Ape and Essence*: "By purely natural means, using human beings and their science as His instruments, [Belial] created an entirely new race of men, with deformity in their blood, with squalor all around them and ahead, in the future, no prospects but of more squalor, worse deformity and, finally, complete extinction" (132–33). Allied with nations, churches, and political parties, Poole is told, Belial "used their prejudices. He exploited their ideologies. By the time they'd developed the atomic bomb, he had people back in the state of mind they were in before 900 B.C." (184).

Near the conclusion of the novel, however, Poole is certain that ultimately Belial will lose because he "can never resist the temptation of carrying evil to the limit. And whenever evil is carried to the limit, it always destroys itself. After which the Order of Things comes to the surface again," thus making it possible for individuals to live meaningfully by working in concord with it (197–98). According to John Atkins, "The point of [*Ape and Essence*] is that we know that we are committing suicide and do nothing to stop it. . . . Man's only hope [in Huxley's view] is that Belial, or the evil in us, always goes to the limit and defeats itself. And then the Order of Things comes to the surface again—but," Atkins asks, "how much destruction will have taken place in the meantime?"[8]

Huxley's idea of an alternating cycle in time may be traced to his earliest poetry, for example, "The Wheel" and "Mole," both first published in 1916. In "The Wheel," alternation is represented in terms of burning energy and stasis rather than chaos and order, as in *Ape and Essence*:

> Weary of its own turning,
>
> . . .
>
> The Wheel must strain, through agony
> On agony contracting, returning
> Into the core of steel.
>
> . . .
>
> But the yearning atoms, as they grind
> Closer and closer, more and more
> Fiercely together, beget
> A flaming fire upward leaping,
> Billowing out in a burning,
> Passionate, fierce desire to find
> The infinite calm. . . .
>
> . . .
>
> And as it burns and anguishes it quickens,

> Begetting once again the Wheel that yearns—
> Sick with its speed—for the terrible stillness
> Of the adamant core and the steel-hard chain.
> And so once more
> Shall the wheel revolve, till its anguish cease
> In the iron anguish of fixity. . . . [9]

The imagery with which Huxley depicts this alternation is a stunning anticipation of billowing atomic flame generated by the atoms of the wheel as they grind closer and more fiercely together; moreover, it makes instantaneous the transformation between the two extreme conditions of existence, the mythic phoenix already dying at the peak of its fiery life. Sybille Bedford, Huxley's chief biographer, sees this poem, among the others in *The Burning Wheel* (his first collection of poetry, 1916), as "the verse of a young man who—after private tragedy—had to begin life in 1914, and is charged with a sense of the moral and physical suicide of the world."[10] This "charged . . . sense" doubtlessly remained with Huxley throughout his life. By the time he drafted *Ape and Essence*, however, his perception of individual limitations in the face of incipient global suicide had diminished his capacity to foster universal moral action through his writing.

The other of these two early poems, "Mole," represents the "old mole-soul" tunneling alone and blindly from ages of oblivion into a brief period of light, then "through the sunset's inmost core," and finally, as Necessity dictates, into further ages of oblivion. Huxley's sense of isolation and foreboding as a young man is apparent. "Mole" was first published in a small literary journal called *The Palatine Review*, which Huxley began with a few schoolmates at Balliol early in 1916 as the war was killing off their friends. A short anonymous preface identifying its purpose seems both to foreshadow the oblivion theme of Huxley's poem and to bridge the gap between the world of chaos and that of the poet. Although later, in *Point Counter Point*, Illidge tells Spandrell, shortly before they kill Webley the reactionary, "You can't compare poetry and politics" (*Point*, 467), that first number of *The Palatine Review* shows that one can. "The present catastrophe, some have dreamed," says the editor, referring to the war, "is the last storm of adolescence beyond which humanity will advance with a graver and more secure soul. Yet it is with equal possibility the bloody sunset of our civilisation."[11]

It was not until the late 1920s, however, notably in *Point Counter Point* (1928), that Huxley began taking serious issue in print with the practice of resorting to large-scale violence and war as a means of achieving one's aims. In *Brave New World*, he devised an easy way to avert violence in a controlled but not rigorously policed society through the use of soma, a combined hallucinogen and sedative. It is at once comic and serious in the novel, and Huxley would seek its equivalent for many years thereafter in life to help ordinary people cope effectively with tension over ordinary problems. The occasional inhabitants of the brave new world who cannot be made happy through the use of soma are sent to isolated communities to live more satisfying, more fulfilling lives without endangering the rest of society. In this respect, they are comparable with the Hots in *Ape and Essence*, those post-holocaust Californians who either cannot or refuse to conform to the rigid sexual prohibitions of the other Belial worshipers. Both societies are totalitarian, although a grotesque irony pervades the latter work in that it is allegedly a democracy that is being described; the inhabitants are persistently reminded that they have chosen to serve the state. Of course, if they choose otherwise, they become social heretics, traitors, and they are treated accordingly.

Between *Brave New World* in 1932 and *Ape and Essence* in 1948 occurred the rise and fall of Hitler and the development and dropping of the Atom Bombs. In a Foreword to a new edition (but not a revision) of *Brave New World* in 1946, Huxley refers to both of these atrocities, attributing the first to the "nationalistic radicals [who] had their way,"[12] a point that the Arch-Vicar would develop in *Ape and Essence*. Also in this Foreword he first discusses atomic power in a book, acknowledging its omission in *Brave New World* as "[o]ne vast and obvious failure of foresight [that] is immediately apparent" (ix). Late the preceding year, he had written to Anita Loos in response to her questions on making a film from *Brave New World*: "Something about the atom bomb will of course have to be brought in. But the point of the original story must be kept—namely, that the really revolutionary changes will come about from advances in biology and psychology, not from advances in physics" (*Letters*, 534; 13 October 1945). In the new Foreword, he explains this and his original lapse by indicating that he was focusing in that novel on the effects of the life sciences rather than the physical sciences because although the latter can have prodigious effect on the way life is lived and even destroy it altogether, genetic engineering, psychological conditioning, and other life sciences can "modify the natural forms and expressions of life itself." "The release of atomic energy makes a great revolution in human history," he states, "but not (unless we blow ourselves to bits and so put an end to history) the final and most searching revolution" (Foreword, x). He concludes that unless we reverse our priorities so that we use applied science, "not as the end to which human beings are to be made the means, but as the means to producing a race of free individuals, we have only two alternatives to choose from: either a number of national, militarized totalitarianisms, having as their root the terror of the atomic bomb and as their consequence the destruction of civilization; . . . or else one supranational totalitarianism . . . [evoked by] technological progress in general and the atomic revolution in particular, and developing . . . into the welfare-tyranny of Utopia" (Foreword, xiv). To Victoria Ocampo early that same year, he wrote emphasizing this confusion of priorities as he would develop the idea in his forthcoming *Science, Liberty and Peace*; he tells her—in a stylistically clumsy manner uncharacteristic of Huxley—that this book will remind people of simple matters which scientists often "like to forget because it is such enormous fun enquiring into the processes of nature and designing bigger and better gadgets that they do not wish to realize that human beings are being sacrificed to applied science" (*Letters*, 541; 28 March 1946).

From the 1930s on, Huxley was increasingly concerned with the relation of hunger to totalitarianism, observing that under-nourishment and over-population inevitably lead nations to the loss of freedom. In his Santa Barbara lectures of 1959 he elaborated upon this point by drawing from Bertrand Russell, whose perceptions of short-range military and political prospects at the time seemed to him "extremely realistic and sensible." Russell had posited three alternatives: human extinction through nuclear warfare, reversion to barbarism through the breakdown of the industrial system, and the creation of "a single world state" through either the victory of one side in a nuclear war or the persistent threat of force (*Human*, 98–100). Huxley dramatized the first two of these alternatives in *Ape and Essence*, in which monstrous births are progressively more pronounced and numerous because of gamma radiation; therefore, the Belial-worshipping dystopia, without the industrial capability, energy, or agriculture to improve or even sustain itself, is doomed to extinction.

Given his concern and fears over nuclear armament as he expressed them in the late 1940s, one might think that Huxley would have emphasized the matter more than he actually did in the years that followed, but, strange to say, he seemed to regard nuclear arms as little more than another facet of the war-making mania among nations. It is true that he called for a ban on nuclear tests in 1959 or perhaps earlier (*Human*, 89), and he was endlessly amazed at the American government's suicidal development of more complex and powerful armament systems—all at the cost of applying science to the improvement of physical and social conditions for distressed humanity. In 1952, for example, he described to his brother, Julian, a trip he had recently made to a naval research center about two hundred miles from his home in Los Angeles, an enormous station, rich in scientific paraphernalia of all kinds—and in the midst of a desert wilderness. He wrote: "The whole [is] directed exclusively to the production of bigger and better rockets. It was the most frightening exhibition of scientific and highly organized insanity I have ever seen. One vaguely thought that the human race was determined to destroy itself. After visiting the China Lake Research station, one feels quite certain of it. And the whole world is fairly crawling with physicians in barbed wire compounds working three shifts a day *ad majorem Diaboli gloriam*" (*Letters*, 645; 20 May 1952). In the summer of 1962, a little over a year before his death, he wrote to Dr. Humphry Osmond, the psychiatrist who had overseen his mescaline experiments, that a few days earlier he had visited the North American Aviation plant, at which he saw how "fabulously well-organized" is the current armament "insanity." He went there to see "the Apollo moon-shot capsule and the latest plane-to-ground missiles, which can turn at right angles, skim along the ground, shoot perpendicularly up into the air to avoid interception and finally be guided, warhead and all, to whatever orphanage or old people's home may have been selected as the target" (*Letters*, 936; 19 August 1962). Reference to the orphanage here echoes a similar usage in *Ape and Essence*, which suggests that although he clearly retained an interest in the folly of the arms race, whatever vital personal investment he had made in combating it was by now more in the memory than in the forefront of his mind.

As an illustration, one may note that although Huxley traveled extensively, he apparently had little interest in seeing first-hand the horrifying effects of the two Atom Bombs in Japan. When he had the chance to return to that country, he wrote to his son, Matthew, from India in November that they would go there "perhaps for a few days" (*Letters*, 926; 7 November 1961). In fact, he went only to Tokyo for what evidently amounted to little more than a stopover (Huxley to Humphry Osmond, *Letters*, 926; 2 January 1962). The following spring, he lectured to the scientists at Los Alamos, a site which should have held a double significance for him. First, it was roughly the setting of the Malpais savage reservation in *Brave New World*, and second, of course, it was the center of Atom Bomb research in the early 1940s. According to Ronald W. Clark, advances on nuclear arms were still being developed there when Huxley visited.[13] Ironically, in his lecture that day he spoke not about nuclear armament but on "Visionary Experiences." He did go to the laboratories and make notes on the radiation experiments in progress, but he apparently wrote nothing on research for atomic weapons.[14]

Perhaps Huxley had come to terms somehow with the prevailing fear and horror of the Bomb. In a limited way, the interest was there, but the persistent presence of nuclear weapons in contemporary life did not grip his imagination as at first it seemed to have done in the immediate aftermath of Hiroshima and Nagasaki, especially while drafting *Ape and Essence*. Yet, even then, one cannot be entirely sure of his intentions in that novel, didactic and pointed as his message appears to be. His letters of the period create an aura of doubt. For example, early in 1947, as the idea of his novel was germinating, Huxley wrote to Anita Loos that he had in mind a futuristic work "about, among other things, a post-atomic-war society in which the chief effect of the gamma radiations had been to produce a race of men and women who don't make love all the year round, but have a brief mating season. The effect of this on politics, religion, ethics etc [sic] would be something very interesting and amusing to work out" (*Letters*, 569; 26 March 1947).

This letter suggests that aberrant sexuality rather than nuclear holocaust was his starting point, an implication that gains strength when he speaks of composing the fiction as something not only "interesting" but "amusing" to work out. After completing the novel by February of the following year, he explained to his correspondent at Harper's, who published it, the source of his title from *Measure for Measure* and speculated over the possible use of illustrations (*Letters*, 581; 24 February 1948). Early in 1949, he told Victoria Ocampo that he had already completed a dramatization of *Ape and Essence* which he thought "might be very effective on the stage" (*Letters*, 589; 9 January 1949), although he said nothing about what kind of effect he wished to achieve. Later the same year, he wrote in French to Georges Neveux (his wife Maria's brother-in-law, who had translated and adapted for the French stage both *The Diary of Anne Frank* and Huxley's own *The Gioconda Smile*) in response to the producer's request for changes in *Ape and Essence* before staging it in France. The producer, Huxley said,

> wants me at all costs to add scenes "with human interest"—that is, scenes in which Poole and Loola's romance would be treated with much greater unction and other scenes in which the incentives for their elopement would become more "idealistic." In a word, De Leon [the producer] wants me to underscore the "positive" side of the play, to proclaim more clearly its spiritual message etc. . . . I hesitate to take his advice, for I am finding that a bigger dose of "human interest" could destroy the plausibility of the phantasy as a whole—that in trying too hard to reassure the public, one risks spoiling the play. On the other hand maybe he is right in wishing to mitigate a little what you call the atomic-bomb impression that the play gives. But I believe that this mitigation can be produced by means of judicious cuts and the introduction of the spectacle and music. Tell me very frankly what you think. . . . Not knowing very well what I've written, I am not attached to it and I can envisage no matter what surgical intervention with complete sang froid [*Letters*, 598–99; 2 June 1949].[15]

The closing lines of Huxley's paragraph constitute an extraordinary confession—that he is relatively ignorant of what he has written, that he feels detached from it, and that he is willing to make whatever revisions Neveux thinks advisable; no matter what may be cut, he would not feel it, and that letter was written only about a year after the book was first published. The nuclear horror—"the Thing"—as the Belial worshipers call it—seems diminished in the author's imagination. It is as if we were back to the novels of the early 1920s in which Huxley jabbed at his characters with barbed points of wit but always from a distance, satirizing the foibles, intellectual and otherwise, of that ever-chatting coterie. Surely, his closing remarks to Neveux offer no evidence of commitment to the strong anti-nuclear message that seems to glow ominously from the pages of *Ape and Essence*. By the time he became involved with staging an English version of the novel, he appears to have lost sight of any purpose more serious than a commercial one. At the end of January 1956, he wrote to Matthew and Ellen that the man who had adapted *After Many a Summer* to the stage is also working on the dramatization I did of *Ape and Essence*—a dramatization which was much too short for practical purposes and which he is re-shaping in the form of a music drama with ballets. Quite a good idea, I think. I count no chickens, but hope none the less that some of these eggs may hatch out. It would be very nice to get something without having to do any work, for a change! (*Letters*, 789–90; 30 January 1956)

Such remarks inevitably leave one uncertain over how seriously Huxley took his anti-war novel as an admonition to begin with and how fearful he actually was over the likelihood of nuclear holocaust during the post-war years. First, the letters pertaining to *Ape and Essence* at least suggest that it originated more as an entertainment than a warning and that the effect he sought in the staged versions was similar, more a matter of amusement and spectacle than frightful prophecy. Whatever his intent, however, the dire admonition is clearly present, and if the reviewers criticized the aesthetic quality of the work, they had no trouble recognizing the significance and impact of his post-holocaust dystopia. However, an apparent lack of forceful commitment makes it also difficult to determine how genuinely fearful he was over the possibility of nuclear holocaust in the foreseeable future. If Huxley asked early for a ban on nuclear testing and often remarked on the organized insanity of nuclear-weapon production in concert with assertive nationalism, he gave to the subject considerably less attention than to the life sciences, integrative education, individual development, and visionary experience. This is readily apparent in his two novels that followed *Ape and Essence*—*The Genius and The Goddess* (1955) and *Island* (1962)—the latter of which he considered his *chef d'oeuvre*; he gave little heed to nuclear matters in either.

One of the lectures that Huxley presented at Santa Barbara in 1959 may explain this apparent lack of commitment and suggest clarification for both uncertainties. In discussing humanity as a single personal being, Huxley observes that in the midst of social upheaval and tumult even on a colossal scale, the individual is not much engaged with them. He acknowledges that this is no less true for the deeply thinking person than for the ordinary one: "Although at certain moments we may be painfully involved," he says, "for the most part we can continue to live our intensely private lives" (*Human*, 117). Even when considering the impact of "technology and scientific invention," he adds, "we shall find that . . . there is a very small part of history which is felt subjectively to be of supreme importance" (*Human*, 121). There is no reason to believe that this general observation does not apply to Huxley himself. This personal revelation necessarily distances him from the globalism, humanistic complicity, and universal social correspondence with which he has usually been associated from the late 1920s on even as it largely explains Huxley's seemingly detached attitude at times toward atomic weapons and the possibility of nuclear holocaust. Through the post-war years, he showed concern but never preoccupation over these matters, not even, as comments in his letters suggest, in *Ape and Essence*; despite his remarkable breadth of knowledge, intelligence, awareness, and foresight, he did not permit the obvious overriding danger of misusing atomic energy to interfere with his deep social and psychological interests. To the end he remained, then, very much the human amphibian he had so often described—the "full-blown" man making the most of his capacities as both a social participant and a discrete physical organism with a unique psycho-intellectual complex that he attempted to employ to the advantage of society as well as toward the gratification of his own insatiable curiosity.

Nevertheless, Huxley seemed ultimately to deny the reality, and certainly the effectiveness, of his own social message, the counsel he expressed through dozens of lectures and publications over more than three decades preceding his death in 1963. It is as if his admonitions were not supported by his faith in social possibility, as if he knew instead that his voice and pen were conveying an academic truth only, one that would not and could not have a vital impact because every person's sense of relation to history was too limited. Individually, Huxley professed, people were insufficiently engaged in existence beyond "their intensely private lives," and like everyone else, he shared this common human predicament.

Huxley's telling observation explains not only why his repeated warnings about the bleak future of civilization went largely unheeded, but it also illuminates, perhaps unexpectedly, at least one reason that the character portraits in his early fiction are so remarkably effective. The idiosyncrasies of his characters usually predominated over whatever serious messages they conveyed through lengthy conversations, monologues, and diaries or journals.[16] When this priority was reversed and theme predominated over eccentricity of character, the fiction flattened out and became too overtly didactic.

This point suggests one source of both the strengths and weaknesses of *Ape and Essence* as fiction. At once comical and horrifying, that novel too effectively undermines through humor Huxley's anti-nuclear warning for it to be accepted with the urgency it demands. Poole and Loola are so amusingly sympathetic that they draw too much attention to themselves and their plight, and the frightfulness of the underlying theme loses its efficacy.[17] Unlike *Brave New World*, which ends tragically as the reader is forced to realize the danger of subordinating individualism to social stability, *Ape and Essence* presents a post-atomic horror show but gratifies the reader with a relatively happy ending in which the naive lead couple is saved. Interesting and amusing, as Huxley originally intended it to be, *Ape and Essence* is not compelling, and in this respect it adumbrates the limited impact of his calls for peace.

Notes

1. Aldous Huxley, *Letters of Aldous Huxley*, ed. Grover Smith (London: Chatto & Windus, 1969), p. 532. Hereafter cited parenthetically as *Letters*.

2. Aldous Huxley, *Science, Liberty and Peace* (London: Chatto & Windus, 1947), p. 36. Hereafter cited parenthetically as *SLP*.

3. Donald Watt, ed., "Introduction," *Aldous Huxley: The Critical Heritage* (London: Routledge & Kegan Paul, 1975), p. 26.

4. Anthony Bower, review of *Ape and Essence*, in Watt, pp. 369–70.

5. Aldous Huxley, *Ape and Essence* (New York: Harper & Brothers, 1948), p. 101. Further references are to this edition.

6. Aldous Huxley, *The Human Situation: Lectures at Santa Barbara, 1959*, ed. Piero Ferrucci (New York: Harper & Row, 1977), p. 85. Hereafter cited parenthetically as *Human*.

7. Aldous Huxley, *Point Counter Point* (London: Chatto & Windus, 1928), p. 144, Hereafter cited parenthetically as *Point*.

8. John Atkins, *Aldous Huxley: A Literary Study*, rev. ed. (New York: Orion, 1967), p. xxviii.

9. Aldous Huxley, "The Wheel," *Oxford Poetry: 1916* (Oxford: B.H. Blackwell, 1916), pp. 32–3. This poem, retitled "The Burning Wheel" and slightly modified in punctuation, opens Huxley's first collection of poetry, under the same title; it was also published by Blackwell in 1916; "Mole," too, appears in this collection, pp. 12–4.

10. Sybille Bedford, *Aldous Huxley: A Biography*, 2 vols. (London: Chatto & Windus, and William Collins Sons, 1973–74), I, p. 67.

11. Anon. [T. W. Earp, ed. (and Aldous Leonard Huxley?)], "Objects," [Preface to] *Palatine Review*, 1 (January–February 1916), [p. 3].

12. Aldous Huxley, Foreword [to] *Brave New World* (1946; New York: Harper & Row, 1969), p. xi. Hereafter cited parenthetically as "Foreword."

13. Ronald W. Clark, *The Huxleys* (New York: McGraw-Hill, 1968), p. 357.

14. Laura Archera Huxley, *This Timeless Moment: A Personal View of Aldous Huxley* (New York: Farrar, Straus & Giroux, 1968), p. 200.

15. This is Grover Smith's translation. The play was never produced.

16. For development of this idea in relation to Huxley's caricatures and animal imagery, see Sanford E. Marovitz, "Aldous Huxley's Intellectual Zoo," *Philological Quarterly*, LXVIII (1969), pp, 495–507.

17. See Jerome Meckier, *Aldous Huxley: Satire and Structure* (London: Chatto & Windus, 1969), pp. 194–95.

Aldous Huxley: The Quest for Synthetic Sainthood

Kulwant Singh Gill

1

Aldous Huxley's interest in psychedelics stems from his deep-rooted concern for the spiritual malaise of modern life. Though he started his literary career on a note of agnosticism,[1] adopted an attitude of "pawky playfulness" toward eternal verities,[2] and debunked mysticism as an ideal,[3] his later writings affirm his belief in the Ultimate Reality. His analysis of the human situation brought about the conviction that modern man is spiritually sick because he has alienated himself from the Divine Reality or the Godhead that, according to Huxley, is "the unmanifested principle of all manifestation" and that "to realize this supreme identity is the final end and purpose of human existence."[4] As an advocate of mysticism, Huxley suggests meditation as a method "for acquiring knowledge about the essential nature of things, a method for establishing communion between the soul and the integrating principle of the universe."[5] But his experience also showed him that contemplation, as J. B. Coates puts it, "becomes increasingly more difficult in an age whose tempo is determined by the machine."[6] So, he tried to explore the avenues of spiritual reality through psychedelics with a view to discovering an easy means to self-transcendence for modern man. He recorded his psychedelic experiences in *The Doors of Perception* (1954), which, according to Bernard S. Aaronson and Humphry Osmond, "marks the beginning of the modern psychedelic movement."[7] Because he was the first well-known writer to assert that chemicals can lead to self-transcendence, his assertions have raised the most fundamental question about the possibility of synthetic sainthood.

Laura Archera Huxley points out that "One of Aldous's chief aims in life was the extension of consciousness."[8] He experimented with mind-manifesting drugs only to ascertain their impact on consciousness. His conclusions, however, led some critics to brand him as the prophet of LSD who

From *Modern Fiction Studies* 27 (1981–82): 601–12. Reprinted with permission of the author and The Johns Hopkins University Press, Baltimore/London.

found God in a bottle and whose advocacy of LSD led to the promotion of hippie culture. R. E. L. Masters and Jean Houston observe that the "contemporary quest for the artificial induction of religious experiences through the use of psycho-chemicals became a controversial issue with the publication of Huxley's *Doors of Perception* in 1954."[9] This paper is an attempt to examine Huxley's assertions with regard to the spiritual nature of a chemically-induced experience and to ascertain the possibility of synthetic sainthood.

The idea that chemical means to transcendence are perhaps as good as the traditional methods of fasting and prayer also occurs in Huxley's early fiction. As an agnostic, Huxley believed that the fruit of spiritual life was ecstasy and that to induce ecstasy one need not sit on the gazelle skin and squint at the top of one's nose for hours, because ecstasy can be chemically produced. He comments on the artificial production of the state of mystical trance: "Every symptom of the trance, from the 'sense of presence' to total unconsciousness, can be produced artificially in the laboratory."[10] Miles Fanning, the central character in the story "After the Fireworks," echoes his author's idea that opium is "as good a way of becoming supernatural as looking at one's nose or one's navel, or not eating, or repeating a word over and over again."[11]

Moreover, it was Huxley's intense longing to seek eternity that made him experiment with drugs that, at least temporarily, led to some kind of self-transcendence. In *Antic Hay* (1923) Huxley raises the question: "Who lives longer; the man who takes heroin for two years and dies, or the man who lives on roast beef, water, and potatoes till ninety-five? One passes his twenty-four months in eternity. All the years of the beef-eater are lived only in time."[12] Because drugs induce a state of timelessness, bring elation to the user, and lead to an experience that shares some attributes of the mystical experience, it has been assumed by the advocates of psychedelics that these drugs lead to a genuine spiritual experience. The modern neophyte need not undergo the traditional ascetical discipline to prepare himself for the mystical experience; the pharmacist can help him seek the experience of the Divine Reality without all those physical discomforts that have been regarded by mystics as the most indispensable requirement for such experience.

Huxley goes back to the religious rites of primitive peoples to show that intoxicants had been an essential part of their religious worship. He points out that "the drug-induced experience has been regarded by primitives and even by the highly civilized as intrinsically divine."[13] R. G. Wasson and V. Wasson certify in their monumental study *Mushrooms, Russia and History* (1957) that the plants containing psychedelic substances have been a part of the religious worship of peoples belonging to cultures widely distributed over the world. There is no denying the fact that the intoxicants have been an important part of the religious rites of ancient peoples. But the drug alone was never considered sufficient to generate the required

mystical experience. It merely acted as a stimulant to make the mind suggestive to religious prayers. *Soma* was, of course, used by the Aryans as a help
to mystical experience, and the drug is addressed in the highest strains of
adulation and veneration in the *Rigveda*. But *soma* alone was never sufficient
to give them the experience of Ultimate Reality. Adolf Kaegi aptly observes
that "Indra, the ruler of battles, takes no pleasure in the Soma offered
without prayer; he scorns the sacrificial food prepared without a song."[14]
Even in Vedic times, prayer, or the mortification of the self, was considered
an essential precondition to attain a union with the *Brahman*. Moreover, the
Vedas are a record of the mystical utterances of the ancient Aryans, and some
of the sublimest utterances are mixed with the superstitious character of
these archaic people. When we come to the *Upanishads*, which mark a more
philosophical and speculative stage of Indian thought, we do not find any
specific importance given to *soma* as a means of mystical experience. In the
Bhagavad-Gītā, *soma* is referred to only in a single *sloka* (IX:20),[15] and it
does not enjoy any specific importance as a means of God-realization. The
Bhagavad-Gītā stresses three ways to seek the mystical experience: the *Karma
Mārga* (the way of action), the *jñāna marga* (the way of knowledge), and the
Bhakti Mārga (the way of love). Huxley, too, in his anthology of mysticism,
The Perennial Philosophy (1946), nowhere talks about drugs as *the* valid means
of seeking salvation. No doubt the use of certain hemp derivatives such as
hashish, bhang, or ganja is still prevalent in India. These intoxicants form
a part of the religious worship of certain tantric cults. For instance, hashish
is smoked by the Shaivites who worship Shiva, the Creator and Destroyer,
Who Himself is said to have smoked hashish. Similarly, the *Nihangs*, a
militant sikh sect, use bhang as a part of their daily ritual. But it is difficult
to justify Masters and Houston's claim that "an estimated ninety percent of
the Indian holy men use hemp, often along with other drugs."[16] And then,
there is no evidence to suggest that the tantric yogis or the *Nihangs* undergo
any kind of spiritual transformation by taking hashish or bhang.

2

Huxley was not the first Western intellectual to experiment with mind-
changing drugs. Before him William James and Havelock Ellis had tried
these drugs to learn about their impact on consciousness. Writing about his
own experience under nitrous oxide, James asserts that his experience was
one of reconciliation, with all conflicts melting into unity. It brought him
"intense metaphysical illumination." James writes: "The centre and periphery of things seem to come together. The ego and its objects, the *meum* and
tuum are one."[17] James, however, does not try to interpret his experience in
religious terms. As an empiricist, he states just facts as he finds them. Like

Huxley, he does not attempt to equate his experience with the genuine mystical experience.

There are, of course, a number of important writers to whom the psychedelic experience seems of utmost spiritual significance. Allen Ginsberg insists that marijuana consciousness shifts attention from "second-hand ideological interpretations of experience to more *direct, slower, absorbing, occasionally microscopically minute, engagement with sensing phenomena* during the high moments or hours after one has smoked."[18] Alan Watts also points out that during the LSD experience he found himself "going through states of consciousness that corresponded precisely with every description of major mystical experience."[19] John W. Aiken, the founder of the Church of the Awakening, also claims that "a properly oriented psychedelic experience can be a deep and genuine religious experience."[20] Walter N. Pahnke's laboratory experiments with drugs suggest that some subjects under the drug reported that they had undergone profound spiritual experience.[21] Masters and Houston also observe that "out of their total of 206 subjects, six have had the mystical experience."[22]

There are also writers who claim that the drug can never promote any genuine religious experience. It is difficult for them to accept Timothy Leary's claim that the "LSD kick is a spiritual esctasy" and the LSD trip "a religious piligrimage."[23] For example, R. C. Zaehner does not give any credit to drug-induced experience because his own mescalin experience ushered him into "a world of non-sensical fantasy." He experienced neither esctasy nor eternity during his mescal experience. Zaehner says that "the experience was in a sense 'anti-religious' and that 'self-transcendence' of a sort did take place, but transcendence into a world of farcical meaninglessness."[24] The effort here has been made to suggest that there is no unanimity among the intelligent with regard to the nature of psychedelic experience.

3

Huxley took mescalin because it had always seemed possible to him that "by means of systematic meditation, or else by taking the appropriate drug, I might so change my ordinary mode of consciousness as to be able to know, from the inside, what the visionary, the medium, even the mystic were talking about."[25] He admits that the experience proved of infinite value to him. Under the impact of the drug, he realized that being and becoming, *nirvāna* and *samsāra*, are one and the same thing. Mescalin gave him a peep into that "other world" about which he had been writing so emphatically for so many years. Huxley says, "The Beatific Vision, *Sat, Chit, Ananda*, Being-Awareness-Bliss—for the first time I understood, not by inchoate hints or at a distance, but precisely and completely what those prodigious syllables referred to" (*Doors*, 18).

He describes his experience under mescalin as "the sacramental vision of reality" (*Doors*, 22). Whereas the first experience showed no interest in human affairs, the second experience has "a human content, which the earlier solitary experience with its Other Worldly quality . . . did not possess."[26] Another mescalin experience made him realize that love is the fundamental cosmic fact, that *Nirvāna* apart from the world, apart from *Mahakaȓuña* for sentient beings, is as terrible as the pains of hell. As his experiences under the drug increase, the generalizations about experience become more bold, and the earlier cautious attitude is replaced by confident, assertive statements. Moreover, he is more emphatic about it in his private correspondence than in his literary writings. About the psychedelic experience, he wrote to his friend Dr. Humphry Osmond: "What emerges as a general conclusion is the confirmation of the fact that mescalin does genuinely open the door and that everything including the Unknown in its purest, most comprehensive form can come through" (*Letters*, 771). In a letter to Victoria Ocampo, Huxley affirms that mescalin took him "beyond the realm of vision to the realm of what the mystics call 'obscure knowledge,' insight into the nature of things." He admits that the drug also brought him "the realization that, in spite of pain and tragedy, the Universe is all right, in other words that God is Love" (*Letters*, 802). Father Merton wrote to Huxley, raising a number of objections to the validity of the psychedelic mystical experience. Like Dean Inge,[27] Merton found it hard to accept drugs as a means to religious experience. Huxley's reply to him again affirms his positive attitude toward the drug-induced experience. He writes:

> In the course of the last five years I have taken mescalin twice and lysergic acid three or four times. My first experience was mainly aesthetic. Later experiences . . . helped me to understand many of the obscure utterances to be found in the writings of the mystics, Christian and Oriental. An unspeakable sense of gratitude for the privilege of being born into this universe. . . . A transcendence of the ordinary subject-object relationship. A transcendence of the fear of death. A sense of solidarity with the world and its spiritual principle . . . an understanding, not intellectual, but in some sort total, an understanding with the entire organism, of the affirmation that God is Love. (*Letters*, 863)

Similarly, in a letter to Margaret Isherwood (*Letters*, 874), Huxley reiterates his stand on mescalin. He tells her that he was able to go beyond vision into the genuine mystical experience. From his correspondence, it becomes quite evident that his psychedelic experiences confirmed his conviction that drugs can generate a genuine mystical experience. It is precisely for this reason that he advocates psychedelics in his "pragmatic dream,"

Island, which, according to Huxley, contains "practical instructions for making the imagined and desirable harmonization of European and Indian insights become a fact" (*Letters*, 944). In this novel, Huxley seems to give his valedictory message to his readers. He exhorts people to try LSD, which he names "the *moksha*-medicine, the reality-revealer, the truth-and-beauty pill."[28] The inhabitants of *Island* use this *moksha*-medicine to get experience of Divine Reality, the Clear Light of the Void. Robert MacPhail, the chief spokesman of the philosophy of *Island*, is, like Huxley, quite anxious to defend the use of psychedelics by the inhabitants of the island. He asserts that they are not "a set of self-indulgent dope-takers, wallowing in illusions and false *samadhis*."[29] He urges Will Farnaby, the neurotic, Western journalist who is totally skeptical about the existence of Ultimate Reality, to try the drug to know its effect. Will takes the *moksha*-medicine and experiences a new level of consciousness. From the description of his experience, it seems that Will gets a direct, unconceptual understanding of Ultimate Reality. Such an assertion raises the most fundamental question: can we place Will Farnaby and Huxley in the category of mystics because they describe their psychedelic experiences in religious terms?

4

Huxley's advocacy of psychedelics in *Island* has been bitterly criticized by the Establishment, which has accused him of corrupting youth. Masters and Houston observe that, to some extent, the responsibility for the seduction of the innocent lies with authors like Huxley and Alan Watts who "in their various writings imposed upon the psychedelic experience essentially Eastern ideas and terminology."[30] Huxley had absolutely no intention of misleading anybody. His chief mission in life was to dispel ignorance and to make men aware of the light within them. His refusal to appear on television in connection with drugs shows that he never wanted to be the prophet of LSD.[31] But the fact remains that he came to believe that drugs are potent enough to generate a mystical experience. To justify his claim that psychedelics really lead to a genuine religious experience, he offers a scientific explanation of the mystical experience.

Huxley accepts the Bergsonian theory of memory and perception, which states that the function of the brain and nervous system is in the main eliminative, not productive.[32] Man is at each moment capable of remembering all that has ever happened to him, and he can perceive everything that is everywhere happening in the universe. The function of the brain and nervous system is to save man from being overwhelmed by useless and irrelevant knowledge, by allowing only as much perception to come to surface as is essential for his biological survival. The enzymes regulate the supply of glucose to brain cells and enable the brain to work as an efficient reducing valve to check the full and free flow of perception. Mescalin inhibits the production of enzymes, and this lowers the amount of glucose needed by the brain and thus impairs its efficiency. The result is that strange things seem to happen to the drug-taker. Huxley says: "In some cases there may be extra-sensory perceptions. Other persons discover a world of visionary beauty. To others again is revealed the glory, the infinite value and meaning-fulness of naked existence, of the given, unconceptualized event. In the final stage of egolessness there is an 'obscure knowledge' that All is in all—that All is actually each" (*Doors*, 26).

If rational consciousness is just a fragment of that larger consciousness, of which we become aware at certain levels—aesthetic, visionary or mysti-cal—and if the lowering of the biological efficiency of the brain can give us entry into that larger consciousness, then the whole matter depends on the change in one's body chemistry. Huxley says that Yogic practices—fasts, prayers, flagellation, and other physical and mental austerities that the tradi-tional mystics advocated as the most important requirements of the seeker of truth—were just the means to change body chemistry. Because drugs are available now, the novice need not undergo rigorous ascetical discipline. What he needs is a pill that will produce the required change in his body without any physical discomforts. Huxley gives a rationale of yogic breathing exercises: "Practised systematically, these exercises result, after a time, in prolonged suspensions of breath. Long suspensions of breath lead to a high concentration of carbon dioxide in the lungs and blood, and this increase in the concentration of CO_2 lowers the efficiency of the brain as a reducing valve and permits the entry into consciousness of experiences visionary or mystical, from 'out there.' " [33]

The psalm singing of the Christians, the mantra intoning of the Bud-dhist monks, and the *japam* of the Hindus have one aim—to increase the concentration of carbon dioxide in the lungs and blood, which results in the lowering of the efficiency of the cerebral reducing valve, which allows the doors of perception to open wide. Huxley observes that the "way to the super-conscious is through the sub-conscious and the way . . . to the sub-conscious is through the chemistry of individual cells" (*Heaven*, 63). In defense of the chemically-induced experience, and as an answer to those who would not cherish a scientific explanation of fasting, hymn singing, and mental prayer, Huxley suggests:

A similar conclusion will be reached by those whose philosophy is unduly "spiritual". God, they will insist, is a spirit and is to be worshipped in spirit. Therefore an experience which is chemically conditioned cannot be an experience of the divine. But, in one way or another, *all* our experiences are chemically conditioned, and if we imagine that some of them are purely "spiritual", purely "intellectual", purely "aesthetic", it is merely because we have never troubled to investigate the internal chemical environment at the moment of their occurrence. Furthermore, it is a matter of historical record that most contemplatives worked systematically to modify their body chemistry, with a view to creating the internal conditions favorable to spiritual insight. . . . Today we know how to lower the efficiency of the cerebral reducing valve by direct chemical action, and without the risk of inflicting serious damage on the psycho-physical organism. (*Heaven*, 73–74)

If spirituality means just a change in the body chemistry, then surely the vast, degenerate majority could be brought back to the path of peace and joy. And that this is not so raises one's doubt with regard to the possibility of synthetic sainthood. Huxley's conclusions are, however, in conformity with the findings of the specialists in the fields of psychology and pharmacology. William Sargant, for instance, suggests the possibility of mechanical sainthood. He observes that if political indoctrination is a success, and if human reflexes can be reconditioned, then a lecutomy operation could bring about a religious conversion. But such conclusions are at variance with the tenets of all religions. Man is said to be superior to animal creation because he has a will, which is the true mark of his freedom. If chemical or mechanical conversion can bring about an involuntary change in man's religious beliefs, human will then loses its entire significance. Sargant stresses the point that "little scientific support has been found that any individual can resist for an indefinite period the physiological stress imposed on his body and mind." He suggests that we "only delude ourselves if we think that any but the most rare individuals can endure unchanged to the very end."[34]

To identify a psychedelic experience with a genuine mystical experience is perhaps to go too far. To justify Frank Barron's claim that "chemical technology has made available to millions the experience of transcendence of the individual ego which a century ago was available to the disciplined mystic,"[35] it is necessary to look into the nature of a genuine mystical experience. The only empirical test a student of mysticism can apply to ascertain whether a particular mystic's experience is genuine or not is to see the effect such an experience produces upon the mystic's personality. "Wherefore by their fruits Ye shall know them" (St. Matthew 7:20), not by their roots. There can be no objection to chemicals as means of transcendence if the experience under them can bring saintliness, the most coveted fruit of a mystic's pursuit. The mystical experience brings equanimity, resignation, fortitude, humility, and unbounded love and compassion to the mystic. There is no evidence to suggest that the drug user suffers such a transformation of personality. Psychedelic experience brings elation, but falls short of the ecstasy of a mystic. The drug-induced experience merely intensifies the senses, but the mystical experience is essentially supersensuous in nature. If the true test of a genuine mystical experience is the annihilation

of the ego, as Huxley emphasizes in *The Perennial Philosophy*, then the psychedelic experience fails to qualify as a genuine mystical experience because it
inflates the self rather than effaces it. The psychedelic experience does not
prove of much value because it does not provide any new outlook on life.
P. J. Saher aptly observes that mysticism "through mescalin resembles paper
currency during inflation; it was valid, yet its validity was a joke for it was
without value."[36]

W. T. Stace, however, employs the "principle of Causal Indifference"[37]
to ascertain whether a psychedelic experience can be classed as a genuine
mystical experience. According to this principle, if the phenomenological
descriptions of the two experiences, the drug-induced and the mystical, are
similar, then the two experiences are certainly one, and the drug-induced
experience is as valid as the experience of those who have attained it after
years of arduous mental and moral discipline. It has been noted earlier that
the descriptions of the various drug-induced experiences are not similar.
Whereas some claim that they had the experience of ineffable bliss, others
brand their experiences as mere hallucinations, nonsensical fantasy. On the
other hand, mystics all over the world are unanimous with regard to the
outcome of *their* religious experience.

The psychedelics, it seems, are potent enough to give us a peep into
the world of enhanced beauty and wonder that our senses are not accustomed
to perceive in their ordinary way. At the most, these can produce a kind of
visionary experience, but "visionary experience," as Huxley puts it, "is not
the same as mystical experience. Mystical experience is beyond the realm of
opposites. Visionary experience is still within that realm" (*Heaven*, 56).
Drugs, it seems, can never provide a genuine mystical experience. J. Krishnamurti questions "the necessity of taking drugs at all—drugs that promise
a psychedelic expansion of the mind, great visions and intensity," and emphasizes that "no golden pill is ever going to solve our human problems."[38] To
attain to a level of mystical consciousness, the disciplining of the apelike,
restless mind is an imperative necessity. The effort is a costly one and requires
years of mental and moral struggle. In this context S. Radhakrishnan affirms
the oriental stance: "No tricks of absolution or payment by proxy, no greased
paths of smooth organs and stained glass windows can help us much."[39]
Surely no golden pill can take man to the City of God. It may be an aid to
the goal, but it cannot be an exclusive means of attaining saintliness. Even
Walter Pahnke concedes that "the drug is only a trigger, a catalyst or
facilitating agent," and that "mystical experiences are hardest, certainly not
automatic, even under optimal conditions."[40]

While on his death bed, Huxley took LSD, perhaps to facilitate his
entry into what he often termed the Clear Light of the Void. Under the
impact of LSD, Huxley, however, realized that he had been wrong in claiming that drugs can produce a genuine mystical experience. His tape-recorded
conversation seems to be a confession of his failure. He was wrong when he

thought that he was making an absolute "cosmic gift" (psychedelics) to the world and that he had a sort of "star role" (as the advocate of psychedelics) (*TM*, 268). He realized that "when *one thinks one's got beyond oneself, one hasn't*" (*TM*, 269). Huxley realized his error and concluded that "there must be no magic tricks," that we must learn to "come to reality without the enchanter's wand and his book of words" (*TM*, 289–90). Huxley's last words, comments R. C. Zaehner, "are his recantation and his last will and testament, a warning [against the belief] . . . that psychedelic experience is not merely similar to mystical experience but is identical with it."[41] Surely, the psychedelic "magic trick" will never do, and there can be no short cut to eternity.

Huxley had never had any first-hand genuine mystical experience. Julian Huxley testifies that "Aldous was never a mystic in any exclusive or wooly sense, though he was keenly interested in the facts of mystical experience."[42] Jerome Meckier also observes, "To Huxley himself, the consciousness of being no more separate, of having attained union with the Divine Ground, probably never came."[43] He could never attain to the state of nonattachment that he advocates as the precondition for God-realization. He was never able to rise above the ordinary worldly level and was often disturbed by the failures and successes of temporal life. This is quite evident from his correspondence in later life, which expresses his professional anxiety for what early theatrical success could never gain.[44] Laurence Brander also suggests that Huxley is "like most Westerners, incapable of that 'holy indifference' to which he often refers."[45] He did genuinely knock at the doors of the Kingdom of Heaven, but the Kingdom of Heaven never revealed its celestial glory to him. He was a pilgrim who was encumbered by heavy intellectual baggage he could never throw away to enter the straight and narrow gate of this kingdom. He could never renounce his formidable intellect, which always came between him and the Beatific Vision. Drugs simply revealed to him a world of visionary beauty, and the visionary experience affirmed his belief that beyond the visionary world there lies a world of spiritual experience. LSD is no panacea for the spiritual maladies of mankind. Huxley's quest for mystical experience through psychedelics fails, and there seems to be, for him at least, no possibility of synthetic sainthood.

Notes

1. In the essay "One and Many" Huxley concedes that, officially speaking, he is an agnostic. Aldous Huxley, *Do What You Will*, Collected Edition (1929; rpt. London: Chatto & Windus, 1956), p. 1.

2. Aldous Huxley, *Proper Studies*, Collected Edition (1927; rpt. London: Chatto & Windus, 1957), p. 175.

3. In a letter (22 August 1939) to Dilipkuma Roy, Pondichey, Huxley wrote that his early interest in mysticism was "predominantly negative" and that he "read a good deal of Western and Eastern writing, always with intense interest, but always with a wish to

'debunk' them." Sisirkumar Ghose, *Aldous Huxley: A Cynical Salvationist* (Bombay: Asia Publishing House, 1962), p. 187n. This letter is not found in *Letters of Aldous Huxley*, ed. Grover Smith (London: Chatto & Windus, 1969).

4. Aldous Huxley, *Time Must Have a Stop* (1944; rpt. London: Chatto & Windus, 1946), p. 289.

5. Aldous Huxley, *Ends and Means*, Collected Edition (1937; rpt. London: Chatto & Windus, 1957), p. 286.

6. J. B. Coates, *The Critics of the Human Person: Some Personalist Interpretations* (London: Longmans, Green, 1949), p. 41.

7. "Introduction," *Psychedelics: The Uses and Implications of Hallucinogenic Drugs*, ed. Bernard S. Aaronson and Humphry Osmond (London: The Hogarth Press, 1971), p. 10. Hereafter to be cited as *Psychedelics*.

8. Laura Archera Huxley, *This Timeless Moment: A Personal View of Aldous Huxley* (London: Chatto & Windus, 1969), p. 11. Henceforth referred to parenthetically in text as *TM*.

9. R. E. L. Masters and Jean Houston, *The Varieties of Psychedelic Experience* (London: Turnstone Books, 1973), pp. 252–253.

10. Aldous Huxley, *Jesting Pilate*, Collected Edition (1926; rpt. London: Chatto & Windus, 1957), p. 191.

11. Aldous Huxley, *Brief Candles: Four Stories*, Collected Edition (1930; rpt. London: Chatto & Windus, 1957), p. 246.

12. Aldous Huxley, *Antic Hay* (1923; rpt. New York: The Modern Library, 1951), p. 293.

13. Aldous Huxley, "Appendix," *The Devils of Loudun* (London: Chatto & Windus, 1952), p. 362.

14. Adolf Kaegi, *The Rigveda: The Oldest Literature of the Indians*, trans. R. Arrowsmith, Indian Edition (New Delhi: Amarko Book Agency, 1972), pp. 78–79.

15. *The Bhagavad-Gītā* (Gorakhpur: Gita Press, n.d.).

16. Masters and Houston, *The Varieties*, p. 37.

17. William James, *The Will to Believe, Human Immortality and Other Essays on Popular Philosophy* (New York: Dover Publications, 1956), p. 295n.

18. Allen Ginsberg, "First Manifesto to End the Bringdown," *Voices of Revelation*, ed. Nancy H. Deane (Boston: Little, Brown and Company, 1970), p. 345.

19. Alan Watts, "Psychedelics and Religious Experience," *Psychedelics*, p. 133.

20. John W. Aiken, "The Church of the Awakening," *Psychedelics*, p. 174.

21. Walter N. Pahnke, "Drugs and Mysticism," *Psychedelics*, p. 162.

22. Masters and Houston, p. 307.

23. Timothy Leary, *The Politics of Ecstasy* (London: Palladin, 1970), p. 286.

24. R. C. Zaehner, "Appendix B," *Mysticism Sacred and Profane: An Enquiry into Some Varieties of Praeternatural Experience* (Oxford: Clarendon Press, 1957), p. 226.

25. Aldous Huxley, *The Doors of Perception* (New York: Harper & Brothers, 1954), p. 14. Hereafter to be cited parenthetically in text as *Doors*.

26. Aldous Huxley, *Letters of Aldous Huxley*, p. 720. Hereafter to be cited parenthetically in text as *Letters*.

27. W. R. Inge, *Mysticism in Religion* (London: Rider & Co., 1969), p. 36.

28. Aldous Huxley, *Island* (London: Chatto & Windus, 1962), p. 136.

29. *Island*, p. 140.

30. Masters and Houston, p. 260.

31. In a letter to Dr. Humphry Osmond, Huxley suggests his friend maintain secrecy about the LSD experience and its effects. See *Letters*, p. 803.

32. Huxley accepts the Bergsonian model of the human mind. See his letter to Humphry Osmond, *Letters*, p. 668.

33.   Aldous Huxley, "Appendix I," *Heaven and Hell* (New York: Harper & Brothers, 1956), p. 62. Hereafter to be cited parenthetically in text as *Heaven*.

34.   William Sargant, *Battle for the Mind: A Physiology of Conversion and Brain Washing* (London: William Heinemann, 1957), p. 231.

35.   Frank Barron, "Motivational Patterns in LSD Usage," *LSD, Man and Society*, ed. Richard C. Debold and Russell C. Leaf (London: Faber and Faber, 1969), p. 9.

36.   P. J. Saher, *Eastern Wisdom and Western Thought: A Comparative Study In the Modern Philosophy of Religion* (London: Allen & Unwin, 1969), p. 172.

37.   W. T. Stace, *Mysticism and Philosophy* (London: Macmillan, 1961), p. 29.

38.   J. Krishnamurti, *The Only Revolution*, ed. Mary Lutyens (London: Victor Gollancz, 1970), p. 175.

39.   S. Radhakrishnan, *An Idealist View of Life*, 2nd ed. (London: Allen & Unwin, 1957), p. 113.

40.   Walter Pahnke, "LSD and Religious Experience," *LSD, Man & Society*, p. 65.

41.   R. C. Zaehner, *Drugs, Mysticism and Make-Believe* (London: Collins, 1972), p. 109.

42.   Julian Huxley, ed., *Aldous Huxley 1894–1963: A Memorial Volume* (London: Chatto & Windus, 1965), p. 21.

43.   Jerome Meckier, *Aldous Huxley: Satire and Structure* (London: Chatto & Windus, 1969), p. 152.

44.   George Woodcock, *Dawn and the Darkest Hour: A Study of Aldous Huxley* (London: Faber and Faber, 1972), p. 265.

45.   Laurence Brander, *Aldous Huxley: A Critical Study* (London: Rupert Hart-Davis, 1969), p. 154.

Accepting the Universe: The "Rampion-Hypothesis" in *Point Counter Point* and *Island*

Keith May

Huxley commented in a letter that "Rampion is just some of Lawrence's notions on legs. The actual character of the man was incomparably queerer and more complex than that."[1] The obvious truth of this remark invites us to consider why Huxley chose to reduce the complexity of Lawrence's personality and ideas in exactly the way that he did. Probably Huxley could not have contrived a sound approximation to the real Lawrence, but why out of the tangled web that was Lawrence did he pick the Rampion thread?

Huxley evidently discerned in Lawrence a quality of great relevance to his own explorations, and this quality, I suggest, was connected with Lawrence's confident, intuitive rejection of Platonic idealism. This was the element in Lawrence that Huxley wished—or, rather, needed—to make use of. It would be superfluous here to discuss Lawrence's anti-idealistic attitudes in detail, but a few observations will be useful. In chapter nine of *Sons and Lovers* Paul Morel, expressing the author's own belief, announces to Miriam Leivers: "God doesn't *know* things. He *is* things." In the foreword to *Sons and Lovers* (the famous letter of 1913 to Edward Garnett) Lawrence maintains that Flesh rather than Spirit is primordial; that in the beginning was the Flesh, not the Word.[2] Lawrence argues in *Psychoanalysis and the Unconscious* that life is not a general force but is simply a general term for myriads of individual life-processes. There is no Life-Force behind these palpable phenomena.[3] Lawrence's reverence for the mystery of life, his distaste for science, his search for a new way to God, did not controvert his fundamentally anti-idealistic beliefs, but on the contrary confirmed them; for he continued to apprehend God as the *being* of each individual plant or creature, existence rather than essence, yet quite beyond analysis or explanation. It is also to the point that Lawrence regarded concepts, not indeed as dispensable, but as mere guidelines that should be modified at the dictates of the "blood." Abstractions or universals were less real in his view than particulars. As a

From *Studies in the Novel* 9 (1977): 418–27. Copyright © 1977 by North Texas State University. Reprinted by permission of the publisher.

consequence of these beliefs Lawrence, it seems, was never troubled by a sense that his consciousness was divorced from the world of nature. In Huxley's terms Lawrence was the complete "pagan."

In Huxley's writings a pagan is one who accepts the world. But of course in both fiction and life there are crude pagans whose acceptance is a product of unawareness and who can often adapt themselves to bad social conditions as well as to the laws of nature. Much more rarely there are pagans of fine intelligence and exquisite sensibility for whom adaptation to an imperfect social milieu is at best a complicated, and perhaps an arduous, business. In life Frieda Lawrence, though socially an aristocrat, seems to have been a crude pagan, and Huxley said of her not only that "she was profoundly matter-of-fact, accepting events as they were given, in all their painful or delightful confusion,"[4] but also that "being with her makes me believe Buddha was right when he numbered stupidity among the deadly sins."[5] Lawrence, unlike his wife, possessed supreme, mercurial awareness, yet he too accepted the universe and felt himself to be part of the great natural process. He was at odds with much of the man-made world, precisely because he saw it as the product of perverted idealism.

It is clear that even at the stage of *Crome Yellow* Huxley had an ambivalent attitude toward his own idealistic tendencies. To begin with (taking only the novels into account), Denis Stone envied Anne Wimbush her crude paganism. After that, in *Antic Hay*, Gumbril, comic and tormented, sensed the "crystal quiet" that lay behind the cacophony of daily life; yet Myra Viveash remained enticing, even in her ennui. In *Those Barren Leaves* Francis Chelifer sneered at Wordsworth's "sense sublime of something far more deeply interfused," but Chelifer's attitudes were cautiously opposed, rather than defeated, by Calamy's concluding reflections. That was in 1925: by 1929 Huxley had written three anti-idealistic works, *Proper Studies*, *Point Counter Point*, and *Do What You Will*. In a letter of December 1929, he remarked with Chelifer-like dismissiveness: "All we've perversely gone back on since Homer's day! All the beastly things from tragedy and spirituality to disgust and *ennui* that we've invented! Plato's at the bottom of it all, I suppose."[6]

However, it would be inaccurate to say that in four years of the late twenties Huxley put aside the aspirations he had expressed through Calamy and went some of the way over to Chelifer's side. What actually happened, as we can tell from *Point Counter Point*, was that Huxley grew capable of defining his problem more precisely. His observations of Lawrence apparently reinforced his own conjectures that an individual should be many-faceted, a succession of states rather than a fixed character, and that it might be possible to accept a purely phenomenal reality without confining oneself in a prison of banalities. This is the working hypothesis in *Point Counter Point*, and indeed it is not misleading (though of course it is a simplification) to see the novel as an elaborate experiment set up to test what may as well be called the "Rampion-hypothesis."

It is evident that Huxley entertained doubts only about the ultimate validity of the Rampion-hypothesis, for he was quite certain of its superiority over other modern attitudes to life. The disdain for all the attitudes in the novel other than Rampion's remained to the end of Huxley's career, though it was moderated here and there by charity. The fault with every character, except Mark and Mary Rampion is, as Rampion tirelessly (and to some, tiresomely) points out is the character's onesidedness. Huxley was animadverting, not chiefly against evil or stupidity, but against living by one ruling principle. The flaw in every flawed attitude is its partiality, its exclusiveness, its failure to take account of even the most obvious facts and arguments that fail to uphold it. None of the numerous unsatisfactory characters adequately conducts an internal dialectic, but is content with a straightforward thesis— the fascist thesis, the communist thesis, the hedonist thesis, and the rest. This deficiency alone renders each attitude false and ridiculous. Huxley, on the other hand, was aiming for a totalization in which every thesis would be confronted by its antithesis and finally transcended. The right answer would therefore be a grand synthesis, overlooking nothing.

Rampion and the views he expresses constitute such a synthesis, but they do so, as I have said, only in an experimental way. In order to test the Rampion-hypothesis it was necessary, from Huxley's point of view, to confront Rampion with something or someone representing spirituality; something ecstatic, unalloyed, harmonious, beyond good and evil, apparently lying outside time. To appreciate this juxtaposition it is helpful to recall Shelley's image in "Adonais": "Life, like a dome of many-coloured glass / Stains the white radiance of Eternity." In effect, Rampion is content with the dome of many-coloured glass and either denies the reality of the white radiance or, at all events, deplores man's efforts to glimpse it. On the other hand, a part of Beethoven's A minor Quartet according to Spandrell (and perhaps according to Huxley himself) delivers to us an assurance that there is such a white radiance and that it is supremely valuable.

There are at least two interesting features of the disputation between Spandrell and Rampion: first, the character of Spandrell, and secondly the indecisiveness of the outcome. Why should Huxley have given to Spandrell the task of casting doubt on what would otherwise have been the positive message of the book? (It is certainly the positive message of *Do What You Will*, which was published in the year following *Point Counter Point*.) Plainly there was the technical advantage of the melodrama in the final chapter to take into account, but this cannot have been Huxley's sole consideration. The point is that Spandrell, a "pervert" in Rampion's sense of the word and in the everyday sense, a satanist, a death-worshipper, is the only character in the book who effectively stands up to Rampion. Yet it was the author who desired to question the Rampion-hypothesis and who at some time, either in reality or in daydream, might well have argued with Lawrence rather as Spandrell argues with Rampion.

Apart from Walter Bidlake and Philip Quarles the characters of this novel are largely products of external observation. It has always been clear that Spandrell derives in part from Baudelaire and Dostoevsky's Stavrogin in *The Devils*, but his fascination with degradation and decay, together with his paradoxical but convincing desire for purity, are not qualities that Huxley merely discerned in others. We can detect the author's comparatively intimate understanding of this figure.

Spandrell is a distinctly Freudian conception (though this is not to suggest that he was in part borrowed from Freud's works). First, plainly, there is his Oedipus complex, so fully brought out in the conversation with Mrs. Knoyle in chapter thirteen. Next, he has that preference for the "lower type" of woman which Freud analyzes in his essay, "The Most Prevalent Form of Degradation in Erotic Life."[7] Finally, he is driven by what Freud called the "death instincts" which further "the most universal endeavour of all living substance—namely to return to the quiescence of the inorganic world."[8] Spandrell as a death-worshipper is the extreme representative of the tendency which Rampion condemns, the tendency to narrow the self down to a single principle. Philip Quarles's exclusion of feeling, Burlap's sentimentality, Walter's infatuation with Lucy, Lord Edward's preference for his laboratory, and the similar unifying traits of other characters, constitute a desire for unity at the expense of life. These people are "characters" because they have eliminated all but one mode of response, while Rampion is a "character" largely in his endless recommendations that all one's potential selves should be actualized. Spandrell, whose desire for unity is so great that he actively seeks death, is the proper person to put up against Rampion. But—and this is the telling point—in the final argument with Rampion, as the A minor Quartet is played, Spandrell comes near to triumphing over Rampion.

At the beginning of the scene Rampion is cocksure. "Where's Beethoven?" he asks. "Where's the famous proof of God's existence and the superiority of Jesus's morality?" (594). Spandrell responds by playing his record from the moment at which the *helige Dankgesang* begins. Spandrell has to change the record over just after the end of the first "Lydian" part and while doing so he asks, "Isn't it a proof?" Rampion's reply is that the music is the "art of a man who's lost his body"; it's a "hymn in praise of eunuchism" (596).

Spandrell persists by playing the second side of the record and now Beethoven's harmonies begin to work their magic more effectively upon Rampion, so that his subsequent comments are less confident. "You're quite right," he says. "It *is* heaven, it *is* the life of the soul" (597). But he insists that this life of the soul is diseased, a cancerous growth consuming the healthy cells of the body. By now Spandrell is disheartened, but he makes

Rampion listen to the last and best part of the movement. The music grows ever purer until at last it achieves the "miraculous paradox of eternal life and eternal repose," and Rampion confesses "Almost thou persuadest me" (598). Rampion's final comment that the music is "too good" smacks slightly of obduracy. Spandrell has fought for his very life in this scene and now he is finished. But Rampion has been diminished in the process.

What we have here is surely the dramatization of a debate within Huxley himself. A part of the author that both theoretically and practically desires life, with all its manifest imperfections, is checked, though not overwhelmed, by another part that longs for a heaven of stasis and serenity. The life-worshipping Huxley who sounds so tub-thumpingly sure of himself when he speaks through Rampion and when in *Do What You Will* he conducts his criticisms of Baudelaire and Pascal, is counter-balanced by the Shelleyan Huxley for whom purity, albeit deathly, is still the goal. Thus *Point Counter Point* represents an impasse, and much of the rest of Huxley's career was devoted to finding the way ahead.

It has often been assumed that the way ahead was found in the mid-thirties and that it took a "spiritual" form. A more discerning view of Huxley's progress sees *Point Counter Point*, along with other works of his "life-worshipping phase," as a diversion, a loop-line from the main track. I do not aim to refute this opinion, but to qualify it by suggesting that *Eyeless in Gaza* and the "American" novels up to *The Genius and the Goddess* constitute progressive corrections or refinements of the Rampion-hypothesis until it will stand the test of Beethoven's music and Spandrell's assertions about the Beatific Vision. In other words, Huxley's life-worshipping attitudes loomed large in a particular period but just as they were present at the beginning of his career, so they continued to the end.

To be sure the process of correction took the form of a prolonged (though never uniform) spiritual excursion, as if Huxley were saying to Rampion: "Until you have fully understood and acknowledged the importance of spirit, you cannot grow into what you should be—the rounded man. You also are incomplete, pugnacious, uncharitable. Yet the ideal of which you are a blueprint must sooner or later be realised." Thus, at or near the beginning of Huxley's spiritual excursion he caused Anthony Beavis in *Eyeless in Gaza* to conclude that Lawrence had wished to work up the raw material of life merely to the animal level, whereas it should be worked up to the level of spirit.[9] But by the time of *Island* Huxley offered a different emphasis, a commingling of spirituality and animality. Similarly, at the end of *Eyeless in Gaza* Anthony contemplates "Goodness beyond the possibility of evil,"[10] a condition which the Palanese in *Island* know to be impossible and no longer desire.

In his last novel Huxley either reached or very nearly reached the goal of understanding the rounded man. Dr. Robert MacPhail (though not MacPhail alone) is what Huxley obscurely had in mind when he simplified

Lawrence into Rampion, and Will Farnaby's growth in understanding as he listens to Bach constitutes a reconciliation of Spandrell's metaphysical views with Rampion's. *Island* is the synthesis which Huxley could not find at the time of *Point Counter Point*. In *Island* Huxley conquered his Platonism, elements of which had lingered through the years, and came down to earth again; but this time the earth was shot through with celestial gleams.

The best way to see the truth of this thesis is to recall Will Farnaby's vision as, under the influence of the *moksha*-medicine, he listens to Bach's Fourth Brandenburg Concerto. The parallel with Beethoven's Quartet in *Point Counter Point* is plain: in each instance the music purports to offer to a sceptical man the Beatific Vision, and the vision is vouchsafed just before a violent dénouement. But these formal and thematic similarities are less interesting than one notable difference: the music in *Point Counter Point* is severely qualified by its aftermath, while the catastrophic conclusion of *Island* does not negate the *moksha*-vision. If Huxley at the time of the earlier novel was tempted by Spandrell's view that the purest music proves the existence of another world, a God who stands apart from His universe, by the time of *Island* he was sure that such music proves just the occasional heavenliness of earth itself. Likewise, the purity of the music is no longer regarded as the antithesis of evil (the "Essential Horror") but as a quality that somehow flows into evil. Good and evil are not finally separable. So in Huxley's final understanding there is no Manichaeism, no Platonic idealism, no "white radiance of eternity," no unknowable God, but only Eckhart's God of "Is-ness," and an eternity of "non-stop, perpetual creation."[11]

It should not be overlooked that throughout *Island*, alongside references to the "Buddha-nature" and the "Clear Light of the Void," there are concomi-tant (not contradictory) references to the undesirability of Calvinism and recurrent attacks on other-worldliness. The emphasis is upon present, percep-tible reality. "Good Being" is knowing who one is; knowing the real, variegated processes of consciousness rather than entertaining relatively fixed self-images. The recommendation is thoroughly existentialistic and may in fact be compared with Sartre's recommendations in *Being and Nothingness* to cultivate continual awareness of one's own consciousness.[12] Interestingly enough Sartre in another work, *The Psychology of the Imagination*, anticipates Huxley's later view of the significance of music. Sartre writes: "The symphony [Beethoven's Seventh Symphony] accordingly appears as a perpetual else-where, as a perpetual absence. We must not think of it (as Spandrell does in Huxley's *Point Counter Point* and as so many Platonists do) as existing in another world, in an intelligible heaven. It is not only outside of time and space (as are essences, for example), but is also outside of the *real*, outside of existence. I do not hear it really, I hear it imaginatively."[13]

Presumably it is because the later Huxley, the Huxley of *Island*, agreed with this view that he made Will Farnaby stop listening to Bach and observe the actual world—the furniture, the praying mantis and the face of Susila.

God is both the imaginatively heard music and the actually perceived woman. As Rampion says in *Point Counter Point*, "God's not apart, not above, not outside. . . . He's in the very body, in the blood and bowels, in the heart and skin and loins" (587).

At the end of *Island* Will Farnaby is in a position to become the complete man of whom Mark Rampion was an unsatisfactory sketch. Critics have normally regarded the presentation of Rampion as a technical failure, but he is a failure in conception as well. He is genuinely idealized throughout *Point Counter Point*, so that his inability to carry off the palm at the end is not a deliberate irony but a sign of the author's puzzlement: Rampion is right, but somehow he cannot be altogether right.

Huxley's advance in understanding of what he had intended by Rampion seems to have been aided in the last decade of his life by acquaintanceship with the psychologist, Abraham H. Maslow.[14] Maslow, whose major book, *Motivation and Personality*, came out in 1954, claimed to have discovered empirically the phenomenon of the "self-actualizing" individual. These persons, Maslow insists, are rare (and may be growing rarer), but they exist. In the past such figures as Goethe, Keats, Franklin, and Whitman may well have been self-actualizers. Among contemporaries Maslow lists Einstein, Eleanor Roosevelt, Albert Schweitzer, and Huxley himself. Such people are characterized by breadth of development: instead of being readily definable (like most characters in even the best fiction and many in real life) they are remarkably diverse, tending to realize all or most of their potential capacities. They are supremely realistic, nonegotistical, spontaneous, creative (in some fashion), and relatively independent of cultural and environmental influences. They have a capacity for continuingly fresh appreciation of the world around them, a clear moral sense (which is not necessarily conventional), and a "democratic character-structure." Many of them are liable regularly to have "peak experiences," or periods of great joy, shading upwards into mystical experiences. However, they are not by any means devoid of vices or incapable of occasional bad behavior. But perhaps the feature of self-actualizing individuals that most confirms the Rampion-hypothesis is their marked tendency to reconcile psychological dichotomies. To take examples, they cannot be classified as either extrovert or introvert, as aggressive or submissive, as ascetic or sensual, as cerebral or emotional. It is not that they exemplify some golden mean, but that they display any of these traits according to circumstances and inclination. In particular, for our purposes, they seem to disprove the epigraph to *Point Counter Point*: passion and reason are not inevitable causes of self-division.[15]

Maslow's assertions, like the assertions of *Island*, may be regarded as speculative, and, in any event, it was Huxley's uncertainty about these matters in the late twenties that provided some of the driving-force behind *Point Counter Point*. The small degree of tension in *Island* is purely dramatic, whereas the tension in *Point Counter Point* expressed the author's own state of mind. Presumably this partly explains the superiority of *Point Counter Point* over *Island* as a novel.

Point Counter Point stands as Huxley's main contribution to the twentieth-century literature of metaphysical uncertainty. (Such literature was a signal feature of the twenties especially, but plainly it was not confined to that decade.) The Huxleyan qualities of irony and harsh, elegant clarity are brought to bear on the problem of how to live in the absence of some transcendent scheme of meaning and values. By the twenties the positivist and scientific certainties, which had so recently replaced religious certainties, were breaking down. The existentialist vision, though represented by nineteenth-century figures such as Kierkegaard, Dostoevsky, and Nietszche, had not yet permeated Western consciousness.[16] *Point Counter Point* contains the quasi-existentialist attitudes of Rampion, but, as we have seen, such a vision of fragmentariness was not yet thoroughly acceptable to Huxley. For the most part, therefore, the novel is an attack on what Thomas Mann, writing at about the same time, called "all the premature apparent harmonies and pseudo-perfections of life that rest upon certain and morally inadequate awareness."[17]

The chief mode of attack was to arrange a series of tragic nemeses or comic comeuppances (not forgetting the gratuitous, nontragic catastrophe of the death of Little Phil), so that a variety of "premature apparent harmonies" would be shown up. However, this was more than a mode of attack, and certainly more than an architectural or polemical device: it embodied Huxley's cast of mind.

In this respect, as in others, Huxley differed from Philip Quarles. Philip is much more of a Pyrrhonist than his creator, and when, in chapter thirty-two, Philip outlines his plan for a novel of ideas he omits the element of nemesis. But Huxley was less interested than perhaps even he realized at the time in producing structural or other brilliancies and more urgently concerned to show up contemporary errors. It is as if he keenly desired, for example, to get hold of John Bidlake (which is to say, any voluptuary) and demonstrate to him that the body is decaying as well as beautiful. Likewise, he wished to show the Illidges of this world the logical outcome of their political theories; or, more lightheartedly, to bring the Sidney Quarleses to an appropriate humiliation.

Such vehemence belies Pyrrhonism in the author. Indeed it seems likely that in 1928 Huxley—who was not adept at introspection—failed to appreciate the extent to which his Pyrrhonic stance had crumbled and that he had produced a remarkable novel out of a clash between some Quarlesian habits of mind and a more energetic moral engagement.

Notes

1. Grover Smith, ed., *Letters of Aldous Huxley* (London: Chatto & Windus, 1969), p. 340.

2. Aldous Huxley, ed., *Letters of D. H. Lawrence* (London: William Heinemann, 1932), pp. 95–102.

3. D. H. Lawrence, *Fantasia of the Unconscious and Psychoanalysis and the Unconscious* (Harmondsworth: Penguin Books, 1971), pp. 212 ff.

4. *Letters of Aldous Huxley*, p. 831.

5. Ibid., p. 335.

6. Ibid., p. 322. Cf. the remark given to Philip Quarles: "Plato wrote marvellously well, and that's why people still go on believing in his pernicious philosophy" (See *Point Counter Point* [London: Chatto & Windus, 1928], p. 439. Subsequent references are to this edition).

7. See Sigmund Freud, *Collected Papers*, vol. 4, trans. under the supervision of Joan Riviere (London: Hogarth Press, 1925), pp. 203–16.

8. Freud, *Beyond the Pleasure Principle*, trans. James Strachey (London: Hogarth Press, 1950), p. 86. First published in German in 1920.

9. Aldous Huxley, *Eyeless in Gaza* (London: Chatto & Windus, 1936), pp. 357 ff.

10. Ibid., p. 617.

11. Aldous Huxley, *Island* (London: Chatto & Windus, 1962), p. 269.

12. Sartre makes this recommendation in various works, but see especially *Being and Nothingness*, trans. Hazel E. Barnes (London: Methuen, 1958), Part 2, chap. 3 on "Transcendence."

13. Robert Denoon Cumming, ed., *The Philosophy of Jean-Paul Sartre* (London: Methuen, 1968), pp. 95 ff.

14. The British writer, Colin Wilson, has informed me about Huxley's friendship with Maslow in this period, and Maslow's influence is discernible in *Island*.

15. See Abraham H. Maslow, *Motivation and Personality* (New York: Harper and Row, 1954), chap. 11.

16. The early twentieth-century philosophers of existentialism, Husserl, Jaspers, and Heidegger were formulating, or had already formulated, their views, but these were not fully accessible, even to so "advanced" and erudite a person as Huxley.

17. See Thomas Mann, *Past Masters and Other Papers*, trans. H. T. Lowe-Porter (London: Secker and Warburg, 1933), p. 198.

Selected Bibliography

◆

Primary Works

NOVELS

Crome Yellow, 1921.
Antic Hay, 1923.
Those Barren Leaves, 1925.
Point Counter Point, 1928.
Brave New World, 1932.
Eyeless in Gaza, 1936.
After Many a Summer Dies the Swan, 1939.
Time Must Have a Stop, 1944.
Ape and Essence, 1948.
The Genius and the Goddess, 1955.
Island, 1962.

OTHER WORKS

The Burning Wheel, 1916 (poetry).
The Defeat of Youth, 1918 (poetry).
Limbo, 1920 (short stories).
Leda, 1920 (poetry).
Mortal Coils, 1922 (short stories).
On the Margin, 1923 (essays).
Little Mexican, 1924 (short stories).
Along the Road, 1925 (essays).
Two or Three Graces, 1926 (short stories).
Jesting Pilate, 1926 (travel).
Proper Studies, 1927 (essays).
Arabia Infelix, 1929 (poetry).
Do What You Will, 1929 (essays).

Brief Candles, 1930 (short stories).
Vulgarity in Literature, 1930 (essay).
The World of Light, 1931 (play).
The Cicadas, 1931 (poetry).
Music at Night, 1931 (essays).
The Letters of D. H. Lawrence, 1932.
Texts and Pretexts, 1932 (essays).
Beyond the Mexique Bay, 1934 (travel).
The Olive Tree, 1936 (essays).
Ends and Means, 1937 (essays).
Grey Eminence, 1941 (biography).
The Art of Seeing, 1942 (essays).
The Perennial Philosophy, 1945 (philosophy).
Science, Liberty and Peace, 1946 (essay).
Themes and Variations, 1950 (essays).
The Devils of Loudun, 1952 (history).
The Doors of Perception, 1954 (essay).
Heaven and Hell, 1956 (essay).
Adonis and the Alphabet, 1956 (essays).
Collected Short Stories, 1957.
Brave New World Revisited, 1958 (essays).
Collected Essays, 1959.
Literature and Science, 1963 (essay).
The Human Situation, 1977 (lectures).

Secondary Works

Baker, Robert S. *Brave New World: History, Science, and Dystopia*. Boston: Twayne, 1990.

———. *The Dark Historic Page*. Madison: University of Wisconsin Press, 1982.

Bedford, Sybille. *Aldous Huxley: A Biography, Volume One: 1894–1939*. London: Chatto & Windus, 1973; *Volume Two: 1939–1963*, 1974.

Birnbaum, Milton. *Aldous Huxley's Quest for Values*. Knoxville: University of Tennessee Press, 1971.

Bowering, Peter. *Aldous Huxley: A Study of the Major Novels*. London: Athlone Press, 1969.

Bradshaw, David, ed. *The Hidden Huxley: Contempt and Compassion for the Masses, 1920–1936*. London: Faber, 1994.

Clark, Ronald W. *The Huxleys*. New York: McGraw-Hill, 1968.

Dardis, Tom. *Some Time in the Sun: The Hollywood Years of Fitzgerald, Faulkner, Nathaniel West, Aldous Huxley, and James Agee*. New York: Charles Scribner's Sons, 1976.

Firchow, Peter. *Aldous Huxley: Satirist and Novelist*. Minneapolis: University of Minnesota Press, 1972.

———. *The End of Utopia: A Study of Aldous Huxley's Brave New World*. Lewisburg, Penn.: Bucknell University Press, 1984.

Henderson, Alexander. *Aldous Huxley*. 1936. Reprint, New York: Russell and Russell, 1964.

Holmes, Charles M. *Aldous Huxley and the Way to Reality*. Bloomington: University of Indiana Press, 1970.

Huxley, Aldous. *Moksha*: *Writings on Psychedelics and the Visionary Experience (1931–1963)*. Edited by Michael Horovitz and Cynthia Palmer. New York: Stonehill Publishing Co., 1977.

Huxley, Laura Archera. *This Timeless Moment*: *A Personal View of Aldous Huxley*. New York: Farrar-Straus-Giroux, 1968.

Kuehn, Robert E., ed. *Aldous Huxley*: *A Collection of Critical Essays*. Englewood Cliffs, N.J.: Prentice-Hall, 1974.

Kumar, Krishan. *Utopia and Anti-Utopia in Modern Times*. Oxford: Basil Blackwell, 1987.

May, Keith. *Aldous Huxley*. New York: Barnes & Noble, 1972.

Meckier, Jerome. *Aldous Huxley*: *Satire and Structure*. London: Chatto & Windus, 1969.

Philipson, Morris, ed. *Aldous Huxley*: *On Art and Artists*. New York: Harper & Brothers, 1960.

Sexton, James, ed. *Aldous Huxley's Hearst Essays, 1931–1935*. New York: Garland, 1994.

Smith, Grover, ed. *Letters of Aldous Huxley*. New York: Harper & Row, 1969.

Stevens, Jay. *Storming Heaven*: *LSD and the American Dream*. New York: Atlantic Monthly Press, 1987.

Thody, Philip. *Aldous Huxley*: *A Biographical Introduction*. New York: Charles Scribner's Sons, 1973.

Wasson, R. Gordon. *Soma*: *Divine Mushroom of Immortality*. New York: Harcourt Brace Jovanovich, 1968.

Watt, Donald, ed. *Aldous Huxley*: *The Critical Heritage*. London: Routledge & Kegan Paul, 1975.

———.*The Collected Poetry of Aldous Huxley*. London: Chatto & Windus, 1971.

Watts, Harold H. *Aldous Huxley*. New York: Twayne, 1969.

Woodcock, George. *Dawn and the Darkest Hour*: *A Study of Aldous Huxley*. New York: Viking, 1972.

Index

♦